Violence in God's Name

Violence
in
God's Name

Religion in an Age of Conflict

OLIVER McTERNAN

ORBIS BOOKS
Maryknoll, New York 10545

Founded in 1970, Orbis Books endeavors to publish works that enlighten the mind, nourish the spirit, and challenge the conscience. The publishing arm of the Maryknoll Fathers and Brothers, Orbis seeks to explore the global dimensions of the Christian faith and mission, to invite dialogue with diverse cultures and religious traditions, and to serve the cause of reconciliation and peace. The books published reflect the views of their authors and do not represent the official position of the Society. To learn more about Maryknoll and Orbis Books, please visit our website at www.maryknoll.org.

First published in Great Britain in 2003 by
Darton, Longman and Todd Ltd
1 Spencer Court
140-142 Wandsworth High Street
London SW18 4JJ
Great Britain

First published in the USA in 2003 by
Orbis Books
P.O. Box 308
Maryknoll, New York 10545-0308
U.S.A.

Printed and bound in Great Britain.

Library of Congress Cataloging-in-Publication Data

McTernan, Oliver J.
  Violence in God's name : religion in an age of conflict / Oliver McTernan.
      p. cm.
Includes bibliographical references.
  ISBN 1-57075-500-0
1. Violence--Religious aspects. I. Title.
  BL65.V55M38 2003
  291.1'78--dc21

2003011804

For Martha

Contents

Foreword

In the past twenty years the world has witnessed a dramatic increase in the number of conflicts where religion has become a salient factor. Regrettably it took the awful events of September 11, 2001 for the world to realize that we could no longer afford to ignore what were once dismissed as 'ancient hatreds', hostilities far beyond the international community's ability to resolve them. The subsequent attacks in Bali and Mombasa reinforced the message that no sector of the human community is immune from the side effects of this form of violence.

To single out one religion as the sole perpetrator of terror in the world would be to distort the historical record and contemporary reality, as well as to misjudge the extent and the complexity of the problem. There are currently numerous conflicts in different parts of the world in which adherents of all the major world faiths can be found justifying atrocities on the grounds that their cause is righteous. All of them hold in common the belief that those who die defending their faith will be immortalized. From Indonesia to Northern Ireland, the Middle East to Kashmir, India to Nigeria, the Balkans to Sri Lanka, Christians, Buddhists, Jews, Hindus, Muslims and Sikhs justify the use of violence on the grounds that they are protecting their religious identity and interests.

In the immediate aftermath of the terrorist attacks on the United States western political leaders were anxious to stress that their war was not against Islam, a religion they hailed to be peace loving and tolerant. Muslim leaders in the United States and Europe were quick to endorse this perception of their faith by disassociating themselves from co-religionists, who had claimed responsibility for the atrocities. Extremists, they claimed, had hijacked Islam for political purposes. The more liberal arm of the media endorsed this prevailing mood, declaring that grievance, and not creed, was the rationalization behind the carnage.

Laudable as these reactions may appear at first, and especially in so far as they undoubtedly helped to curtail mindless revenge attacks on the migrant Muslim communities in western societies, none do justice to the complexity of the growing phenomenon of faith-based violence. Who can claim to understand fully the minds and motives of those young, educated and talented men, all of whom spent the last months of their lives meticulously planning the destruction of themselves and thousands of others? Who can claim with certainty that it was grievance, real or imagined, and not their profoundly held religious beliefs that motivated their use of commercial aircraft to commit mass murder on the working communities of New York and Washington?

The US-led coalition appears to have succeeded in ousting Osama bin Laden and his Al Qaeda network from their strongholds in the mountains of Afghanistan, an action that undoubtedly helped to disrupt, at least temporarily, their ability to inflict similar large-scale atrocities. This success should not delude us into thinking that the war against terrorism, and in particular terrorism that is religiously motivated, can be won on the battlefield alone. It would be foolhardy to think that the world has seen the last of religious terrorists like Mohamed Atta, the suspected leader of the 9/11 hijackers, and Richard Reid, the British 'shoe bomber' and self-confessed member of Al Qaeda, who attempted to blow himself up with his fellow passengers on a flight from Paris to Miami. These two young men, who came from completely different ethnic and social backgrounds, were united in their readiness to sacrifice their own lives, evidently believing themselves to be on a sacred mission and acting on God's authority in the ultimate battle between good and evil.

Given this mindset, I doubt if the world will ever succeed in completely eliminating the threat of the faith-inspired terrorist. The killing of Osama bin Laden may satisfy the thirst that some have for revenge or for what others perceive to be justice. His demise is equally likely to serve as a rallying call for other self-designated messiahs to pick up his mantle of leadership and to pursue what they see, albeit misguidedly, as a divinely authorized mission of terror against the enemies of their God. The present Israeli counter-terrorist strategy aimed at targeting and eliminating leaders as well as punishing relatives seems to have failed to deter the recruitment of suicide bombers. To curtail the spread of religiously inspired terror will require a greater willingness for self-critical reflection by both political and religious leaders than we have witnessed so far. An essential first step would be for them to acknowledge that religion can be an actor in its own right and should not be dismissed as a surrogate for grievance, protest, greed or political ambition.

It will also require a more decisive and comprehensive plan to alleviate chronic poverty that annually robs millions of human beings of the basic right to life. The world's political leadership needs to acknowledge that gross inequalities that exist between and within states do indeed matter. The rich G8 countries need to develop urgently the collective political will to partner with the world's poor to eradicate the systemic poverty that currently mars the lives of millions and provides religious and secular extremists with a fertile recruiting ground. The poverty gap that has grown wider in recent years needs to be bridged sooner rather than later, if peace and security are to be guaranteed anywhere in the world. The 9/11 attacks on New York and Washington have taught us that there are no impenetrable fortresses.

Religious leaders also need to reflect more critically on their own failure to provide more effective leadership and witness to the true fundamental values of their respective faiths. During the conflict in Bosnia, the UN Secretary General, Kofi Annan, spoke of the need 'to restore religion to its rightful role as peacemaker and pacifier'. It is true that all religions aspire to peace but it is questionable whether religion has ever fulfilled that role. The fact that all major world faiths have at times sanctioned the use of violence to protect or to promote their own sectarian interests allows religious terrorists today to claim moral justification for their actions. Faith-inspired terrorists can find in their religious tradition role models that give legitimacy to their own use of violence. It is not enough, therefore, for religious leaders to disown the murderous actions of their co-religionists and to denounce these terrorists as misguided fringe groups. To justify the taking of human life whatever the circumstances seriously questions religion's claim that human life is a sacred gift. Until each faith group is prepared to promote actively a respect for the gift of life above all other beliefs, dogmas and interests, religion will always have the potential to be an exclusive, divisive and destructive force in the world.

To speak of the need for tolerance is in my opinion a wholly inadequate response to the terror that is now perpetrated in the name of God. Tolerance is an essentially negative concept that was developed more as a rejection to than an endorsement of pluralism in religious belief and practice. The current crisis in our global human relationships demands a more pro-active response to cultural and religious diversity. It requires willingness from those with faith and with none to acknowledge and to protect more vigorously the right of others to believe and to act differently.

When I took up the invitation to be a Fellow in the Weatherhead Center for International Affairs at Harvard University in August 2000, I had already opted to focus my research on the role of religion in conflict. In the mid

1970s, I became actively involved in the work of the peace movement Pax Christi International. I was convinced that religion had an important role to play in promoting global peace and reconciliation. As the co-ordinator of the international movement's efforts to establish within the framework of the Helsinki Agreement a confidence-building dialogue, I was a frequent visitor to the Soviet Union and to the other Eastern Bloc countries. The euphoria that I shared with so many others when I began to see the hope of Helsinki realized with the collapse of the Berlin Wall was soon to evaporate, however, as I read the weekly press reports of religious-related conflict in diverse parts of the world. It became clear to me that religion can be as much a part of the problem as a part of the solution in resolving conflict, and that the phenomenon of faith-based violence presents a challenge equally as vital as the old ideological divide between East and West.

The problem one encounters when trying to access the role of religion in conflict is the lack of data. Facts and given conditions are just not there because of the consensus among political scientists that for the past two hundred years or so religion has ceased to be a cause of conflict. In addition, most scholars tend to believe that people no longer battle over beliefs; and even where religion appears, at least on the surface, to be a con-tributing factor, as in the Arab-Israeli conflict or India-Pakistani conflict, they would still claim that the real cause for such armed struggles is merely the contest for land or political power. In most of the literature on conflict ethnicity or religion is looked upon purely as a recruiting and motivating factor for what is essentially a political or economic cause. The fact that for a major part of the twentieth century conflicts were viewed solely through Cold War lenses has only helped to endorse the irrelevancy of religion.

Jonathan Fox is one of the few scholars who is beginning to address the deliberate omission of religion in the current statistics. In his article 'The Salience of Religious Issues in Ethnic Conflicts' Fox uses data collected from 268 politically active ethnic minorities worldwide for the 1990 to 1995 period to access the significance of religion in ethnic conflict. His results show that religious issues are 'more than marginally relevant' in about 15.5 per cent and are 'among the dominant issues' in 4.5 per cent of all ethnic conflicts.[1] His conclusion is that, although religion does play a role, the figures in-dicate that its role is less common than anecdotal evidence taken from the media would suggest. I have no means of testing his results but from my own travel and in-depth interviews in conflict situations and from my read-ing of the current literature my observations would suggest that, contrary to Fox's conclusions, religion is a more salient factor in a larger number of contemporary conflicts than even our media cares to acknowledge.

The Department of Peace and Conflict Research at Uppsala University publishes an annual report entitled 'States in Armed Conflict'. The statistics for 2001 show that during the period from 1989 to 2001 there were 115 armed conflicts in which twenty-five or more were killed in battle. In 2001 thirty-four of these conflicts in twenty-eight countries were still active and at least seventeen of them had begun before 1989. The Uppsala figures do not identify whether or not religion plays a role in any of these conflicts. My own estimate is that out of the 115 listed since 1989 religion has been a relevant factor in at least twenty-nine, and that over half of the current conflicts have a significant religious component.[2]

Neither of these sets of figures should provide comfort to religious leaders, and this is especially true in light of the fact that these percentages represent some of the most protracted and bloodiest conflicts currently raging. In 1980 the United States Department of State's roster on international terrorist groups included scarcely a single religious group. By 1998 it was estimated that at least half of the thirty most dangerous groups in the world were religious.

The bomb attacks last year that killed holidaymakers in Bali and Mombasa and the more recent attacks in Riyadh and Casablanca underscore the fact that the barbarous consequences of antagonisms, in which people feel their ethnic and religious identities threatened, transcend borders. Understandably people import their sense of grievance and prejudices as they seek refuge from the fighting in lands far from home. Even before the atrocities of 9/11 there were serious tensions among migrant and refugee communities in Europe and North America arising from conflicts in their homeland. In London I frequently found myself judged as being naïve by Sudanese, Nigerian and Iraqi Christian asylum seekers who dismissed any suggestion of engaging in dialogue with their Muslim neighbours as being foolhardy. Despite their common status as migrants in a foreign land, prejudices, stemming from years of conflict and grievance, were too deeply ingrained to allow trust to develop among them.

The excessive media attention given to the millions of Muslim migrants and refugees living in the United States and Europe in the immediate aftermath of the terror attacks on New York and Washington exposed a deep sense of alienation and isolation that many of these communities felt in the host society. It also highlighted the tensions that exist within the Islamic diasporas between those who believe in an accommodation between Islam and life in the West and those who regard any attempt at such integration as the equivalent to apostasy. This is particularly true in Britain where a number of young Muslims saw the war in Afghanistan as an attack on Islam and who without the knowledge of their families secretly slipped away to fight for the Taleban.[3]

The escalation of the conflict in the Middle East, it is claimed, led to the worst spate of anti-Jewish violence experienced in France since the Second World War. In April 2002 pro-Palestine sympathizers firebombed a synagogue in Marseilles, and thousands of Arab protesters took to the streets of Paris and other French cities denouncing the Israeli and American policy towards the Palestinians.[4] In the United States Arabs became the victims of Jewish and Christian anger. In California the chairman and another member of the Jewish Defence League were charged with plotting to set off pipe bombs at one of Los Angeles' famous mosques and at the office of a congressman of Middle Eastern descent. The Christian right used the breakdown in the peace process and the increase in suicide-bombing attacks to denigrate Islam as a violent religion. The volume of anti-Muslim comments by Christian TV evangelists reached such a level that the US Secretary of State, Colin Powell, condemned the Christian Coalition for propagating hatred against Muslims.[5]

The fallout from the Middle East also impacted on life on university campuses across the United States as tensions grew when students and faculty members allied themselves with either pro-Palestinian or pro-Israeli factions. The hullabaloo at Harvard over a Commencement Day speech by a young American Muslim illustrated the depth of anger and passion that is felt by sympathizers on both sides of this ethno-religious conflict. Reportedly, more than five thousand students, faculty, alumni, parents and other interested parties signed an online petition calling on the authorities at Harvard either to replace the speaker or to insist on the inclusion in his speech of a full condemnation of terrorism, violent jihad and organizations that support terrorism, directly or indirectly.[6] The fact that none of the protesters had read what Zayed M. Yasin intended to say seemed not to matter. The title 'American Jihad' that had been chosen not by him but by a member of the selection committee was considered sufficient cause for the uproar. In the end his speech had in fact nothing to do with 'holy war'. His traditional use of the word 'jihad' was to exhort his privileged classmates to fight against social injustices in their society.

These are just a few examples of the reverse side of globalization, and how conflicts that involve ethnic and religious differences in what we may regard as some remote part of the world can impact on life in our urbanized western societies. The global village is a reality, and no sector of the human community is immune from the side effects of the violence perpetrated beyond our boarders. Sectarian violence in Nigeria, Northern Ireland, Kashmir, Sri Lanka or the Middle East should concern us, if for no other reason than that it can threaten our own security. Failure to address and to help resolve these conflicts can inadvertently undermine the efforts of western countries to transform themselves into genuine pluralistic, multicultural, multi-faith societies.

Violence in God's Name is the product of my research at Harvard as well as the collective and diverse experiences of my own unusual career. For over twenty-five years I have combined my work as a priest in a busy multi-ethnic, socially diverse inner-city London parish with my role as a regular broadcaster and peace activist in the international arena. Each one of these commitments has, I have found, greatly enriched the other. My combined responsibilities as a parish priest, broadcaster and peace activist allowed me to function concurrently in three distinctively different worlds or sub-cultures, each with its own mindset and language, a fact which I found so often hindered one subculture from understanding the other.

For the past two and a half years I have lived and worked in an exclusively academic environment. Here I have been introduced to yet another sub-culture, which like the others has its own language and idiosyncratic outlook on the world. It too has similar problems in understanding and interrelating with the worlds of the practitioner and the priest, a fact that became all too obvious to me when I took part in a series of seminars in which eminent economists and political scientists from different parts of the world attempted to interpret data drawn from various religious communities. The experience alerted me to the real risk of creating, albeit unintentionally, new myths when one subculture tries to interpret what is happening in the other. I mention this as I fear part of the problem in the current discourse on religiously motivated violence is that few political and social scientists have either the language or understanding to analyse accurately what is happening in the world of religion.

My goal in writing this book is to try to bridge the gap between the worlds of the theorist and the practitioner. I have endeavoured to use a language and style that will help to make the current debate on the connection between religion and conflict more accessible to the non-specialist reader. My argument is that the religious factor in contemporary conflict does matter, and that it should not be dismissed as an epiphenomenon, a proxy for some other cause. Religion needs to be acknowledged as an actor in its own right. Initiators of peace processes who fail to address the religious concerns and interests of a wider constituency, seriously risk unravelling the underlying mode of operation and dialogue as some of the protagonists left out of the 'track one' negotiations refuse to buy into agreements that they fear may have compromised their fundamental beliefs.

The nerve-gas attack on the Tokyo subway in March 1995 by members of Aum Shinrikyo, a Buddhist fringe group, and the destruction of the Twin Towers and part of the Pentagon on 9/11 alert us to the destructive potential of a religious fanaticism that feels it is being persecuted or ignored. My hope is that the observations and reflections recorded in this book will provide some useful markers for discussion and act as a paradigm or framework that will stimulate further reflection and debate on an issue of such vital importance for the security of our planet. This book is very much a work in progress. How can it be other, given the breadth, the seriousness and the complexity of the subject matter under debate?

A question I had to address in writing this book was, how important is it to define what I mean by religion? It is difficult to find a definition that is totally inclusive and reflects how adherents of each of the religions referred to in the book would describe their own beliefs and practices. In the United States alone it is estimated that there are between four and twelve hundred different Christian denominations. Muslims are divided by the Sunni and Shia traditions, Buddhists by the Theravada and Mahayana traditions. Even the choice of the book's title, *Violence in God's Name*, was problematic in the sense that I include Buddhists among the groups who justify their use of violence, and yet Buddhists do not believe in a creator God in the same way that Jews, Christians and Muslims do. The origins of religion I believe are rooted in the transcendent and point to a reality beyond our world of time and place. I would accept, however, that religious rituals, practices and dogmas are a human construction in so far as these are part of what the Swiss theologian Karl Barth described as 'a human response to revelation'.[7] Each of the world religions referred to in this book share a number of characteristics. In practice, however, each of these traditions give different emphasis or priority to the place of doctrine, to their founding myths or sacred narratives, ethics, ritual, spiritual experience, and social institutions. Buddhists, for example, give priority to doctrine and spiritual experience, whereas for Hindus ritual is all important.[8] Part of the difficulty we encounter in defining religion is the fact that religion is more dynamic than the political or academic worlds have hitherto acknowledged.

My focus is solely on that form of religiously inspired violence that is targeted at civilian populations, other faith communities and state institutions with the aim of attracting maximum public attention in order to affect political change or power shifts in favour of the perpetrators' cause. I want to acknowledge at least in passing the seriousness of the violence suffered in God's name by the victims of religious sects that use mind control techniques to prey on vulnerable people, as well as the victims of the child sexual abuse that seems to have thrived for several decades under a clerical culture of denial within the Catholic Church. A discussion of these forms of violence, although it is associated with religion, is beyond the limits that I had set for myself in writing this book.

Chapter one profiles three competing theories on the causes of conflict – creed, grievance and greed. In *The Clash of Civilizations* Sam Huntington argues that globalization has created more opportunity for interaction, making people more conscious of their differences. He believes that religion is possibly the most profound difference that can exist between people, and that 'beliefs in different gods' therefore enhance the likelihood of conflict along the fault lines where people have to compete for resources and influences. Ted Gurr plays down the religious factor as a cause for conflict and argues in favour of a causal link between grievance and revolt. The greater the inequalities among groups in heterogeneous societies, he contends, the greater are the chances for conflict. Paul Collier disagrees with both these theories. In *Greed or Grievance* he argues from the results of his research that greed considerably outperforms grievance as a cause for civil strife. For him the presence of 'lootable' commodities like diamonds, oil, timber or drugs greatly increases the risk of conflict.

Chapter two identifies examples of contemporary conflicts in which the link between violence and at least one of the major world religions is substantial. I question the academic 'givens' of the past century, and especially the 'reductionist' mindset that is rooted in a secularist world view that excludes religion as a cause of conflict. This received wisdom of the post-Enlightenment period has put political and social scientists, politicians and journalists at a serious disadvantage in their efforts to understand and to address the rising phenomenon of faith-related violence, which essentially questions modern society's legitimacy. A common complaint of the religious terrorists, whatever their faith tradition, is the absence of values in a world that has excluded God. Their common goal is to make religion the 'foundation' of a new social order.

Chapter three traces the long, perplexing history of religion and violence. The overview helps to demonstrate how today's religiously motivated terrorists of whatever religious tradition can invoke numerous exemplars to justify the violence that they set out to perpetrate in the name of God. It describes the activities of the Zealots, the Assassins, the Crusaders and the Thugs, all of whom believed their killing to be divinely authorized and their roles, as agents of God's vengeance, legitimate. The chapter emphasizes the need for religious leaders to recognize that past ambivalence towards violence is a major contributing factor to the present-day problem.

Chapter four examines three contemporary conflicts – Northern Ireland, Sri Lanka, and Israel/Palestine. I have chosen to limit the focus of this chapter to the religious component of these conflicts that has been deliberately overlooked in the peace processes initiated by the international community. I do not believe that religion is the sole or prime cause of the ongoing communal strife in these countries. I recognize that colonial, economic, social, and political factors are also at play. Drawing on extensive interviews that I have had with some of the protagonists in these conflicts, my goal is to illustrate that religion per se is a part of the contemporary problem and as such needs to be addressed if durable solutions are to be found. Competing claims on land that are rooted in religious identity and belief have complicated the search for durable solutions. Sacred turf matters enough for some to battle over and, if needs be, to die for.

Chapter five focuses on what part poverty, tolerance and leadership plays in exasperating or resolving conflicts. As the world grows wealthier it has also become less equal. My argument is that inequality matters. Extreme poverty is not the prime cause for the rise of fundamentalism but social injustice, unemployment and illiteracy help to create a fertile recruiting ground for high-minded and idealistic young religious entrepreneurs who believe that it is their religious or sacred duty to act decisively in favour of the downtrodden. The political will to tackle poverty can help to reduce but not completely eliminate the threat of faith-based terrorism. To underestimate the power of religious conviction is to misjudge the seriousness of the threat that religiously motivated terrorism poses.

I argue that the crisis facing the world today calls for a more imaginative response from the world's faith communities than we have witnessed to date. It examines the different traditions' attitudes towards tolerance. It outlines the thoughts of the second-century Christian writer Tertullian who rooted his arguments for freedom of conscience and religious liberty in the nature of the human person and religion itself. It notes how once the Christian Church had secured its own freedom, it justified the use of violence and even the death penalty to deprive others of freedom of thought and practice. The chapter argues for the need for all the main faith traditions to adopt what the French existentialist philosopher, Gabriel Marcel, calls 'counter intolerance'[9] or a more proactive approach to pluralism in belief and practice. It also examines the qualities of religious leadership required at this defining moment in human history.

Chapter six lists recommendations for the international community, religious leaders and secular peace organizations based upon my own extensive experience in inter-faith dialogue and conflict resolution. My hope is simply to stimulate a debate that can help to move us to a new level of dialogue and action in tackling the threat that religious terrorism poses to the security and well-being of our global society. New initiatives promoting confidence building and understanding among peoples of different political cultures and faiths, and especially between Islam and the West, are urgently required to lessen the risk of religiously motivated violence.

Internationally sponsored programmes drawing upon the expertise, beliefs and experiences of people from different cultures and faith traditions and aimed at promoting a sea change or paradigm shift in political thinking are essential if the international community is to curtail an intensification of religiously motivated violence and to develop more creative approaches to conflict resolution and prevention. The training of religious and community leaders in the skills needed to work across the restrictive boundaries that currently divide them would be an important first step in the battle against religiously inspired strife.

The picture on the cover of this book is a reproduction of a Salvador Dali painting titled 'Atavism at Twilight'. Those who are familiar with 'The Angelus' by Jean-Francois Millet will immediately recognize that Dali has reinterpreted Millet's composition of the praying couple at the end of their working day. Dali uses Millet's religiously comforting image to demonstrate his theory that the artist should 'perceive and paint different images within a single collection of shapes'.[10] Dali believed that everything one saw had the potential to be something else. He saw in Millet's reassuring image of a woman in prayer 'a resemblance of a post-copulating female praying mantis about to eat her mate'. I chose Dali's picture because both the title and composition help to illustrate the underlying theme of this book. Dali saw in Millet's comforting and uplifting religious composition a potentially destructive force. Some of his reinterpretations of Millet's 'Angelus' are too gruesome to reproduce on the front cover of a book.

Dali's title 'Atavism at Twilight' reminds the viewer that in any generation the primitive characteristics of ancestors can unexpectedly re-emerge. This I believe is what we are witnessing in the present spate of religiously motivated violence. Each tradition's past ambivalence towards violence has come back to haunt us. The willingness of religious leaders, at different periods in history, to compromise their own transcendent values for the sake of personal gain and unchecked licence, regrettably, provides today's religious militants with sufficient role models to warrant their own acts of violence.

I would like to express my gratitude to the Executive Committee and staff of the Weatherhead Center for International Affairs at Harvard for the two wonderful years I spent there while researching the subject of this book. I owe particular gratitude to the former Director of the Fellows Programme, Steven Bloomfield, and to Donna Hicks, the Assistant Director of the Program on International Conflict Analysis and Resolution for their friend-ship and encouragement during the writing of this book. I am also grateful to the numerous people whom I interviewed during my research visits to Sri Lanka, Israel/Palestine and Northern Ireland for their hospitality and generosity with their time. I have deliberately chosen not to identify some of my interviewees for the reason that they are still living in situations of unresolved conflict and I have no wish to complicate their role as leaders and potential mediators. My thanks to the John Anson Kittredge Educational Fund and to CAFOD, the UK Agency for Overseas Development, for their grants which contributed to the cost of my field research, and to those close friends, especially Frank and Sabina Wong and Karine McCall, who provided me with the financial support that enabled me to take the time out to research the causal link between faith and violence and to write this book. I also wish to acknowledge my gratitude to James Chichetto of Stonehill College for his helpful comments on the text.

OLIVER McTERNAN
March 2003
Cambridge, Massachusetts

1

The Clash of Paradigms

On 7 February 1993 *The New York Times* carried the headline 'As Ethnic Wars Multiply, US Strains for a Policy'. Most of the thirty violent conflicts raging in the world at the time, the article claimed, were ethnic and sectarian in nature and were having a devastating impact on the lives of ordinary people. This notable rise in ethnic and sectarian clashes prompted a greater interest on the part of academics and political powers to study the causes of such widespread conflict. The intervening decade has produced a number of conflicting hypotheses. In this chapter I have set out to provide a summary of the main theories under the headings of creed, greed and grievance. I have chosen the writings of Sam Huntington, Paul Collier, Ted Gurr and Jack Snyder whom I consider to be the leading advocates of the paradigms that are widely accepted as models for interpreting communal conflict. Whilst I do have a number of observations to make, it is not my intention to provide an in-depth analysis of these different and sometimes clashing theories. My purpose is to provide the non-specialist reader with an overview of the debate that is taking place within academic and political circles. It is within this broader context that I hope to stimulate a wider discussion on the role that religion can and does play in both fermenting and preventing conflict.

In the wake of September 11 many commentators hailed the controversial theory of Samuel P. Huntington, the Harvard-based political scientist, to be 'prophetic'. In the summer of 1993 Huntington published an article in *Foreign Affairs* claming that in the post Cold War era, cultural and religious differences would replace ideology as the more probable cause of conflict. When others were celebrating the demise of communism and what they believed to be the inevitable emergence of liberal democracy as the universal political system of the future, Huntington predicted that the old divisions of the first, second and third worlds that were drawn up along ideological lines would give way to new civilizational differences that could prove to be even more menacing.

In his book, *The Clash of Civilizations and Remaking of World Order*, Huntington expands his hypothesis and argues for a new paradigm or framework to grasp the shifting focus in international relationships. In this new emerging post Cold War world Huntington identifies eight major civilizations or cultural blocs – Chinese (Sinic), Japanese, Indian, Islamic, Western, Orthodox, Latin American and, possibly African – that he believes will play a significant role in shaping the new world order. He accepts that people can and do redefine their identities, but his basic premise is that, 'Civilizations are nonetheless meaningful entities, and while the lines between them are seldom sharp, they are real.'[1] His second premise is that globalization created greater opportunity for interaction among these diverse civilizations, making people conscious of their differences, and as a consequence people have become more anxious about where they fit into this new global design. His conclusion is that the possibility for conflict, and especially along what he describes as the 'fault lines' where different civilizations meet and have to compete for resources and influence, is greatly enhanced.

Nationalism and communism were essentially artificially constructed belief systems, whereas culture, the defining factor in a civilization, Huntington argues, is about identity itself; it shapes the basic perceptions that people have about life and their understanding of their relationships with God, with each other, with authority, with the State. The differences between the major cultures that are re-emerging as key players in the reshaping of the contemporary world are more profound therefore than those created by the discarded ideologies of the twentieth century. This is particularly true of religion, which Huntington regards as 'possibly the most profound difference that can exist between people'. Conflict between states of different civilizations is 'greatly enhanced', he claims, 'by beliefs in different gods'.[2]

Pivotal to the Huntington argument is the claim that as globalization, the process of social, economic and cultural modernization, swept around the world in the second half of the twentieth century, so too did a religious revival. By the mid 1970s secularism, he argues, was in the decline and religion began to re-emerge as an actor in its own right. Citing Gilles Kepel's *Revenge of God* he declares that 'the theme was no longer *aggiornamento* but "a second evangelization of Europe", the aim was no longer to modern-ize Islam, but to "Islamize modernity".'[3] Christianity, Islam, Judaism, Hinduism, Buddhism, Orthodoxy have, according to Huntington, all experienced a new relevance as people sought to fill the vacuum in their cultural identity created by the onslaught of globalization and the collapse of the communist ideology. Western ideas of individualism, liberalism, constitutionalism, human rights, rule of law, democracy, free market, and the separation of Church and State often have little resonance, he claims, in Islamic, Confucian, Hindu, Buddhist and Orthodox cultures.

Huntington gives particular attention to the role of Islam in the remaking of world order. He refutes the argument that the West does not have a problem with Islam itself but only with violent Islamist extremists. Relations between Islam and Christianity, he maintains, have often been 'stormy'.[4] Islam is the only civilization, Huntington argues, that has twice threatened the survival of the West. The cause of what he sees as an 'on-going pattern of conflict' is deeper than any transitory phenomena and is rooted, he believes, in the nature of the two religions, Christianity and Islam, and the civilizations based on them. It is a product of the difference and the similarities between these two world faiths, he argues. On the one hand Christianity separates the realms of God and Caesar, whereas Islam recognizes no separation between religion and politics. The two religions, however, are monotheistic, and see the world in dualistic 'us-and-them' terms. Missionary in nature, both these religions aim to convert non-believers to their version of 'the one true faith'. 'From its origins Islam expanded by conquest and when the opportunity existed, Christianity did also,' Huntington argues.[5]

In support of this hypothesis Huntington claims that nineteen of the twenty-eight 'fault-line' conflicts between Muslims and non-Muslims in the mid 1990s were between Muslims and Christians. He identifies four major contributing factors for this:

> First, Muslim population growth has generated large numbers of unemployed and disaffected young people who become recruits to Islamic causes, exert pressures on neighbouring societies, and migrate to the West. Second, the Islamic Resurgence has given Muslims renewed confidence in the distinctive character and worth of their civilization and values compared to those of the West. Third, the West's simultaneous efforts to universalize its values and institutions, to maintain its military and economic superiority, and to inter-vene in conflicts in the Muslim world generate intense resentment among Muslims. Fourth, the collapse of communism removed a common enemy of the West and Islam and left each the perceived major threat to the other.[6]

In the decade between 1980 and 1990, according to Huntington, Muslims came to regard western secularism, irreligiosity and immorality as worse evils than the western Christianity that produced them. In their eyes the

West replaced 'godless communism' as the opponent of Islam. In the same period the West became concerned over what was perceived as the 'Islamic threat'. Huntington concluded, 'something very much like a war is under-way' and that 'the futures of both peace and Civilization depend upon understanding and cooperation among the political, spiritual and intellectual leaders of the world's major civilizations'.[7]

It is Huntington's focus on Islam, and more especially his claims that Islam and the West are in a state of war and that Islam poses the greatest threat to western civilization that have angered moderate Muslim leaders, and especially those already active in promoting inter-faith dialogue. Sheikh Zaki Badawi, the Egyptian scholar and head of an Islamic Institute in London, denounced Huntington's hypothesis, arguing in the wake of September 11 that *The Clash of Civilizations* is being used by extremists to justify their self-proclaimed jihad between Islam and the West. Prince Hassan of Jordan, another renowned activist in promoting inter-faith dialogue, was equally critical.[8]

The most widely shared criticism of Huntington's paradigm is that he por-trays the different civilizations as being more homogenized and integrated than they are in reality. Huntington rejects this accusation by pointing out that he acknowledges that cultures can overlap and interact, and that people can and sometimes do redefine their identities. He also argues that a whole section of his book deals with divisions, and especially within the Islamic world.[9] This is true, but none the less *The Clash of Civilizations* fails to convey the depth of diversity and the dissonance that is to be found and especially in the Muslim world.

Whatever the depth of the desire among Islamic activists and religious scholars for a common and unanimous agreement on how the funda-mentals of their faith should be interpreted and universally applied, there is neither a consistent voice nor unanimity in observance among Muslims today. Opinions and practices on issues ranging from the role of women in society to attitudes towards authority vary from country to country. The Qur'an and the Sunna are frequently interpreted by different religious fig-ures to favour one political system over another. While some Muslims see the creation of an Islamic state in the absence of the successors of the Prophet as abhorrent, Ayatollah Khomeini, for example, taught that an Islamic state could be justified on religious grounds provided that a learned clergyman, a *faqih*, guided it. This *faqih* would have 'the knowledge of the law and justice' and could therefore act as a representative of the imam and, by implication, of Allah.[10]

Again the differences reflected in the writings of, for example, Sayyid Qutb, the Egyptian radical executed by Nasser in 1966, and Abdullah

Ahmed An-Na'im, the Sudanese Islamic scholar and human rights advocate, could not be more fundamental. Qubt believed that the absolute sovereignty of God could not be usurped by human powers and that Islam had a universal vocation. Society for him had to be Islamic in its foundation and its structure.[11] It was the religious duty of every Muslim, Qubt believed, to revolt and to overthrow apostate and corrupt leaders. Political revolution he declared as a necessity before the sharia, the divine law that governs all aspects of daily life, could be genuinely applied in a society. Disillusioned by his short stay in western society he declared that Islam was God's answer to western materialism and decadence, writing,

> Any system in which the final decisions are referred to human beings, and in which the sources of all authority are human, deifies human beings by designating others than God as lords over men ... to proclaim the authority and sovereignty of God means to eliminate all human kingship and to announce the rule of the Sustainer of the universe over the entire earth ... to establish God's rule means that His laws be enforced and that the final decision in all affairs be according to these laws.[12]

An-Na'im sees the challenges facing Islam as radically different. For him the claims of human rights and the claims of Islam are not incompatible. He believes that it is possible to be a good Muslim and at the same time to live in a contemporary pluralistic society. The sharia he regards as the consequences of human choices and that as such these laws can and should be re-examined. However, he acknowledges that, for this to happen, it will require a radical transformation within Islam itself. An-Na'im accuses Muslims of shying away from taking responsibility. He claims that they prefer to delegate the choices to others by seeking *fatwai*,[13] forgetting the fact that they are also morally responsible if they act on the advice given. All Muslims, he argues, have a right to engage in discourse and to make up their own minds without fearing for their lives if their opinions differ from those of the *ulama*, the body of recognized religious scholars. Unlike Qubt, An-Na'im believes in constitutionalism, which in his view 'encompasses not only limitations on the powers of government but also the imposition of positive obligations on government to maintain and enhance the life, liberty, and dignity of its citizenry'.[14]

Even though Sayyid Qubt's teachings remain extremely influential today and especially among militant Islamic organizations,[15] it is important to acknowledge the diversity of thought and that Muslims, in common with other believers, can and do hold dynamically opposing positions on such fundamental questions as the meaning and application of their beliefs in contemporary society. The scars of past schisms and doctrinal disputes, sectarianism and human personalities can equally impede their ability to work together in harmony. In his book *The Failure of Political Islam* the French orientalist Olivier Roy claims, 'despite Tehran's effort to make headway in Sunni milieus, the opposition between Shiites and Sunnis remains a key aspect of the contemporary Islamic world'.[16] It is because of this division, he argues, that the impact of Islam on the political and social life of Afghanistan, Algeria, Egypt, Indonesia, Iran, Jordan, Saudi Arabia, Sudan, Turkey and Uzbekistan differs greatly.

What Roy calls 'an imaginary solidarity' may still have the power to rally popular support, but ethnic, religious and national divisions among Muslims remain stronger, he believes, than calls for Islamic solidarity. The fact that, despite the pro Saddam Hussein street demonstrations, more Muslim countries joined the United States led coalition to liberate Kuwait than rallied to the defence of Iraq would seem to indicate that Roy is right when he states that 'Islamo-nationalism' wins out over 'pan-Islamism'. The Gulf War and the more recent campaign against the Taleban and the Al-Qaeda network in Afghanistan seem to confirm that for many Muslim governments geopolitical interests still transcend cultural and religious differences.[17] Even though it is true that a number of militant Islamic groups advocate violence in their efforts to reverse what they see as the godless influences of western secular society, it would be a distortion of contemporary evidence to look upon the Muslim world as a political bloc united by a common religious ideology, and therefore presenting a viable threat to alternative civilizations. Islam may have 'bloody borders', as Huntington claims, but so too have other major religious traditions whose adherents are currently engaged in violent battles over identity and land.

The dissonance and diversity that mark contemporary Islam are equally evident within other major world religions. Fundamental disputes over the interpretation of sacred texts, political involvement, the use of authority and the role of women deprive these other-faith communities also of a sense of common purpose. This is particularly true of western Christianity. In North America there are at least 400 to 500 different Christian denominations, although some estimate it to be as many as 1200.[18] There is also evidence to suggest that the traditional practice of separating religion from politics, which Huntington sees as one of the essential differences between Christianity and Islam, is becoming more blurred. In recent years it seems that Americans are shifting away from the traditional custom of defining each other by their ethnic and theological differences, and are forming new political alignments that transcend the old denominational divides.

Traditional and conservative members in one denomination are forming political alliances with like-minded people in other denominations to pursue common political goals on abortion and other contentious issues. The progressive members of the different denominations are forming similar alliances. As a consequence the previous predictable voting patterns of religious groups that tended to vote according to their ethnic, racial and denominational ties are beginning to unravel.[19] A similar trend can be observed among European Christians. This new interplay between faith and politics is likely to cause further divisions within the western Christian world, which already lacks any real sense of homogeneity, either in the interpretation or practice of the Christian faith.

The theory that 'Europe ends where western Christianity ends and Islam and Orthodoxy begin'[20] leads Huntington to claim that the historic line which runs from the Russian–Finnish border in the north to the Croatia–Bosnia border in the south and which marked the division of the Roman Empire in the fourth century into East and West, has re-emerged as a 'fault line' between what he perceives to be two distinctly separate civilizations – the western Christian and orthodox Christian worlds. The open clashes that have marred relationships between Rome and Moscow since the collapse of communism, and especially the hostilities that surrounded the visit of Pope John Paul II to the Ukraine in June 2001 would seem to vindicate this claim. The Russian Orthodox Patriarch Aleksie II has frequently condemned Catholic efforts to gain new converts in Russia, accusing them of intruding on what was traditionally regarded as the 'canonical territory'[21] of the Orthodox Church. Real as these current tensions are, I do not agree with the Huntington analysis that would interpret this conflict as the clash of fundamental differences in culture and belief between the Orthodox and Catholic worlds. The cause is as much a clash of personalities, as memories of historical injustices.

Since the Great Schism in 1054 the relationship between the Churches of East and West has been marred by suspicion and mutual mistrust. The sacking of Constantinople by western Crusaders on route to the Holy Land in 1204 left a deep scar on the Orthodox memory. After the annexation of Red Ruthenia, the Ukraine, to Poland in 1569 Catholic missionaries worked to bring the Ruthenian Orthodox Church under papal jurisdiction. In 1596 a Synod was convened in Brest where it was formally agreed that the Ruthenians would accept papal authority but would be allowed to retain their Byzantine Liturgy and married clergy. In 1946 when Stalin revoked this agreement and forcibly reunited the Byzantine Rite Church to Moscow's jurisdiction, many Western Ukrainian (Uniate) Catholics chose to continue their church life underground. When communism collapsed these Catholic Byzantine-rite Christians resurfaced to reclaim their churches sometimes by force. The deep-seated hostilities and suspicions between Rome and Moscow were rekindled despite the fact that during the years of Soviet oppression both Churches had grown closer in understanding and respect.

I was present in the mid 1990s at a private meeting in London between Patriarch Aleksie II and Cardinal Hume, the former Archbishop of Westminster. The purpose of this meeting was to help defuse the growing tensions and misunderstandings between our respective Churches. Metropolitan Kyrill of Smolensk and Kaliningrad, who was also present, expressed in the course of the discussion the belief that relationships between the Catholic and Russian Orthodox Churches had been so good during the Cold War period that some Orthodox hierarchs had thought that a formal reunion between the Churches was conceivable before the end of the century. That desire had been shattered, he claimed, with the appointment of Cardinal Angelo Sodano as the Vatican Secretary of State. It was Sodano's aggressive policy of expansionism and endorsement of Catholic proselytizing in Russia, according to Metropolitan Krill, that led to the rapid deterioration in relationships between the Churches in the mid 1990s.

Based on my own twenty-five years of active engagement with the Russian Orthodox Church I believe it would be wrong to allow the existing state of inter-church relationships and in particular the tensions and open hostility that mars the contemporary climate to overshadow the fact that Russia is part of Europe. It has developed different characteristics from western European countries but it was born in the cradle of a common faith. Orthodox Christian beliefs are rooted in the same philosophical and theological traditions as western Christianity. Georges Florovsky, the renowned Russian Orthodox theologian who taught at the Harvard Divinity School in the 1920s, affirms this when he writes: 'The Orthodox theologian does not feel lost among colleagues of different thought or faith ... But he refers directly or indirectly to the Ecumenical Councils and to the Holy Fathers, that is to authorities and moments which essentially transcend historic disagreements and ought to have determining value for all Christians.'[22] To confine Europe to the borders of western Christendom, as Huntington suggests, would be to rob European civilization of its true identity and full spiritual and cultural potential. Since the Great Schism of 1054[23] the Churches of East and West have behaved more like estranged sisters, living independently but at the same time never losing that sense of family identity. The symbolic image of Europe having 'two lungs' has been used in recent years to express the essential unity of a continent that has developed from a common Christian heritage.[24] It is true that the reality of Europe today, both East and West, is more of a multicultural multifaith society. None the less Europe retains a core identity that is rooted in a common philosophical and faith heritage. To claim otherwise is to risk distorting both historical and contemporary fact.

In various empirical studies, a number of scholars have challenged Huntington's prediction that conflicts between 'civilizations' and especially between Islam and the West would increase in the post Cold War period. Some would argue that Islam does not pose the threat that Huntington fears,[25] and others claim that he mistakenly identifies conflicts caused by other factors as civilizational clashes.[26] According to these scholars, the predicted increase in conflict appears to be more 'within' rather than 'between' civilizations. For example, between the Cold War and post Cold War, Jonathan Fox found little change in the level of conflicts between Islam and the West.[27] The slight increase recorded, he argues, may seem important to western eyes but from a global and Islamic perspective it reflects nothing more than a general rise in ethnic conflicts.

The Henderson and Tucker study, which over a three-year period immediately following the Cold War examined the clash of civilizations hypothesis in relation to civilization membership and the likelihood of inter-state war, reached the opposite conclusion. They found 'that states of different civilizations are less likely than states of the same civilization to fight one another'.[28] Huntington, they claim, relies too much 'on anecdote and selective [in]attention to the historical record'.[29] They criticize him for taking 'the mutterings of political leaders' at face value and for failing to examine how much 'blood and treasure' these same leaders devote to civilizational interests.

The Huntington hypothesis, however, is not without its supporters. In his book *The New Cold War? Religious Nationalism Confronts the Secular State* Mark Juergensmeyer notes a rise in religious nationalism, which he interprets as a reaction to the failure of secular nationalism to deal with corruption, excessive materialism, the decline in moral values and state inefficiency. The religious nationalist, Juergensmeyer claims, sees no divide between faith and politics or need for the separation of Church and State. Islamists, Buddhists, Sikhs, militant Hindus, Christians and Zionists all seek to root the legitimacy of political authority in religious principles. The conflicts that this fundamental divide can engender between communities can be impossible to resolve according to Juergensmeyer as they are based on value systems that are contradictory.

My own assessment is that Huntington's paradigm, as he himself acknowledges, was aimed primarily at reshaping western and in particular the United States' foreign policy.[30] This end goal, I fear, led him to present his argument in an over-simplified manner. The lack of nuances and the questionable assumptions on both the conflict-enhancing differences *between* and the homogeneity *within* the civilizations distracts from the more valuable insight that *religion* is indeed a salient factor that can increase the risk of conflict. On this point Huntington displays the intellectual courage to challenge the reductionist mindset that dominated the social and political sciences for the best part of the twentieth century and that has refused to recognize religion's capability to have an impact on its own. In overstating the argument that the religious factor needs to be taken more seriously as a potential cause of conflict Sam Huntington has allowed his critics to avoid addressing their own neglect of such a crucial factor in conflict analysis, resolution and prevention.

Paul Collier, the Director of the Development Economics Research Group at the World Bank, offers an equally controversial but radically different analysis for the causes of conflict and civil strife. He claims that conflicts are far more likely to be caused by economic opportunities, the chance to get rich, than by grievance or religious divisions. He draws this conclusion from the research that he and a team of fellow economists have done on some 160 countries and 78 civil wars between 1960 and 1999. Testing what they call their 'greed theory' that focuses on a group's ability to finance rebellion and to benefit from it, against a 'grievance theory' that looks at ethnic and religious divisions, political repression and economic inequality, they conclude that the greed motive for rebellion considerably outperforms grievance.[31]

The greed theory is based on a statistical analysis that identifies low income, a slow rate of economic growth and a dependency on primary commodities such as diamonds, oil, timber and even drugs as the most powerful explanations for the likelihood of civil war. The evidence that conflicts occur overwhelmingly in countries with low income, a high dependence on their natural resources and large numbers of young men that have little or no opportunity to better themselves leads Collier to conclude that the best way to reduce the likelihood of conflict is to promote rapid economic change in these countries,[32] and to prevent rebel groups from growing rich through export of looted commodities.

For a rebellion to be viable, he argues, insurgents need to be able to finance their military campaign. The three most common sources of funding he identifies are the extortion of primary commodity exports such as diamonds, donations from compatriots living abroad that are sympathetic to the rebel cause but who themselves do not have to suffer the direct consequences of the violence, and support from countries who for ideological or other political reasons are hostile towards the indigenous government. It is the presence of 'lootable' commodities, large quantities of natural resources, he found, that provides the best opportunity for financial viability and increases substantially therefore the risk of conflict.[33] The fact that these commodities are tied to a single spot, a diamond mine or a coffee plantation, makes them an easier target for rebels to commandeer. It is this ability to seize, loot and to export such resources that explains for Collier many of the current and former civil conflicts. He quotes the capture of rich diamond mines by rebels in Sierra Leone as an example. Their ability to sell their looted diamonds abroad, he maintains, was one of the main reasons why the rebels were able to prolong the internal conflict that claimed so many lives in that war-torn country. The fact that civil wars create economic opportunities for a minority to get rich quick and often at the expense of the majority leads Collier to conclude that the main motivation behind rebellion is simply greed. The claim that they are fighting to right grievances Collier sees as providing rebel organizations with a convenient cover for their true motives. It allows them to recruit more easily and to enjoy a better public image at home and abroad. 'Hence, even where the rationale at the top of the organization is essentially greed, the actual discourse may be entirely dominated by grievance.'[34] The only way to discover their true motivation, he claims, is to observe their behaviour.

Statistical evidence, he argues, does not support at least globally the commonly held presumption of a strong correlation between income and land inequality or political repression and an increased risk of civil conflict. Moreover, according to his findings, the more a society is fractionalized into different ethnic and religious groups, the less the likelihood of conflict. A rebel force that fails to achieve a sense of common identity and internal unity within a short period of time risks defeat by a government that can use the powerful rhetoric of nationalism to rally its troops. The need for cohesion Collier sees as a real constraint on the ability of a rebel group to recruit within an ethnically and religiously diverse society.

However, the presence of a high proportion of young men in a society increases the risk of conflict as, according to Collier, it makes recruitment easier. This is especially true if they have no other opportunity to earn an income. Collier illustrates this point by looking at what happened in the Russian civil war in which both the White and Red armies had huge problems with recruitment and desertion. The desertion rate rose by ten times in the summer because their recruits, who were mainly peasants, could earn much more during harvest time than during winter. Today Collier's findings indicate that it is education that can make a significant difference to the rebels' ability to recruit among young men. Each year of education reduces the risk of conflict by around 20 per cent.

Collier's reason for claiming that the grievance theory is so out of tune with what he sees as the actual pattern of conflict is simply that it overlooks what social scientists call the 'collective action problem'. He argues that there are three dimensions to this problem. First is the free-rider mentality: no matter how angry people may feel about their grievances against those in authority, the human tendency is to 'free ride' and to leave the fighting to others. People are happy to enjoy the benefits of change without having contributed to the process. Second is what he calls the problem of 'co-ordination' in the sense that rebellions usually start small but many people are reluctant to join them out of a fear of punishment until they seem large enough to be assured of success. Third is the awareness that a rebel leader may promise more than he is prepared to deliver when he gains power. The fact that they have to fight before they can put this to the test may mean that many would-be recruits may be reluctant to trust him to keep his word. Collier sees the combination of these three factors as posing a formidable obstacle to rebellions that are motivated purely by grievance.

The only way, according to Collier, that a rebel leader can overcome the collective action problem is by building what the social scientists call 'social capital'. This simply means that one has to develop trust between people by forming networks and clubs that will give them the opportunity to socialize and work together. Collier sees this problem as an added reason why ethnic and religious diversity in a society reduces the risk of rebellion. Social capital building, he claims, does not usually span ethnic and religious divides. In highly fractionalized societies, therefore, it is much harder to mobilize large numbers of people than in homogenous societies. He acknowledges that it may be possible to mobilize the people within a par-ticular 'ethnic-cum-religious' group, but if this is only a small part of the overall population, the prospects of victory are poor and so the prospects of rectifying grievances are poor. Grievance-motivated revolts by small minorities are in his judgement likely to be 'quixotic', in other words completely out of touch with reality, and therefore unlikely to succeed.

The greed theory assesses the odds for civil conflicts primarily on eco-nomic factors. If there is a real opportunity to grow rich quick and the price is right; if there is sufficient loot in terms of natural resources to make the risk worth taking; if the local economy is dysfunctional and there is a large population of unemployed and uneducated young men that can provide low cost labour, then the likelihood of civil war in a country is increased significantly. Some of Collier's colleagues, however, have challenged his findings. A subsequent World Bank report *How Much War Will We See?* examined the statistical analysis upon which the greed theory is based, and concluded that more importance should be given to political rights than Collier acknowledges. The authors of this report advocate that the best way to prevent future civil wars is to act simultaneously to promote political reform, poverty reduction and economic diversification. But given the unlikelihood of achieving all three at once, they conclude that it is more important to prioritize political liberalization rather than economic development as a strategy for preventing future civil wars. Their reason for this is that the starting conditions in the countries that are most vulnerable to civil wars are such that the effects of any economic reforms would take a long time to be felt by the population at large. The pace of political reforms toward better governance and improved political rights, however, could be accelerated more easily.[35]

The Collier-Hoeffler paradigm, despite the reservations expressed in the follow-up report by their colleagues form the World Bank, has a seductive sense of simplicity and logic that appeals to that most basic human instinct – self-interest. Rebellions need money as well as people who have something to gain from their involvement. The greed theory, though, fails to address in my opinion the critical question of how do you judge motivation? Collier and Hoeffler recognize this problem, at least implicitly, when they acknowledge in their report that the question of whether the opportunity to seize natural resources directly motivates rebellion or simply provides the critical finance that facilitates the violent pursuit of other objectives, is beyond the scope of their study. Despite this shortcoming they stand by their conclusion that the evidence points in favour of the greed motive as the presence of exportable primary commodities greatly increases the likelihood of civil conflict in a country.[36]

Those religious leaders that may be tempted to take comfort from the greed theory in the sense that it exonerates religion from being a primordial cause of conflict, need to keep in mind that the Collier-Hoeffler research limited itself to conflicts which fit within the accepted definition of a civil war.[37] Conflicts, for example, like Northern Ireland or Israel where religious differences are a pertinent factor were not included. Those tempted to accept greed paradigm as the most plausible cause for conflict – the belief that the selfish gene trumps any sense of self-sacrifice for a higher cause – still need to explain what motivated the perpetrators of the September 11 attacks on New York and Washington. It would be difficult to comprehend their actions if they and the network behind them were motivated solely by greed and by a sense of grievance and not religious conviction, misguided as these may be.

Ted Gurr, the Director of the Minorities at Risk Program at the University of Maryland that monitored 275 politically active ethnic and communal groups in the 1990s, rejects both the primordial and instrumental explanations for the explosion of post Cold War conflicts centred on ethnicity. The primordial explanation is based on the view that ethnic identities are more fundamental and persistent than loyalties to larger social units. The instrumental explanation holds that ethnic identities are no more salient than any other kind of identity: they only become significant when mobilized by political entrepreneurs in the pursuit of material or political benefits for the group or the region.[38] Single factor explanations that focus on ancient hatreds or cultural differences should be avoided, Gurr argues, as their significance lies solely in the fact that they are invoked by contemporary ethnopolitical leaders seeking to mobilize support. For him there is a clear causal link between grievance and rebellion.

'Discrimination and repression against national and minority peoples are a pervasive source of poverty and resentment and provide strong incentives for ethnopolitical mobilization, protest and rebellion,' Gurr maintains. He identifies economic and political discrimination, cultural restrictions, loss of autonomy, government repression, group capacity for collective action, territorial concentration, external support, regime instability, and democratic, autocratic and incoherent policies as significant risk factors for conflict in a heterogeneous and multi-ethnic society.

In the fifty-two most serious ethnopolitical conflicts that Gurr studied in 1993–4, he identified the main issue to be the contention for state or political power among communal groups. He found this was especially true in the immediate aftermath of major political changes. In all of these conflicts Gurr discovered one or more of the contenders defined themselves by communal criteria.[39] Their claims, made on behalf of the collective interests of their group reflected their material, political, cultural, linguistic and religious concerns. He rejects the argument that the significance of cultural identity is unimportant as what really motivates the leaders and group members is a personal quest for material benefits and power. A decisive factor for Gurr is that ethnopolitical groups organize around their shared identity and seek gains or redress grievances for the collectivity or the group as a whole. People who follow the likes of Slobodan Milosevic do so, he argues, because they feel that militant nationalists best serve their collective interests.

Gurr accepts that identities based on a belief in common descent, shared experiences and cultural traits are social constructions that can vary over time; they can be created as well as recreated by force and differential treatment. These identities, he claims, are none the less real and not only endure over time but also provide the bases for mobilization and action to redress grievances or to protect self-interests. Their salience at a given time depends upon a group's social and political circumstances. 'Treat a group differently, by denial or privilege, and its members become more self-conscious about their common bonds and interests. Minimize the differences, and communal identification becomes less significant as a unifying principle.'[40] The greater the competition and inequalities among groups in heterogeneous societies, he contends, the greater the salience of ethnic identities and the greater the likelihood of open conflict. When conflict erupts, the opposing groups, he claims, become even more conscious of their differences and at the same time more aware of the common interests of their own group. The longer the conflict goes on, the stronger and more exclusive the group identities become. Groups that are proportionately large and are concentrated in a particular region with a history of political autonomy frequently adopt an ethnonationalist agenda as their goal and set their sights on either independence or extensive regional autonomy. Indigenous groups also seek autonomy as, according to Gurr, they see political independence as the most effective way of protecting their land, resources and culture from the state builders and developers.

Gurr examines both Huntington's clash of civilizations hypothesis and Juergensmeyer's fundamental divide between religious and secular nationalism.[41] He asks whether or not ethnopolitical conflicts in which one or both protagonists are religious nationalists have become more frequent and intense. He asserts that he could find no evidence that either religious or civilizational cleavages were becoming more important as a source of ethnopolitical conflicts.[42] The results of more recent research seem to confirm these findings for, although he acknowledges that religious identity leaves less room for compromise and religious minorities are targets for systematic discrimination in a number of Islamic states, he found ' ... no strong supporting evidence, direct or indirect, from studies that there is a connection between religion in general or Islam in particular and the occurrence of severe conflict'.[43] Equally surprisingly he found material inequalities to be an underlying issue in some ethnonational conflicts but not a strong driving force. He warns, though, that it would be unwise all the same to underestimate the importance of economic factors because 'conflicts tend to be more numerous and intense in regions and countries where systemic poverty is greatest'.[44]

Gurr maintains that a key factor determining the dynamics of a communal conflict is the initial response of the regime or government in power. His observation from case studies that escalate from protest to rebellion is that the intervening years are 'mostly characterized by inconsistent and expedient state policies, often a mix of limited and partly implemented reforms with repression'. The problem, according to Gurr, is that governments frequently regard the claims of cultural identity groups for greater recognition or autonomy as a threat to security and the overall identity of the state. Severe repression, he found, may have a short-term effect but it is substantially more likely to intensify than contain conflicts over contested identities; eventually repression gives rise to 'enduring legacies of anger and resentment' that lead to retaliation.[45] Groups that are subjected to repression wait and work for future opportunities to rebel.

It is not always easy, Gurr found, to draw an absolute distinction between protest and rebellion as ethnopolitical groups can alternate or use both of these strategies simultaneously. A group's options are often determined by its salience, the strength of its incentives for action, its cohesion, the authenticity and skilfulness of its leadership, and empowering ideals such as minority or indigenous rights. The interplay between these components can determine the capacity for political action as well as the intensity and length of a communal conflict. The extent to which people differ culturally from other communal groups with whom they interact, their relative social and political advantages or disadvantages, their comparative sense of superiority or inferiority and the intensity of past or ongoing conflicts with rival groups and the State are, in Gurr's model for analyzing conflict, important factors in determining the salience of people's ethnocultural identity at any point in time.[46]

Gurr found that incentive for collective action by ethnopolitical groups is enhanced by a combination of disadvantages and overtly discriminatory policies. A group's resentment is focused on those who are held responsible for such policies. Past losses and the fear of future losses can feed these resentments. The desire for political autonomy and other relative gains he identifies as additional important factors in the causal link from grievance to rebellion. The greater the shared incentives the more likely that the group will support and participate in political action. The range of action can be from conventional politics to strikes, non-violent direct action and demonstrations to open rebellion and conflict. It begins with mobilization, the process by which people are recruited into movements or action groups. What happens next depends on the opportunities for action offered by the political environment and the tactical skills of the leadership.

The role of the leadership throughout the process Gurr recognizes as critical. Skilful leaders are able to utilize a group's cultural identity and values and its common grievances and aspirations to mobilize people for action. He distinguishes between established leaders and entrepreneurial leaders. The former have what he describes as intrinsic authenticity by virtue of their position. They control resources, manage collations and articulate the group's interests and demands. It is easier for them to overcome the collective action problem and to bridge internal divisions. They can strengthen the ties that unite the group and help its members to identify more clearly their shared interests. To retain their authenticity within the group they cannot deviate from or reinvent the established goals for the group's existence. Wrong words or misguided action can lead to a loss of their credibility. Entrepreneurial leaders, whom Gurr describes as more often risk-takers attracting a following by dramatic personal acts of resistance, have a much harder task in achieving group cohesion and inspiring collective action.[47] These leaders, according to Gurr, are more likely to articulate what he calls 'frames'[48] that give people a new sense of hope and power. They are quick to capitalize on errors by their established counterparts and are more likely to appeal to people who are dissatisfied with the longer-established leaders and movements.

Gurr can find no simple explanation for the decline observed in the number and the intensity of ethnopolitical conflict since 1992. Part of the reason he suspects may be that democratic and non-democratic regimes alike have learnt to employ a wider range of techniques to accommodate, deter and co-opt 'communal challengers'. The international community has also been more proactive in its preventative diplomacy and peacekeeping efforts. None the less, Gurr warns that many of the preconditions still persist and others can be reinvented.

In his book *From Voting to Violence*, Jack Snyder, the Chair of the Political Science Department of Columbia University, agrees with Gurr that cultural differences and ancient hatreds are not in themselves responsible for the marked increase in civil conflicts since the end of the Cold War. These explanations provide western politicians, he claims, with the excuse not to get involved on the grounds that such conflicts are hopelessly intractable. In support of his argument he points to the fact that the Serbs and the Croats never fought each other until the twentieth century and then largely because 'the Nazis installed an unrepresentative regime of murderers in Zagreb'[49]. The clash of civilizations theory, he argues, can delude those wanting to promote liberal democracy globally into thinking that the major obstacle in achieving their goal is these 'aged old ethnic prejudices'. The irony of this argument for Snyder is that the process of democratization itself can have violent side effects. The American foreign policy of the 1990s was shaped by the belief that, since no two democracies have ever fought a war against each other, democracy was the antidote to war and civil strife. To promote democracy was to promote peace. What the policy failed to recognize, Snyder argues, were the risks involved in the process itself. Consequently, the 1990s turned out to be 'a decade of both democratization and chronic nationalist conflict'.[50]

The greatest risk in a period of transition from autocratic to democratic rule, according to Snyder's theory, comes from the old military, social and cultural elites who feel threatened by the loss of power and who seek to harness popular nationalist sentiments to thwart the process. These elites commonly seek to exclude their political opponents, the working classes, rival elites and ethnic minorities by alleging that these groups lack 'the proper national credentials' and are a threat to national security as they are in league with foreign powers. They therefore justify the suppression of democratic rights and the freedom of speech on the grounds that they are protecting the nation from its 'enemies within'.[51] This exclusionary nationalism, Snyder maintains, is most likely to prevail in poor countries where people lack the skills to participate in the political process and where political institutions and the standards of journalism are weakest. In such circumstances threatened elites find it easier to use the nationalist ticket to hijack the political discourse and to hold on to power. Conflicts arise, he argues, as a by-product of efforts on the part of elites to persuade people to act upon divisive nationalist ideas.

Snyder's main conclusions from his comparative studies on historical and contemporary transitions to democracy are that 'uncontrolled conflict is more likely when mass participation increases before civic institutions have been extensively developed' and that 'trouble is more likely when elites are highly threatened by democratic change ... than when elites are guaranteed a satisfactory position in the new order'.[52] The way to avoid the risk of conflict, Snyder concludes, is first to establish civic institutions that can help to channel greater participation by the people and to ensure that elites are 'buffered' from the effects of change. To promote democratization without heeding the risks, Snyder condemns as 'self-indulgent idealism'.

Although both Gurr and Snyder acknowledge that there is a religious factor in many conflicts, like Collier neither of them considered religion as a serious enough actor to merit particular interest in their research. Their paradigms reflect the reductionist approach to conflict that prevails within the social and political sciences. Reductionists always seek the simplest explanation for conflict. As religion is considered to be a redundant factor in life, an epiphenomenon that is incapable of having its own independent impact on the social and political level, it does not merit, therefore, being taken seriously as a real cause. In sharp contrast Huntington over-emphasizes the potential of religion to shape contemporary culture and therefore to be a primal cause of conflict. In applying the creed, greed and grievance theories to contemporary civil conflicts it becomes clear that no one theory in itself is capable of providing a convincing explanation for the root cause of these conflicts. Each theory provides an important insight, a piece of the jigsaw that needs to be kept in focus as we navigate the complexities of causes and the interplay of motives that make so many of these contemporary conflicts appear at the very least to be intractable. Economic and political discrimination, injustice, scarce and unequal access to essential resources are 'all factors that make people more receptive to ethnic and nationalistic appeals'.[53]

In *The Myth of "Ethnic Conflict": Politics, Economics, and "Cultural" Violence* Beverly Crawford asks the question, 'Why is it that some ethnic and religious problems are solved peacefully, others remain unsolved but do not erupt into violence, and still others seek resolution in violent conflict?'[54] The fact that Bulgarian Muslims possess different cultural characteristics from Bulgarian Christians, and Ajaris see themselves as culturally different from Georgians and yet they managed to negotiate the political transition and to live peacefully together leads her to reject primordial explanations that claim, 'the urge to define and reject the other goes back to our remotest human ancestors' and 'accumulated hatreds' erupt once the grip of central control is relaxed.

Based on the findings of a comparative study of twelve culturally, politically, socially and religiously diverse countries, she argues that cultural differences such as language, religion, customs and ethnicity lead to conflict only when they have become 'politically charged'. This happens when cultural (religious) identity becomes 'a criterion for discrimination and privilege in struggles over the distribution of political and economic resources, rights and protection'.[55] Her conclusion, therefore, is that state institutions play a critical role in 'easing, perpetuating, or triggering cultural conflict by structuring incentives in ways that either exacerbate or attenuate the political relevance of cultural identity'. 'Weak institutions', she writes, 'permit political entrepreneurs to exploit those divisions in ways that lead to violence.'[56] This is particularly true she found where economic hardships have fallen disproportionately on one distinctive cultural group, thus providing 'a concrete justification for political grievances', and where prior to weakening or collapse states had politicized culture. The two examples given are Abkhazia and Yugoslavia, where ethnic and religious cleavages had been deeply politicized and, as a consequence, violence had been intense and protracted.[57] Strong and supportive institutions that promote social integration, she concludes, can help to prevent violence by channelling cultural claims into non-violent political competition.

The promotion of democracy, power sharing and economic growth will undoubtedly help to lessen the likelihood of ethnic or religious conflict in a multi-ethnic religiously diverse society. These factors in themselves are insufficient, though, to guarantee against the kind of violence that is motivated solely by religious conviction that justifies killing in the name of a higher cause. In the following chapters I will expand on this point with examples of how religion has always demonstrated a propensity for violence regardless of the social and political conditions of its devotees.

2

Religion Matters

People tend to react in one of two ways to headlines that link religion and violence. They either exaggerate religion's role, denouncing it as the root cause of all conflict, or they deny that 'real' religion could be responsible in any way for indiscriminate violence. Those who overstate the religious factor blame religion for the intolerance and sectarianism that so often leads to violence against those labelled as 'other'. They regard religion as a negative force in a secularized society and frequently argue in favour of curtailing or completely eradicating its influence. Richard Dawkins is a good example. He argues the case against religion on what he considers to be the irrational fact that the overwhelming majority adopt the religion of their parents, and yet despite the arbitrary nature of this hereditary factor they believe in their religion 'often with such fanaticism that they are prepared to murder people who follow a different one'. Dawkins is not alone in his scorn. Two days after the 9/11 terrorist attacks on the United States, when the religious motives of the hijackers were evident, I was asked by a presenter on the BBC's *Today* programme, 'Should not all religion be banned from public life as it is clearly a dangerous influence?' The question was asked in earnest. I suspect the presenter who put the question to me felt exasperated by the number of high profile religious and political figures who had appeared on the programme in the previous forty-eight hours wishfully declaring that these atrocities had nothing to do with religion, while the evidence clearly indicated the opposite.

The same week I took part in a seminar at Harvard at which the main speaker was the highly respected Jordanian journalist, Rami Khouri. His rationalization for what had happened on 9/11 was simply Arab anger. The terrorists were, he claimed, a fringe group who acted out of the deep sense of frustration and anger that the whole Arab world feels at what they see as

American arrogance, hypocrisy, self-interest and partiality in dealing with conflicts in the Middle East and elsewhere in the Muslim world. It would be 'immoral', he declared, to allege that these atrocities were motivated by religion. His analysis endorsed the comments of the American Muslim leaders who were keen to disassociate their religion from such unwarranted violence.

The post 9/11 coalitions of liberal commentators, religious leaders and politicians, all of whom were keen to exonerate religion from any form of responsibility for what had happened, reminded me of the response to the first outbreak of sectarian violence in Northern Ireland. In 1970 church leaders were united in declaring that, whatever might be the causes, religion was not to blame. Liberal and academic opinion endorsed this view, pointing to Britain's colonial record in Ireland as the real explanation for the conflict between Catholics and Protestants.[1] It took several hundred deaths before an inter-church working party finally acknowledged that religious identity and centuries of unchallenged sectarianism were, and for that matter still are, a real issue in the Northern Ireland conflict. The secular endorsement of the claim that faith is not to blame for any of the current-day atrocities stems from a deeply ingrained conviction that religion by itself is incapable of inspiring such actions. To focus on religious motives, many political and social scientists would argue, is to risk masking over the real cause, which they would claim is more likely to be a mix of grievance and political ambition.[2]

The eagerness of religious leaders to repudiate and disclaim atrocities committed by their co-religionists is no doubt prompted by an understandable fear that violence linked to religion portrays a distorted image of their faith. The scapegoating of the perpetrators by labelling them as political criminals or misguided fanatics has become a common mechanism used by leaders of all faiths to protect what they believe to be the purity and integrity of their religion. The denial that there is a problem, whether it be consciously or unconsciously, is in itself part of the problem. It allows religious leaders to circumvent the fact that all the main faith traditions have a violent and bloody record that needs to be acknowledged and addressed to avoid the risk of repetition. Today's violent activists, as we will see in a later chapter, have numerous exemplars within their own faith traditions that provide the kind of religious sanction they need to justify their own use of violence.

Reactions that either over exaggerate or underplay the role of religion in conflict fail to do justice to the complexity of faith-linked terrorism. Most of the sound-bite analyses, given in the immediate aftermath of 9/11 were equally far too one-dimensional. Claims that we were witnessing a rejection of modernity and globalization or the pursuit of a kind of 'apocalyptic nihilism' are partial truths that fail to address the core of the problem, which lies within how faith-inspired terrorists perceive their religion, and in particular how they understand the process of revelation that lies behind their sacred texts.

Whatever their particular religious beliefs and customs, today's faith-inspired terrorists hold in common the belief that their scriptural or foundational texts were dictated verbatim by a divine authority and as such are beyond interpretation. The word as it is written must be obeyed. The fact that they are always selective in their choice of texts and tend to focus on passages that underscore their exclusive claim to truth and superiority over others whilst ignoring passages that stress the universal nature of divine love and compassion seems not to perturb them. The documents found in luggage left behind at Boston's Logan Airport by Mohamed Atta, the alleged ringleader of the 9/11 hijackers, clearly reveal that they were acing upon deeply held religious convictions, and that they regarded what they were doing as a sacred duty, aimed at giving glory to God.

One letter reads like a pep talk in which he instructs his co-conspirators how to prepare themselves physically, mentally and spiritually for their murderous mission. They were instructed to shave excess hair from their body, to shower, to wear cologne, to rehearse in their minds their plan of action and above all to read and to reflect upon the traditional war texts in the Qur'an.

> Tame your soul, purify it, convince it, make it understand, and incite it ... bless your body with some verses of the Qur'an – this is done by reading verses into one's hands and then rubbing the hands over whatever is to be blessed – the luggage, clothes, the knife, your personal effects, your ID, your passport ... the rest is left to god, the best one to depend on ... we will all meet in the highest heaven, god willing.[3]

Mohamed Atta's will, that was among the documents found at Logan, indicates that he had been preparing himself for several years to die in the service of God and as a martyr for Islam. Far from being driven by any sense of apocalyptic nihilism, Atta and the others clearly saw themselves as God's secret agents, charged with the task of ushering in a new era of God's rule that would transform the world.

To underestimate the power of religious conviction is seriously to underestimate the threat that religiously motivated terrorism presents. The social injustices, poverty, unemployment and political repression, that leave millions dispossessed, provide unquestionably a fertile breeding ground for militant groups but these conditions are not in themselves the prime cause for why people kill in God's name. The question 'Why do they hate us?', which obsessed the American media for months after the 9/11 attacks, assumed that the prime motive for these attacks was grievance. The perceived partiality of United States policy in the Middle East and its apparent willingness to prop up autocratic regimes that serve America's best interests may well be the root cause of a deep anger and rage among Arab populations but it is not the sole cause for the attacks that we witnessed on 9/11. To accept the common assumption that the hijackers were driven solely by a fanatical hatred rather than the sense of a higher mission is to lose sight of the fact that people were killing in God's name before the coming of modernity, secularism, globalization, cosmopolitanism and even the founding of the United States of America. Religiously motivated terrorism is not a new phenomenon.

The conflict in Kashmir cannot be blamed on globalization or American foreign policy. Likewise the roots of the rise of an intensely intolerant strain of Islam are deeper than just a reaction to the existence of Israel, the autocracy of Arab regimes, illiteracy and widespread destitution in the region. The same is true of other faith traditions currently involved in conflict. The social and political milieu can and often does provide the trigger for sectarian violence but these are not the fundamental causes for religious intolerance and violence in the world today.

The contemporary mindset of the political and academic world of conflict analysis and resolution sees no role for religion as it has been shaped by the belief that the seventeenth-century Treaty of Westphalia combined with the Enlightenment had banished religion once and for all from the international agenda. The 'secularization thesis' that dominates today's political thinking is based on the premise that the decline in religion is an irreversible process. The Enlightenment, secularists argue, challenged the old religious certainties, making science the new paradigm of understanding the world. Religion lingers as a comforting myth providing support in times of personal crisis but in effect, they argue, it has been relegated from 'the mainstream to the backwaters', and it has ceased to have impact on the social or political life of modern society.[4] Religion therefore is seen as an epiphenomenon – it represents something other than what it appears to be – and as such, they maintain, it could not be a real cause for conflict.

The argument that religion is 'other than what it appears to be' is not new in the sense that it even predates the Enlightenment. The Greek philosophers had argued that, unlike 'their own rationally purified concept of the One', other gods were mere projections or objectifications of people's imaginations and desires. The great fourth-century Christian apologist, Augustine of Hippo, used similar arguments to dismiss the pagan gods who he claimed were no more than projections of sexual desires that were used to legitimate 'lascivious' human behaviour. Tibetan Buddhism advised, especially the dying, to look upon 'gods and devils alike' as no more than 'dream images' and 'projections of inner karmic forces' to which one should avoid wanting to hold on.[5]

Thinkers like Marx, Freud and Durkheim who helped to shape modern political and social theory were greatly influenced by the projection theories that saw the gods as nothing other than an objectification of human needs and desires that had assumed an authority and control over the original subject. Religion, they and others argued, is a social construct, the product of particular social conditions, which when changed will eradicate the need for religion. Marx looked upon religion as an economic tool, an ideology that legitimized social oppression. Freud regarded religion as a psychological illness, a neurosis that dehumanized people because, among adults, it was rooted in the wish to be able to feel as an adult the same sense of security against external threats that a father provided in childhood.[6] Durkheim saw in religion nothing other than 'society worshipping itself' – the reality behind religion was not God but society.[7]

The thoughts of Marx, Freud and Durkheim remain influential in shaping contemporary political and social theory and especially on the question of religion. Their psychological and socio-economic explanations still hold sway. The belief that secularization is the inevitable consequence of modernization despite growing evidence that it may be in retreat,[8] is still used to support the 'reductionist' argument that seeks to reduce what appears complex to something more simple. When this theory is used to analyze conflicts religion is measured to be nothing more than a surrogate for political power and ambition, an effective mobilizing force that can help to gain the advantage over rivals in the competition for land or loot but not in itself a cause for conflict.

Some sociologists are beginning to question the secularization thesis, arguing that it is built on the assumption that there once existed a 'golden age' of religion like, for example, the Middle Ages or the nineteenth century for Christianity. Alan Aldridge argues that 'the religiosity of those periods has been greatly overstated in order to point a contrast with an exaggeratedly secular present. In the past many people went to church and obeyed its authority not because they were devout but because they had no choice.'[9] Too much attention, he fears, is paid to formal religious organizations, which he acknowledges have indeed lost many of their social functions, whilst 'latent religiosity' or the 'believing without belonging' phenomenon is overlooked. Aldridge accuses secularists of reinterpreting the evidence to fit their theory. They see, for example, ecumenical co-operation between denominations as a sign of internal weakness and something that will merely accelerate the process of religious decline. Revival movements are dismissed as 'shallow and disruptive'. The collapse of communism, they maintain, robs religion of its protest role, and the resurgence of Islam is dismissed as 'a temporary stage of social development' that will be reversed with the advance of modernization. The treatment of evidence, he concludes, seems to indicate that 'what we are dealing with is not a testable scientific theory after all, but an anti-religious ideology – one that dramatically protects itself against the force of any evidence whatsoever'.[10] This speculation may or may not be true. The fact, though, that religion does not easily fit the standards of 'empirical measurement'[11] to which social scientists are accustomed, makes it difficult to judge their objectivity as well as their ability to interpret religious data.

The extent to which the secularization thesis still prevails in academic circles was clearly demonstrated in the response to a talk given at Harvard in 2001 by the former *Guardian* correspondent in Tehran and author on Islamic fundamentalism, Genevieve Abdo. Her thesis, which was based on her experience of living in Iran for more than ten years and from her prolonged dialogues with many of the main religious and political protagonists, was simply that the main cause for the feuding among members of the government and the tensions on the street that the country was then experiencing stemmed from a fundamental theological dispute between senior religious figures. Her argument was immediately dismissed by those who regarded religion as a distraction and who saw the struggle for power between reformers and hardliners as the real cause for the political unrest. The death sentenced passed a year later on one of Iran's leading academics, Hashem Aghajari, who was accused of apostasy for suggesting 'a Shia version of Europe's Protestant Reformation' seems to verify Abdo's argument that the religious interpretation of texts and tradition is at the core of the current political conflict.[12]

In June 2002, I encountered a similar mindset when I visited the offices of the European Commissioner responsible for the European Union's programmes for conflict prevention and resolution. The suggestion that the EU should consider broadening their criteria to include religion among the causes of ethnic and sectarian strife brought the same response from all the officials with whom I met. Religion, I was told, was a mask and not a real cause for conflict. Jihad, I was informed, was a political creed that had appropriated religious language and sentiments to further its own revolutionary aims. It soon became clear to me that the reductionist theory, either consciously or unconsciously, is still a dominant factor in the minds of those responsible for EU policy on the prevention and resolution of conflict.

The combination of Westphalia and the Enlightenment may have been 'a double whammy for religion' but it certainly was not lethal. The Treaty of Westphalia, signed at the end of the seventeenth century, succeeded in putting an end to the pitch battles over beliefs that had marred inter-state relationships in Europe for most of that century. The claim that it removed once and for all the influence of religion from international politics is more questionable. It could be argued that by domesticating or nationalizing belief – the motto being that the faith of the ruler is the faith of the realm or the state – Westphalia in fact turned religion into a powerful social agent that was used to enforce the cultural identity of the colonizers as European princes and governments expanded their rule to embrace the countries of Africa and Asia. Sinhala Buddhists in Sri Lanka and the BJP, Hindu nationalist party, in India argue that the British colonial policies that favoured one group over another, a practice aimed at restricting the religious hegemony they enjoyed prior to colonization, ultimately sowed the seeds of their present conflicts. Similar arguments have been made to explain the current sectarian violence between Christians and Muslims on the Spice Islands. It is claimed that a root cause of the present conflict stems from the Dutch practice of promoting over other groups locals who converted to Christianity.[13]

The impact of the Enlightenment may also have been over exaggerated in the sense that secularist argument seems to confuse religious practice with faith. In an age when people are no longer obliged to conform to the cultural norms and expectations of society, the phenomenon of believing without feeling a need to belong to a community or to practise a particular faith makes it more difficult for social scientists to evaluate the real impact of religion on community or tribal life. To quote Aldridge, 'Latent religiosity survives as a resource to be mobilised at times of crisis in the lives of individuals or the history of the society.'[14] The scale and form of the public reaction to the untimely death of Princess Diana, it could be argued, was an expression of 'latent religiosity'.

Samuel Huntington's assertion that 'this is the new age of religion'[15] may prove to be a premature exaggeration but without question the mid 1970s marked a turning point for religion as new faith-inspired movements became more aggressive in their efforts to promote their revived brand of Hinduism, Judaism, Christianity and Islam. 'The theme', to quote the French academic Gilles Kepel, 'was no longer *aggiornamento* but a second evangelization of Europe: the aim was no longer to modernize Islam but to Islamize modernity.'[16] Kepel attributes this revival in religion's fortunes to 'a worldwide discrediting of modernism'. In his book The *Revenge of God* he examines the renewal movements that have emerged in the 1970s from the three Abrahamic faiths, the people of the book – Judaism, Christianity and

Islam. He discovered that many of the young educated people who were attracted to these movements are themselves 'the product par excellence of the modernity whose course they now wish to alter'.[17] Despite the diversity in faith, Kepel claims that these groups had much in common. 'They are at one in rejecting a secularism that they trace back to the philosophy of the Enlightenment,' he writes.[18] They question modern society's legitimacy. Their common complaint is the absence of values that they could own in the world that has excluded God. Their common goal is to make religion the 'foundation' of a new social order. Their common belief is that society should conform to the 'commands and values' of their sacred or foundational texts – the Hebrew Scriptures, the Qur'an, the Gospels. It is over the question of the shape of future society that these movements, according to Kepel, diverge and become 'deeply antagonistic'. Each has an identity that has been formed by exclusive claims to truth that could prove to be 'a potential for bitter conflict'.[19]

In his more recent book *Jihad: The Trail of Political Islam*, Kepel set out his controversial theory that militant Islam is in decline, claiming that the violence, which has been responsible for scaring people away from the movement, has proven to be a 'death trap' for Islamists as a whole. He argues that it has prevented Islamists from holding and mobilizing the range of constituencies they need to seize political power. 'The attack on the United States', he writes, 'was a desperate symbol of the isolation, fragmentation and decline of the Islamist movement, not a sign of its strength and irrepressible might.'[20] He supports his argument by giving examples of the movement's failure to maintain its struggle for dominance in countries like Bosnia, Algeria and Egypt. Even in Iran he claims the 1997 presidential elections demonstrated that the zeal for revolution had waned in view of the fact that vast numbers had voted in favour of a more democratic form of society. The failure of the Islamists, he asserts, lies in their inability to address the needs of ordinary Muslims and the emergence within the same group of a vision of Islam that is more compatible with the modern world. The evidence of a change, he asserts, is demonstrated by the growing number of Islamist parties from Indonesia to Morocco, who are prepared to 'set aside the sovereignty of God' and stand for election. 'Today, as Muslim societies emerge from the Islamist era, it is through openness to the world and to democracy that they will construct their future', he writes.[21] Even though he believes that the Islamist movement will find it very difficult to reverse the 'trail of decline', Kepel warns that this does not mean that we have seen the last of acts of terrorism that 'claim the mantle of jihad'.[22]

Even if Kepel is right in predicting the decline of the Islamists' cause, the seriousness of the threat that the core group of activists pose should not be underestimated. Kepel himself acknowledges that we are witnessing the emergence of a new kind of terrorist. The tradesmen, convicts and un-employed with their home-made bombs, he observes, have given away to more sophisticated, university-educated, well-off operators who 'spoke the languages and understood the cultural codes of the Western societies with-in which they moved'.[23] They have what he calls the 'paradoxical ability' to conceal their true selves and to remain deeply rooted in their extremist beliefs even when exposed to all the contradictions of western life. In keep-ing with the secularist mindset that dominates contemporary political and social scientific thought, Kepel attributes this extraordinary level of self-discipline to the ideological brainwashing they received in the Afghan training camps through which thousands of militants have passed.

Not all Islamic terrorists, however, have been trained in the Afghan net-work of camps, and yet they still share an equally strong conviction that sustains their determination to operate within western societies without betraying their fundamental values. An example par excellence is Kamil Daoudi, a young Algerian-born computer specialist who has lived most of his life in France. He has been accused of involvement in a plot to blow up the American embassy in Paris, a charge that he vehemently denies, and yet he is happy to designate himself as a 'terrorist'. Writing from his prison cell, Daoudi explains that it was the combination of anger that he felt at the French for supporting an illegitimate, one-sided regime in Algeria, and the deep sense of alienation he felt as a 'sub-citizen' in Paris that drove him to Islam. He declares that his commitment 'to fight any form of injustice and those who support it' is total. He draws his purpose in life and his inner strength from his newfound faith in Allah. He writes,

> I reviewed everything that I have learned and put all my knowledge into a new
> perspective. I then understood that the only person worth devoting my life to
> was Allah . . . Everything suddenly became clear to me and I understood why
> Abraham went into exile, why Moses rebelled against the Pharaoh, why Jesus
> was spat upon and why Muhammad said 'I came with the sword on judge-
> ment day'. My battle was and will be to eradicate all powers that are opposed
> to the law of Allah, the most high, whatever the price may be, because only our
> creator has the power to make laws and any system based on laws of men is
> artifice and lies . . . my fight will only end in my death or in my madness.[24]

The glimpse he offers into the mindset of a self-designated terrorist demonstrates that even though his rebellion against the society in which he was educated was triggered by a deep sense of grievance, it is his faith that provides the ideology that sustains him in the conviction that it is his task to change the world in accordance with the designs of God.

This incongruous mix of religious piety and homicidal behaviour is not exclusive to Islam. I recall in the summer of 1972, on a visit to friends who lived in a staunchly Catholic area of Belfast, being warned by a local community leader that I should stop talking to the young British soldiers who were on foot patrol in the area. He explained to me that even though they knew that I was a priest, and that the IRA hit men responsible for order in the locality went to mass and communion daily, they would still consider me a legitimate target if they were to suspect that I was passing information to the troops. According to my informant they would have seen no incongruity between their everyday acts of piety and their resolve to commit murder if and when required for the good of the cause. Catholic church leaders had condemned the violence, but the IRA, he told me, had the support of a number of priests who were sympathetic to their cause and who justified their use of violence on the principles of the traditional Christian just war theory that allows for killing provided that the cause is honourable and the use of force is the only option. Given what they saw to be the intransigence of the British government's support for the Protestant Loyalist ascendancy, they considered their acts of terrorism on behalf of the Catholic nationalist minority as morally legitimate.

The claim that at least some Catholic priests were actively involved with the IRA seemed to be substantiated when it was revealed in December 2002 that thirty years previously a former Northern Ireland Secretary, William Whitelaw, and the Catholic Archbishop of Armagh, Cardinal William Conway, had conspired to cover up the role of a priest in one of the worst atrocities of the Northern Ireland conflict. The evidence suggests that in July 1972 a local priest, Father Jim Chesney, played a key role in the bombing of the village of Claudy in which nine people, including an eight-year-old girl and two teenage boys, were killed and dozens more were injured. It seems that Whitelaw and Conway agreed that it would be better to move Chesney to a parish in the Irish Republic than to put him on trial for terrorism and murder.[25]

Catholic clergy are not alone in providing moral and religious justification for violence. The American Protestant clergymen, Michael Bray and Paul Hill, defend their own acts of terrorism, the burning of abortion clinics and the murder of doctors and staff, with the same argument that their cause is just. Not unlike Mohamed Atta they too were steeped in the belief that it is their duty to help establish God's law and kingdom on earth. They argue that their violence is a defensive act that helps to prevent what they regard as the 'killing of babies'. Michael Bray's moral hero is, he claims, Dietrich Bonhoeffer, the German Lutheran pastor and theologian, who was executed for his part in the plot to assassinate Hitler. For Bray, Bonhoeffer is an excellent example of a committed Christian, and yet he was someone who was prepared to condone violence and to break laws in the pursuit of a higher good.[26]

I met with a similar argument on my visit to Sri Lanka during the cease-fire in November 2002 when I was told of a Catholic priest who had given up his position as the head of an educational institute and had gone into the bush to act as advisor to the Tamil Tigers. I also met with another priest in the Jaffna region who told me that he believed that the Tamil Tigers were morally justified in continuing with their armed struggle against the Sri Lanka government if the Danish-initiated peace talks failed to secure for the Tamils independence from Singhalese control.

Christians in Indonesia also have justified the excessive use of violence by ad hoc paramilitary groups on the grounds that these activists are defending Christian interests. Ambon, the capital of the Moluccas, is a 'fault-line' city divided by competing claims of Christians and Muslims. The causes of this conflict are as complicated as elsewhere but the religious differences seem to have fuelled the intensity of the present strife. The followers of Laskar Christus, the army of Christ that is led by Agus Wattimena, a man whom *The Economist* once described as a Jesus lookalike, perceive themselves to be warriors, 'who are defending the faith'. They attribute their survival to the will of God. Their youth counterpart is known as AGAS, or church children who love God, and is also actively involved in the conflict. The youth are said to rush from school to the front line whenever the fighting breaks out between the two communities, as they see the making of bombs as 'their crusade'. In North Maluka the leader of the Christian army, Bernard Bitjara, who is better known by the nickname 'Benny Doro', also claims to be driven primarily by religious motives. He evidently believes that he was appointed to the role of commander by God and that he 'once saw Jesus Christ soaring like a bird above him while he was fighting Muslims'. In the Indonesian island of Sulawesi the 'Black Bats', a Christian paramilitary force, who claim to possess magic properties that make their Muslim enemies powerless, are said to be responsible for the abduction of children and the mutilation of hundreds of Muslims, and yet they are revered by the local Christians who see them as the defenders of 'their ancestral lands'.[27]

In the conflict that led to the NATO intervention in Kosovo the Serb forces were deliberately targeting Islamic religious institutions. It is estimated that 218 mosques and the homes of 302 imams as well as several Islamic libraries and achives were destroyed.[28] Two of the main protagonists in the earlier Balkan wars, Radovan Karadzic and Ratko Mladic, both of whom were subsequently indicted by the international tribunal in The Hague for war crimes, were honoured by the Orthodox hierarchy as examples of those who had chosen to follow 'the thorny path of Christ'. Karadzic was decorated by the Greek Orthodox Church as 'one of the most prominent sons of our Lord Jesus Christ working for peace'. High-ranking Orthodox officials also exalted on several occasions Zeljko Raznatovic Arkan, the leader of the Serb paramilitary group responsible for some of the worst atrocities of the Balkan conflict.[29]

Judaism also has its own modern-day terrorists who are prepared to murder in God's name. When Yigal Amir, the pious and articulate young Jewish university student, was arrested immediately after he had assassinated the Israeli Prime Minister, Yitzhak Rabin, in November 1995, he was said to have had no regrets and to have claimed that he had acted 'on orders from God.'[30] He later revealed that his decision to kill Rabin had been influenced by some militant rabbis who justified the killing on the grounds that the Israeli Prime Minister was putting the interests of the Jewish people at risk.[31] Rabin's chief crime seems to have been his willingness to bargain away biblical lands conquered in the Six-Day War in 1967 for peace with Israel's Arab neighbours. Amir and his supporters believe that the borders of Israel were fixed by the divine promise made to Abraham, borders which today include modern-day Egypt and Iraq. No one therefore, they believe, has the right to settle for 'borders any narrower than these'.[32] Israel, Amir is convinced, must do what it can to secure these borders and that 'God will take care of the rest.'[33] Like their Muslim and Christian counterparts these militant Jewish groups have no problem in using their religious traditions and scriptures to sanction violence in the pursuit of religious goals.[34] In 1984 the Israeli security services foiled a plot by one of these extreme groups, Gush Emunim, the religious driving force behind the settlements, to blow up the mosques on the Temple Mount in Jerusalem. Their intention was to provoke Muslim anger on such a global scale that it would lead to the ultimate war and the coming of the messiah.[35]

The incongruous mix of religious conviction and murderous intent is not confined to the Abrahamic communities of faith – Jews, Christians and Muslims. On 31 October 1984 Indira Gandhi, the Prime Minister of India, was assassinated by two of her Sikh bodyguards. Their motive was to avenge the storming of a Sikh sacred shrine, the Golden Temple at Amritsar, an action that Mrs Gandhi had ordered four months previously in an effort to halt Sikh terrorist activity. The assassination sparked off a three-day orgy of violence during which Hindus were responsible for the killing of thousands of Sikhs.

Although Hinduism with its belief in multiple incarnations of the one God and with no single founder figure or text is less structured than

Judaism, Christianity and Islam, it too in common with other faiths has groups that justify the use of violence in support of their intolerant and exclusive religious and political claims. In December 1992, a Hindu mob with sledgehammers, crowbars and their bare hands razed to the ground the sixteenth-century Babri mosque in Ayodhya, claiming that it had been erected on the site of a Hindu temple that marked the birthplace of Ram, an incarnation of the Hindu god Vishnu. The mosque's destruction and the determination of the World Hindu Council to erect a *mandir* (temple) on the site have fuelled a decade of bloodletting between Hindus and Muslims, costing thousands of innocent lives over the past decade.

Hindutva is a term that has become 'an umbrella for all sorts of right-wing Hindu nationalists groups'.[36] It embraces all those that share in common a supremacist ideology and who are committed to promote a chauvinistic form of Hinduism. Their goal is to ensure that 'The honour and the interests of Hindus will be protected in every manner.'[37] For them Hindu interests are synonymous with national interests. They are committed to protect their culture, heritage and religion from foreign influences. They accuse Muslims and Christians of wilfully demeaning Hindus. They violently oppose religious conversion and are especially weary of what they describe as the proselytizing tactics of 'sari wearing nuns offering food'.[38]

They denounce the legacy of Mahatma Gandhi, who, they claim, robbed their nation of self-respect and pride through his promotion of *ahimsa*, the principle of non-violence. They regard Gandhi's assassin, Shri Nathuramji Geodes as a martyr. They believe that the source of their spiritual energy is from the mother goddess, Bharat Mata, who is manifested in the country itself. The country therefore must be worshipped as a goddess and protected from those who would harm her. They regard it as their sacred duty to restore her to her rightful place as the mother of all nations.

A modern-day faith-inspired terrorist group that succeeded in manufacturing and in using a chemical weapon is the Japanese-based Aum Shinrikyo cult that was responsible for the gas attack on the Tokyo subway in March 1995. Asahara Shoko, the founder of the sect that has its spiritual roots in Buddhism and was originally founded as a yoga and meditation group, believed that it was their 'sacred duty' to wreak vengeance on their enemies who had thwarted the sect's ambition to transform a materialistic and corrupt world by purifying it of its 'negative karma'. The need to protect the sect's sacred mission was used to justify the killing of group members who questioned the leaders' methods and the subway atrocity that resulted in the leaders' arrest and imprisonment.[39]

The situations described above are just a few examples of where religion has either directly contributed to or exacerbated civil conflicts. When reporting on the activities of these distinctly different groups of religious extremists, the media branded them all – Hindu, Sikh, Jewish, Christian, Islamic, Buddhist – fundamentalist. The late Rabbi Hugo Gryn, a good friend and colleague, who had survived the horrors of Auschwitz and spent the rest of his life campaigning against all forms of intolerance frequently complained to me about the media's use of this word. Hugo would protest that it was an inappropriate use of the word, as all believers should be considered fundamentalists to the degree that they had committed themselves to upholding the core beliefs of their own faith tradition.

The word 'fundamentalist' was first used in 1920 by a Baptist journalist to describe a group of evangelical Christians who were determined to uphold the literal truths of the Bible in the face of the onslaught of Darwinian theories of evolution and German biblical criticism that favoured a less literal interpretation of the Scriptures. In 1987 the American Academy of Arts and Sciences sponsored a six-year research project that brought together academics from around the world to study the global phenomenon of modern religious fundamentalism. After much discussion on the appropriateness of using what was essentially a western term to reflect the cultural and religious diversity of the movements under scrutiny, it was decided that there were sufficient 'family resemblances' among these groups to justify describing them in common as fundamentalist.[40] Not everyone in the academic world agreed with this decision, and certainly today an increasing number of scholars have expressed misgivings about the term 'fundamentalist' being used to describe activists and movements that are so different in their origins and goals as the examples given earlier in the chapter clearly indicate.

The American Academy of Arts and Science Project report, edited by Marty and Appleby, provides a valuable insight into the mindset of religious extremists in so far as it helps to identify several ideological and organizational characteristics that these religiously diverse groups hold in common. A concern over the erosion of religion's role in society is uppermost on each of their agendas. Their goal is to reshape society in accordance with their group's credal and ethical beliefs. They reject ideas like relativism and individualism, which they see as threats to their personal, social and religious identity, and yet they make effective use of modern technology to further their causes. They are highly selective in the parts of their tradition, heritage and sacred texts that they choose to highlight, and are absolute about the truthfulness of their interpretation of divine revelation. Their world view is tainted by a dualism that sees a clear-cut division in life between good and evil. They demonize anyone who challenges or who is indifferent to their cause. They imagine themselves as part of a larger cosmic struggle and as being actively engaged in the advent of a new messianic age. Their male, authoritarian, charismatic leaders provide mandatory norms of behaviour for those chosen or elected to belong. The groups' boundaries are clearly defined and separate the members from outsiders. They acknowledge no room for compromise either with wayward co-religionists or with outsiders in their struggle to counteract the threat to their group identity or in their struggle to impose their own monolithic religious structures and norms of behaviour on a global scale.[41]

Most fundamentalists, according to Marty and Appleby, see themselves as interpreters of history. They believe that they have the knowledge and the empowerment to direct the course of events. They perceive themselves to be the chosen ones who have been mandated by the divine to fulfil the instructions found in their tradition's sacred writings. Fundamentalists differ from the normal conservative and orthodox believers who aim to pre-serve the whole of tradition, as they understand it, by the fact that they select only those scriptural texts and episodes of history that support their claim of a divine mandate to act chauvinistically. They seek out the 'warrior deities' from their founding myths or those historical figures in their tradi-tion that justified violence in the name of their God or faith as exemplars for their own actions.[42]

Mark Juergensmeyer provides additional insight. His research findings, based on extensive interviews with many of today's most feared religiously motivated terrorist groups and published in his book, *Terror in the Mind of God*, endorses Marty and Appleby's profile of the faith-based terrorist as one who perceives himself to be engaged in a mission of transcendent importance. Juergensmeyer describes the religious terrorist as a man who is driven by an apocalyptic vision, the belief that he is fighting in that final battle between the forces of good and evil: a cosmic conflict, which allows for no compromise as he is dealing with demonic forces, and which permits him to dispense with everyday moral norms. The victims of his terrorism, Juergensmeyer claims, are simply regarded as symbols, tools, corrupt beings that can be justifiably disregarded. Anyone not belonging to the inner circle of the committed, including moderate and open-minded co-religionists, is categorized as a legitimate enemy. What may appear to be random and capricious acts of violence are constructed events, a 'perfor-mance violence' that is deliberately aimed at provoking revulsion and anger in the onlooker. Without horrified witnesses, Juergensmeyer argues, these acts would be 'as pointless as a play without an audience'.[43]

Juergensmeyer discovered that the immediate goal of the groups he inter-viewed is to demonstrate through their acts of terrorism the inability of secular authorities to control and secure public spaces. In setting out to achieve this goal the religiously motivated terrorist believes that he is reclaiming the ground for the 'spiritual' forces. What can appear to an outsider as a hopeless cause in human terms takes on new significance in his mind as he redefines the struggle in spiritual terms. The ultimate victory, he believes, is in God's hands.[44] The feeling of being part of a greater cause, Juergensmeyer claims, matters more than whether or not they think that their battle is winnable. These terrorists perceive themselves to be victims. They fear that their identity is threatened in a world that is 'stifling, chaotic and dangerously out of control'.[45]

Juergensmeyer avoids the claim that economic or social despair leads automatically to violence. On the contrary he argues that virtually everyone on the planet has experienced such hardship at some stage in his or her life. And yet the findings of his research provide a profile of the religiously motivated terrorist as a young, jobless, unmarried male who sees no way of escaping the conditions that rob him of all sense of honour and respectability. He discovered that regardless of differences in culture, religious beliefs and practices, members of groups as diverse as Hamas in the Middle East and Christian Identity in the United States share in common a sense of humiliation. Even when these terrorists do not fit into the common stereotype of being young and poor, he writes, they are still driven by a fear of being socially marginalized in the future. Religion, Juergensmeyer discovered, provides them with a sense of honour, personal pride, kinship and identity. Violence, he claims, gives them a sense of empowerment. The combination of religion and violence provides the 'antidotes to humiliation', according to Juergensmeyer. He illustrates this point by quoting what Dr Abdul Aziz Rantisi, the political head of Hamas, said regarding the actions of the suicide bombers: 'To die in this way is better than to die daily in frustration and humiliation.'[46]

Mark Juergensmeyer concludes that religiously motivated conflicts differ from their secular counterparts in what he describes as 'the transhistorical scope of their goals'.[47] The idea that one is acting for God, he claims, carries an enormous sense of power as it surpasses all claims of political authority and gives to the struggle a sense of timelessness that makes combatants less willing to compromise. They reconcile themselves to the fact that it may take centuries to achieve their objective of imposing a religious understanding and code on the secular realm. They overcome the fact that they frequently find themselves in conflict with their own faith communities by dismissing the leadership as being too cowardly and comfortable with the establishment. Juergensmeyer's judgement on these movements is that they 'are not simply aberrations but religious responses to social situations and expressions of deeply held convictions'.[48]

The combination of the Juergensmeyer and the Marty/Appleby studies of fundamentalist groups provides a helpful analysis of the religious mindset and group characteristics as well as the psychological and social conditions that attract recruits to such movements, but neither study identifies what it is exactly that ignites the fuse that transforms potential philanthropists into psychopathic killers. Juergensmeyer recognized a sense of humiliation as a common factor shared by all the extremists that he had encountered. His observation, however, does not explain why many people who are subjected to the same humiliating experiences as the terrorists do not resort to violence. I have often wondered how, for example, in Northern Ireland two people brought up in the same neighbourhood, in the same faith community, educated in the same school, with the same limited opportunities in life can respond to the sectarian conflict in distinctively different ways. What is it that attracts one young Catholic or Protestant to join the IRA or one of the Protestant paramilitary forces when another chooses to shun any contact with violence? The same question applies to those young people brought up in Palestinian refugee camps on the West Bank, Tamil-controlled areas of the Jaffna peninsula or the divided city of Ambon in the Spice Islands. Why do some take up arms and others not?

A recent book by the Polish-born psychoanalyst, Alice Miller, *The Truth Will Set You Free*, provides some helpful insights in the search for an answer to this question. She claims that the root of the problem why some people can act so violently, without feeling or conscience, lies in early childhood experiences. Rejecting the concept that some are just born 'bad', she argues that the 'capacity for empathy ... cannot be developed in the absence of loving care'.[49] Based on the neurobiological evidence that acutely traumatized children have 'severe lesions affecting 50 per cent of their brains', Alice Miller claims that when such children grow up they have a psychological need to react to the violence they were subjected to in their youth. The repressed rage of childhood, she believes, is encoded in the emotions leading victims in adulthood to seek positions where they can project similar injustices to those they had experienced on to individuals over whom they have gained power. She sees in the childhoods of both Hitler and Stalin examples that support her argument. They both suffered in their youth from daily beatings by their fathers. Racism, anti-semitism, fundamentalist fascism and ethnic cleansing, Miller argues, have their roots in early parental neglect and cruelty. 'Poverty', she writes, 'may have no adverse effect on the character of a child as long as that child's personal integrity is not damaged by hypocrisy, cruelty, abuse, corporal punishment, or psychological humiliation.'[50]

Through her analyses of the childhoods of public figures like Stalin, St

Augustine, Hitler, the writer Frank McCourt, Milosevic, Pope John Paul II and many others, a study that transcends the boundaries of culture, belief and time, she recognizes common human experiences that determine people's proclivity for good or for evil. 'Children forced to overlook the cruelty born of irresponsibility and indifference on the part of their parents', she writes, 'are in danger of blindly adopting this attitude themselves and staying bogged down in the fatalistic ideology that declares evil to be the way of the world. As adults they will retain the perspective of the helpless child with no alternative but to come to terms with its fate.'[51] The difference, she believes, can be determined by what she describes as 'enlightened witnesses' in the lives of the traumatized. These 'enlightened witnesses' she defines as therapists who have learnt to come to terms with their own history and who are therefore able to champion the cause of the once abused child. They can help the traumatized person to come to an understanding of their unhappiness and by so doing enable them to effect the sort of behavioural change that makes the difference between them becoming psychopaths or philanthropists.

Miller also accuses the religious schools of different denominations of contributing to the problem in the sense that they justify sadistic punishments like child beating as if they were divinely revealed. People who have been bought up to obey without ever being allowed to question those in authority often display, she claims, 'an astounding willingness to espouse the most abstruse ideologies of religious sects, neo-Nazi groups, or fundamentalist communities, and at the command of others (commands from others are indispensable!) will think nothing of destroying human lives and trampling on human dignity'.[52] She attributes the problem to her belief that the Bible was written by a man who was abused by a parent. This explains why God, she believes, is presented in a vengeful sadistic light. It also explains why so many churchmen throughout history have been unable to follow the example of love portrayed by Jesus and have embarked on murderous adventures like the Crusades and the Inquisition. Their actions, she believes, are symptomatic of an abused childhood.

> The image of God entertained by children who have received love is a mirror of their very first experiences. Their God will understand, encourage, explain, pass on knowledge and be tolerant of mistakes. He will never punish them for their curiosity, suffocate their creativity, seduce them, give them incomprehensible commands, or strike fear into their hearts.[53]

Alice Miller offers valuable insights into the psychological conditioning that predisposes one human being to inflict or to rationalize violence on others. St Augustine and Osama bin Laden belong to different periods of history and to different religious traditions. The fact, though, that they share in common the childhood experience of an emotionally remote father and a religious conversion after a period of morally loose living, may be a significant factor in explaining why both Augustine and bin Laden sought to justify death sentences for those judged to be heretical or unorthodox. Further research into why both men have sought to legitimize the use of violence in their personal quest for certainty in life and orthodoxy in faith may help to provide a clearer understanding of the connection between religion and violence.

The results of a research project that was jointly sponsored by the Institute for the Study of American Religion (ISAR) and Center for Studies on New Religion (CESNUR) provide a helpful perspective into the mindset and social circumstances that can trigger or ignite religiously inspired violence. *Cults, Religion and Violence* was a five-year project that focused on the connection between violence and a number of new religious movements, small obscure groups that have their roots in mainstream religious traditions like the Branch Davidians who are Christian and Aum Shinrikyo who are Buddhist in origin. The study revealed that, contrary to received wisdom, distinctly apocalyptic world views, charismatic leadership, tight internal control, intense communal solidarity and high boundaries that isolate members from broader society do not in themselves account for a group or sect's proclivity toward violence. The fact that the vast majority of religious cults and sects share these particular characteristics but do not resort to violence either against their own members or towards the outside world indicates that the causal link is more complex.[54] The report claims that it is the interaction between a number of internal and external factors that triggers the process that leads to collective acts of violence.

The endogenous violent potential of these millennial or apocalyptic type movements is actualized, the authors of the report claim, when the leadership feels under threat from negative media coverage based on accusations of former cult members and over zealous state authorities, who fearing subversion, try to curtail or control their activities.[55] It is then that the group's understanding of the world, which is rooted in a clear division between good and evil, the elect and the damned, begins to dictate their response to what they perceive as a threat to their own survival. They resort to violence in the belief that they can influence historical events. Their 'apocalyptic vision of an imminent and total transformation of the world'[56] leads them to interpret the unfolding crisis as if they were living in the 'last days' and to perceive themselves as the 'spiritual vanguard of the elect whose destiny to survive the transitional turmoil may entail a legitimation of ruthless conduct toward the less favoured worldlings'.[57] The norms and values of the broader society are regarded as irrelevant in the face of the group's 'sacred duty' to stand up and fight for truth and to wreak vengeance on its enemies. The ability of its members to carry out acts of violence and to kill without compunction, the authors claim, is made easier through the process of distancing the people on whom the violence is to be perpetrated. They come to be perceived as 'other', 'abnormal', 'not fully human' or even agents of 'Satan'.

One of the movements featured in the *Cults, Religion and Violence* study is Aum Shinrikyo, the Buddhist cult, which, as mentioned above, was responsible for the nerve gas attack on the Tokyo subway. It began in 1984 as 'a world rejecting movement' whose aim was to develop the 'spiritual consciousness' of its members through the practice of yoga and meditation, but developed within a period of ten years to become a group of paranoid killers who were prepared to annihilate thousands to ensure the success of its own self-conceived spiritual mission. The founder, Asahara Shoko, originally called Matsumoto Chizuo, who had been brought up in a state-run boarding school for the blind, and who is said to have suffered from an early sense of abandonment and discrimination, saw religion as the solution to the world's woes. He came to believe through a spiritual vision that he received that he had a special role to play in the cosmic war, the final confrontation between good and evil.[58] He believed that those who engaged in the maelstrom of ordinary society 'imbibed its negative karma' and were on the road to perdition. It was only through rejecting the world and purifying the body and mind by ascetic practices that one could achieve salvation and help the world to purify itself of negative karma to achieve a spiritual transformation.[59] What was originally perceived as a spiritual struggle, a global mission to bring about the peaceful transformation of a doomed world, took on a more sinister overtone when Shoko felt that as the world had failed to listen to him it merited destruction. He began to prophesy that by the end of the twentieth century there would be a 'catastrophic end time scenario' and that it was only by joining Aum Shinrikyo that one could be saved.[60]

In preparation for the final struggle a 'culture of coercive asceticism' took hold within the movement. He believed that members of the movement had to be made to conform for their own good. To use violence in this way required a paradigm shift because of the negative karma associated with its use. He justified the coercion and beatings on the grounds that when used by an enlightened and compassionate leader the intention was only to achieve the highest spiritual good for the victim.[61] When a follower threatened to expose the cover-up of the accidental death of one of his devotees, who died as a result of the excessive asceticism, he was killed. Asahara

Shoko justified his murder on the grounds that, if he had been allowed to wreck Aum's mission for the salvation of the world by informing the authorities, he would have incurred a terrible karma. The violence perpetrated on its own members was extended to the broader community when Aum Shinrikyo, having formed its own political party, stood for election and was humiliated by the Japanese electorate. Shoko interpreted this public rejection as a justification for taking up arms. He believed that 'the unworthy would be punished in the inevitable war to come'.[62] Everyone who was not a member of the movement was considered an enemy who could be justifiably killed to protect Aum and its mission. The external pressures on the movement in Ian Reader's judgement exacerbated the group's internal propensity to violence and drove the leadership to manufacture and stockpile the chemical weapons they would eventually use against an unsuspecting public.[63] Not all the members of the movement, however, were aware of the leadership's actions.

The report concludes with a very pessimistic prediction that, even though incidents of violence may be rare, in light of the number of groups and people involved in these new religious movements, future episodes will continue to occur and especially as state authorities seek to exercise greater control over such groups. Even though the authors did not include Al Qaeda in their research they none the less expressed the belief that like these other groups the religious dimension is integral to Al Qaeda's operation. 'Religion explains the agenda, the tenacity of its operations, even to the point of suicide.'[64] The evidence to support this assessment of the importance of religion in understanding the rationale of Al Qaeda can be found in documents that were discovered in the rubble of their offices and training camps in Afghanistan. Among the documents there was a collection of Islamic decrees that were apparently being used 'to justify and legitimize' their actions including the attacks on the World Trade Center and Pentagon.[65]

Whatever the psychological, social and political factors that trigger violence in fringe or mainstream religious bodies the religious mindset is itself an important factor that needs to be acknowledged and understood if durable solutions are to be found for many current conflicts. Religion is more than just 'a tool for protest' or 'a useful marketing ploy' to mobilize recruits for a more worldly cause. From Belfast to Belgrade, Jerusalem to Jakarta, Kashmir to Khartoum, religion is an active and potent factor in conflicts that have cost thousands of lives. The battles over dogmas that marred relationships between states in Europe for the whole century prior to the Treaty of Westphalia have modern-day resemblances in the killings perpetrated in God's name on the streets of Ahmedabad in India[66] and Kaduna in Nigeria.[67] People still feel sufficiently passionate about their beliefs to die and to kill for them. Religion is rarely the sole cause but it is central to the meaning of too many conflicts to be ignored or to be regarded as irrelevant in the analysis and search for solutions. Those who have grown to accept uncritically the 'secularization thesis' that has dominated political thinking for the best part of the past century may find it extremely difficult to understand that theology and belief can, and indeed do, shape people's political judgements. Religion is not a passive agent waiting to be ignited into a political flame by some unscrupulous political or tribal chauvinist, as Peter Berger would have us believe when he writes, 'upsurges of religion in the modern era are in most cases political movements that use religion as a convenient legitimation for political agendas based on non-religious interests, as opposed to movements genuinely inspired by religion.'[68] Religious activists are also capable of being opportunist and of using the political ambitions of nationalist or tribal leaders to gain advantage and privilege for their particular beliefs and traditions.

Again, when the author Salman Rushdie writes that 'the restoration of religion to the sphere of the personal, its depoliticization, is the nettle that all Muslim societies must grasp in order to become modern',[69] he fails to recognize that religious people, other than those who follow a distinctively Protestant individualistic concept of religion, do not understand faith to be a private affair. Political power is 'indispensable' to the establishment of Islamic society, and therefore political action in Islam has 'a religious goal'.[70] The separation of Church and State is an incomprehensible concept to even the ordinary believer. The 'religionization' of politics, however, is not a phenomenon exclusive to Islam. From Teheran to Zagreb, Colombo to Bosnia, clerics of various religious traditions have exploited periods of political uncertainty and change to pursue their dream of reviving the social and religious order of a past 'golden age'.[71]

Alliances between political and religious activists were entered into as they were seen to be mutually beneficial. The Bosnian Serb leader, Radovan Karadzic, who has been indicted for war crimes by the International Court at The Hague, claimed that 'not a single important decision was made without the Church'.[72] It may be true that many of those directly responsible for the atrocities committed by all sides in the Balkan wars may indeed have had only a superficial grasp of the beliefs and practices for which they were ready to kill or die, but this cannot be said of those who served alongside them as Orthodox, Catholic and Muslim military chaplains. Paul Mojzes has accused the Orthodox leadership of failing to protest even though they were aware of the threat to other faiths because they had come to see themselves as 'the self-proclaimed guardian of national interests'.

Extremist groups who legitimize the use of violence on the grounds that they are fulfilling a sacred duty may be minuscule in number within the faith traditions that they claim to represent. None the less with today's tools of terror, weapons designed for mass destruction, they have the potential at a regional and global level to be a real lethal threat. Far from rejecting modernity religious terrorists embrace its benefits to further their own religious ambitions. The Internet, cell phones, aeroplanes, chemical warfare and automatic weapons are used to serve their goal to impose a new world order that is based on their religious principles. Right across the denominational boundaries violent religious extremists have displayed a remarkable ability to adapt their tactics and to harness the tools of modernity for their cause.

As Juergensmeyer discovered, what distinguishes the religiously motivated terrorists and extremists from their secular counterparts is among other things the unwillingness to compromise. Secular terrorist movements usually have clearly defined realizable goals such as the attainment of civic rights, regional independence or the seizure of state power. In their struggle to achieve their objectives they frequently display a readiness to engage in ceasefires and talks that frequently require compromises. The Tamil Tigers are a good example of a terrorist movement that seems prepared to forego their original demand for total independence and to settle for regional autonomy. Religiously motivated terrorists or extremists that act out of the deeply held conviction that their cause has been divinely sanctioned regard compromise as a betrayal of their fundamental beliefs. Although I would be reluctant to describe the religious settlers that I encountered in the West Bank as terrorists, some clearly indicated to me that they saw it as their religious duty to kill to protect their claim on those occupied territories which they believed had been bestowed upon their ancestors by God. To compromise they believed would be to betray their religious heritage.

The unwillingness to compromise stems from the belief that they have a total and exclusive monopoly on truth and goodness. Their claim to exclusivity and spiritual superiority can give rise to the belief that they have a divine right to look upon others as less than human. The experience of the Balkan wars shows that when religion is used to demean others, to label them as false, foreign or heretical, it can set in motion a perverse logic that allows ethnic cleansing to become a religious duty. When that happens 'homicide becomes malicide', in other words the perpetrators of violence do not regard their actions as killing people but eradicating evil.[73] At one end of the causal chain from belief to violence is the religious extremists' understanding and attitude towards revelation, the foundational texts or scriptures of their faith tradition, which they frequently use to justify their violence.

In the Abrahamic faith traditions especially, religious extremists are vehemently opposed to anything other than a strictly literal explanation of their sacred texts. This is in part driven by the fear that interpretation is open to error and that error can lead to damnation, and in part by the belief that the words as written in the text were divinely inspired. They are so convinced that God dictated his message verbatim that they remain undisturbed by the inherent textual inconsistencies, contradictions and the anthropological, astronomical or historical errors found in the Scriptures. The concept of biblical criticism that was introduced in the late nineteenth century in the belief that the message of both the Jewish and Christian scriptural texts is 'culturally conditioned' and therefore needs to be subjected to rigorous scrutiny and literary analysis to understand its contemporary relevance is anathema to them. The more recent attempts of John Wansbrough and others to apply similar principles of literary analysis to the Qur'an and other Islamic foundational texts were found to be equally repugnant to Muslim scholars and practitioners.[74] Fundamentalists make no distinction between fact and fable. The text for them is the source of all knowledge. It is God's truth and therefore there can be no room for compromise.

This is not to say that all fundamentalists have a proclivity for violence. The findings of the *Cults, Religion and Violence* study to which I have already referred, indicates the opposite. A literalist understanding and selective use of foundational texts, however, helps to generate an ambience of certainty that feeds the sense of absolutism that allows extremists to kill in the name of their God. Andrew Sullivan made this point more eloquently when he wrote in the *New York Times Magazine* on the Sunday after 9/11, 'the blind recourse to texts embraced as literal truth, the injunction to follow the commandments of god before anything else, the subjugation of reason and judgement and even conscience to the dictates of dogma, can be exhilarating, transformative, comforting'.

The combination of a literalist approach and selective use of foundational or scriptural texts is not a new phenomenon nor is it confined to those who label themselves as fundamentalists. It was not until 1943 that the Catholic Church accepted the principle of biblical criticism and acknowledged that the literal sense of the Scriptures is not always obvious because of the manner in which these books were originally compiled. The encyclical letter *Divino Affante Spiritu*, while upholding the traditional belief that the Bible was inspired by God and therefore free from error, recognized that to understand its message one needed, with the aid of history, archaeology and ethnology, to recapture the spirit of the 'remote centuries' in which it was written. Until that defining moment the literalist understanding of the Bible was used to condemn those who like Galileo dared to question the creationist account of the universe. It was also used to support the doctrinal claims for unity, catholicity and exclusiveness that required the persecution of heretics and were used to justify the horrors of the Inquisition.

A new phenomenon, however, is the tendency particularly among graduates in the hard sciences and information technology to use the Qur'an and other foundational texts as if these were instructional or operational manuals.[75] Unlike their counterparts in law, history or theology who are accustomed to critically evaluating the language of texts, the attitude of some religiously minded technology students appears to leave no room for interpretation. The letter of the text is what matters. It is difficult to assess how widespread this tendency is but it is a disturbing development that is likely to lead to the justification of further violence committed in the name of God.

My aim in this chapter has been to demonstrate that, despite the received wisdom that religion should not be regarded as a serious cause of conflict, there is sufficient evidence to suggest that religion does matter and that it needs to be seen as an actor in its own right. The preciseness of role that religion plays will vary from conflict to conflict. Vjekoslav Perica puts the seriousness of the role of religion in context when he writes, 'from the globally televised scenes of the burning Bosnian government towers in Sarajevo in 1992 to the smoke, fire and death at the World Trade Center in Sept. 2001, the world seems to have experienced some kind of apocalypse rather than a religious renaissance. Religion was a factor instrumental in bringing about both these catastrophic events.'[76]

3

Religion and the Legitimization of Violence

On September 11, in Chicago, a speaker addressing an assembly representing various religious bodies spoke the following words: 'Sectarianism, bigotry and its horrible descendant, fanaticism, have long possessed this beautiful earth. They have filled the earth with violence, drenched it time and again with human blood, destroyed civilization and sent whole nations to despair.'[1] These words were spoken on September 11, 1893. The occasion was the Parliament of Religions. The speaker, a man named Vivekananda, a western-educated disciple of the nineteenth-century Hindu mystic, Ramakrishna. A century earlier the French philosopher Voltaire had reached a similar conclusion. Acutely aware of the injustices and cruelty committed in the name of religion, he concluded from his reading of history that 'the differences between religions constituted the single most important cause of strife in the world'.[2] This chapter sets out to provide vignettes from the history of some of the world's major religious traditions to illustrate why people from different centuries and beliefs came to regard religion as a major factor in communal strife, and how easy it is for today's activists to find exemplars in their own religious tradition to justify their violence in God's name. I am aware that there are different interpretations and perceptions of some of the episodes recorded here. Whether these stories are based on historical evidence or myths, their importance lies in the fact that they are part of the written or oral tradition that can and is used by some to provide legitimization of violence today.

Whilst Hindu commentators were quick to condemn the recent violence perpetrated against Muslims in India, claiming that such actions violate the values and ideals of their tradition, they also acknowledged that violence and non-violence have co-existed uneasily in Hinduism for centuries.[3] In common with other world faith traditions Hinduism extols the divine qualities, *daiva pravritti*, of forgiveness, compassion, the absence of anger and malice, peace and harmlessness, and at the same time sanctions the use of violence under specific conditions. Although violence can never be justified when used aggressively to promote individual self-interests, Hinduism none the less sees it as a sacred duty in situations of self-defence. Violence is not used to terrorize but to protect oneself and the world from evil and injustice. This moral justification of violence is rooted in the belief that God reincarnates on earth to restore order whenever the weak are threatened by the ascendance of evil.

The Bhagavad-Gita, the Hindu holy book, tells the story of Arjuna, the hero king who hesitated to wage war when he recognized friends and relatives among the faces of his enemies on the battlefield. 'It is not right that we slay our kinsmen,' he argued.[4] Sri Krishna, who was serving as his charioteer and whom Hindus believe to be an incarnation of God, warned Arjuna that it would be a sin for him to retreat as he was a warrior, a *kshatriya*, whose sacred duty it was to engage in battle.[5] Krishna consoled him with the argument that physical death does not destroy the essence of the person, the atman:

> Just as a person casts off worn-out garments and puts on others that are new, even so does the embodied soul cast off worn-out bodies and takes on others that are new. Weapons do not cleave this self, fire does not burn him, waters do not make him wet; nor does the wind make him dry. He is uncleavable ... He is eternal, all pervading, unchanging and immovable. He is the same forever. (*The Bhagavad-Gita* 2, 22–4)[6]

'Even without you' Krishna assured Arjuna, 'all the soldiers standing armed for battle will not stay alive. Their death is foreordained by me: you are merely to be the tool' (11, 32–4). But despite the overall sense of fatalism and the disregard for the human body that pervades the story, it establishes the ground rules that demand respect even in battle for the weak, the wounded, prisoners, deserters and non-combatants. The moral of the story is that good must confront evil and, because the soul is immortal, one should therefore never try to avoid one's *dharma*, which requires one to act appropriately in the given circumstances. To die defending one's country in the Hindu belief is to be assured a place in *viraswargam*, the warriors' heaven.[7]

The alleged activities of the Thugs or Phansigars who wanted their victims to experience terror and to show it in order to bring pleasure to Kali, the goddess of terror and destruction, falls completely outside the more orthodox Hindu norms on the use of violence. There is no precise record regarding the origins of this terrorist group but there is evidence to suggest that they were active as early as the seventh century. It is estimated that they may have been responsible for as many as one million deaths before the British curtailed their murderous activities by the mid-nineteenth century.[8] This brotherhood of killers drew their inspiration and the justification for their use of violence from the Hindu myth of the monster that devoured humans as soon as they were created. The goddess Kali, who according to legend is responsible also for sustaining life, is said to have killed the monster with her sword but from each drop of blood that fell to the ground a new monster was formed. Traditional Hindu belief is that Kali resolved the problem by licking the blood of the monsters as she killed them. The Thugs' version of the myth is that Kali created two men from her own sweat and provided them with handkerchiefs made from her garment so that they could help her to avoid the bloodshed by strangling the evil creatures.

The murderous activities of the Thugs are said to have terrorized India for centuries. Disguised as groups of travellers they selected individual fellow travellers as their targets whom they frequently befriended for weeks or months before murdering them. Without pity or remorse they slowly strangled their victims, prolonging the death agony as required by their doctrine. They acted in the belief that through their deception they were in fact helping their victims, who as offerings to the goddess were assured of paradise. They also believed that if they were to be caught and hanged for their crime they too would be rewarded by paradise. If they failed to fulfil their duty, however, they feared impotence and that their family would become extinct. Although they took the property of their victims after killing them, it is believed that this was mainly to pay the local princes who provided them with sanctuary, and there is no evidence to suggest that their prime motive was ever robbery.[9] The ordinary thief, in fact, was judged to be 'morally unfit' for membership of the Thug brotherhood. Their motives it would seem were clearly religious. Their interpretation of the role of Kali in the creation myth gave them both the incentive and method for creating terror. As the descendants of those who helped Kali to destroy the monster that consumed life, they believed that it was their duty to supply the blood that the goddess now needed 'to keep the world in equilibrium'.

The Thugs operated according to strict rules of engagement. Women, vagabonds, lepers, the blind, the disabled and certain craftsmen were all regarded as immune from attack. This was presumably in keeping with the fundamental Hindu belief that God intervenes on behalf of the weak. Once initiated into the brotherhood the individual Thug was expected to partici-pate in their annual killing expeditions until he was physically no longer capable of doing so. They were masters at deception and living the double life. In the intervening months between their murderous expeditions, members of this brotherhood blended into their local community as hard-working, sober, trustworthy and kind individuals. When in the nineteenth century some members of the brotherhood became more interested in the booty than the observance of the religious code, which they were expected to follow, the British persuaded the more tradition-bound members of the brotherhood to inform on the less observant, an action that eventually led to their demise.[10] In recent years some historians have questioned the accounts of the Thugs' activities on the grounds that the only documentation available, apart from some passing references in pre-colonial literature, are the accounts provided by British colonizers. The suspicion is that the British may have exaggerated the treacherous activities of the Thugs to justify the enforcement of their own legal system and their religious motivations to highlight the importance of Britain's 'civilizing' role on the Indian subcontinent.[11] Others argue that, as the Thugs had no specific sacred texts of their own or hierarchical lineage, our knowledge of their activities and beliefs may be 'elusive and limited', but it is not entirely speculative. There is some evidence to suggest that these 'strangler fraternities' included Muslims who were able to maintain their own distinct religious identity.[12]

When we look at India's history and the willingness of Hindus to take up arms to defend their homeland and religious way of life, we soon realize that Mahatma Gandhi was the exception rather than the norm when he insisted that his followers adhered strictly to the Hindu principle of *ahimsa* or non-violence in their struggle to gain independence from British rule. Convinced that violence was a delusion and a folly, Gandhi regarded his policy of non-violent direct action and non-co-operation as legally seditious for their aim was to overthrow the government. He did not consider the non-violent option as 'a resignation from all real fighting against wickedness'; on the contrary as Gandhi himself wrote,

> I seek entirely to blunt the edge of the tyrant's sword, not by putting up against it a sharper-edged weapon, but by disappointing his expectation that I would be offering physical resistance. The resistance of the soul that I should offer would at first elude him. It would at first dazzle him, and at last compel recognition from him, which recognition would not humiliate him but would uplift him.[13]

He was convinced that in the final outcome moral force would prove a greater power than brute force. Gandhi's untimely death at the hand of a co-religionist helped to ensure a return in general to the more orthodox Hindu practice of endorsing the use of violence in the face of evil and injustices.

The spirit of *ahimsa*, the principle of non-violence or non-harming of others that was the hallmark of Gandhi's life, permeates the whole of

Buddhist thought and practice. Among all the world religions Buddhism stands out for its unambiguous commitment, at least as an ideal, to the promotion of peace and pacifism as a way of life. For example, when the Venerable Thich Nhah Hanh was asked during the Vietnam War whether he would rather have peace under a communist regime even if it meant the end of his religion or a democratic victory with the possibility of revival of Buddhism in his country, he is said to have answered in favour of peace at any price. He went on to explain that he did not believe that people should be sacrificed in order to preserve the Buddhist hierarchy, monasteries or rituals. He believed that when the lives of human beings were preserved, and human dignity and freedom were cultivated towards human kindness, Buddhism could always be reborn in the hearts of people.[14] The fundamental principle of not killing requires the followers of Buddhism to develop the kind of spirituality that will enable them to dissolve inner hatred, to acquire patience and to practise *metta* or loving-kindness to all, even in the face of adversity. In traditional thinking the end result of a conflict, be it victory, defeat or compromise, is less important than the way in which that result was reached. Conflict is to be understood as an opportunity to learn more about oneself and others. In theory, the Buddhist belief is that with skill and patience world conflicts can be resolved non-violently.[15]

Not all Buddhists, however, would rule out the use of military force in certain circumstances. The Mahayana Buddhist tradition, in fact, argues that the Buddhist obligation to end suffering, stop harm, foster compassion and to promote peace paradoxically requires violence provided that it is the only way one can prevent further harm. To be morally justified, this limited and specific use of force, however, must be driven by a deep sense of compassion and not the desire for vengeance, greed, hatred or justice. It also requires the perpetrators of the violence to choose their targets with utmost care, as the killing of the innocent can never be justified.[16]

In his book, *Ethics for the New Millennium*, the Dalai Lama, commenting on a quote from Chairman Mao that political power comes from the barrel of a gun, acknowledges that violence can achieve short-term objectives but not in his opinion long-lasting ends. Based on the belief that violence begets violence and that inevitably means suffering, he argues for a whole new mindset that sees war for what it really is, that is, a 'fire' that spreads and whose fuel is living people. While upholding the traditional Buddhist ideals of non-violence and emphasizing the need for everyone to create the external conditions for disarmament by countering one's negative thoughts and emotions, he acknowledges that 'military disestablishment' cannot be achieved overnight. The world cannot hope to enjoy true peace, he fears, as long as there are authoritarian regimes propped up by armed forces who are willing to act unjustly at their bidding. There will always be groups of troublemakers and fanatics who will cause disturbance for others, and it is therefore necessary, he argues, to have ways of dealing with them.[17] His recommendation is the formation of a global police force whose task it would be to protect 'against the appropriation of power by violent means'.[18]

The Dalai Lama's tacit sanctioning of the limited and specific use of violence stands in sharp contrast to the unequivocal endorsement of pacifism that is found in *The Brahmajala-sutra*, one of the Buddhist holy books, which insists that the children of the Buddha should not touch lethal weapons, take part in any kind of war, revolt or rebellion, or give assent, approval or be a party to killing in any way. It even forbids followers to watch a battle.[19] Despite such explicit sanctions against participation of any kind in violence, there is evidence that the practice of non-violence was not always adhered to in the history of Buddhism. In the first century before the Common Era, the Singhalese king, Dutthagamani, is said to have marched to battle with monks at his side and with a relic of the Buddha as his banner. The legend is that, when Dutthagamani was disturbed by the slaughter that had been inflicted on his Tamil Hindu neighbours, his advisors reassured him that these people that had been killed were less than human. In Tibet, a monk, who claimed he was acting out of compassion, assassinated the king Glan Durma, who was openly hostile to the Buddhist faith.[20] Over several centuries Korean monks have been enlisted to resist various invaders of their country. Again, there is evidence of Buddhist monks resorting to violence in both the history of China and Japan.

It was in Japan during the civil war of 1331–3 CE that Buddhist military chaplains were enrolled to assist warriors. They belonged to a special itinerant-mendicant order, known by the name *jishu*, and they were assigned to warriors rather than to a temple. The prime duty of these monks and nuns was to secure the rebirth of their patrons and themselves in a purified land; they achieved this primarily by chanting the ten invocations of Amida Buddha's name before death. In the battlefield, however, their duties expanded beyond burning, burying and praying for the dead to embrace many of the tasks performed by today's military chaplains, namely, the care of the sick, the wounded, non-combatants and the defeated, as well as to entertaining the troops and informing relatives. These monks and nuns were also expected to act as personal servants to their patron. They were expected to do everything in their power to protect their warrior patron but they were not allowed to touch weapons. The practice of military chaplains was phased out by the year 1400 mainly because of a conflict of loyalties that inevitably arose between obeying the requests of their patrons and those of their religious superior. In the sixteenth century the practice of 'camp-priests' was renewed when warlords forced religious schools to provide them with religious who acted as their servants, couriers and body-guards in the field of battle.[21]

The participation of Buddhists in war is not just a matter of historical record. Buddhist monks fought in the Korean War in the belief that they were being faithful to their vows because they were killing in order to save people. Today native Buddhists and Tibetan refugees, who live in the region of Ladakh in the disputed province of Kashmir, are acclaimed to be India's most 'effective fighting force' along the Line of Control that separates the Indian and Pakistani sectors.[22] The Kashmiri Islamic militants are said to have focused their sights on local Buddhists in retaliation for the decisive role the Ladakh Scouts, a 4,000-man paramilitary unit of Buddhist and Tibetan commandos, played in countering the militants' attack on Kargil in 1999. It is alleged that, during one of his visits to the region, the Dalai Lama gave his personal blessing to the Buddhist soldiers caught up in the fighting.[23] This conflict with the Sufi militants of the Kashmir Valley has not disrupted harmonious community relationships between Buddhists and the Shia-Muslims of Kargil. The role Sinhalese Buddhist monks played in inflaming ethnic tensions and their active support of terrorist violence in Sri Lanka will be dealt with in a later chapter.

Buddhist pacifists argue that, even though Buddhist kings in the past have waged war and sometimes claimed that they were acting in the defence of the religion, there has never been a holy war as such in the entire history of the Buddhist religion. They base their argument on the assertion that those Buddhists, who either in history or in the present day, condone the concept of a just war, cannot find a saying of the Buddha or any other canonical source to support their claim.[24] Others dispute this argument and claim that scriptural justification for killing under certain conditions may be found in the Mahayana *Mahaparinirvana Sutra*. It tells the story of how Buddha in one of his former lives killed some Brahmin heretics. He acted to protect the Doctrine or Teaching, the Four Noble Truths that are the instrument of redemption in Buddhist thought, from their continued attacks on it. When the Doctrine is in danger the whole community or Buddhist Order or social life is at risk and therefore the Five Precepts, the rules that govern the everyday actions of a Buddhist and which prohibit killing or doing harm, can be disregarded. There is another story of a Buddhist traveller who was warned by a scout for some bandits of their plan to attack his five hundred travelling companions. He knew if he told his companions they would kill the scout and all of them would suffer in hell for taking his life. If he let him go, the bandits would attack and they would all be killed. The Buddhist, therefore, decided to kill the scout himself, even though he knew he would have to suffer in hell himself for his action, as he thought this was preferable to them all having either to lose their lives or to suffer in hell. The principle of the story is that it is sometimes justified to kill one in order to save two. Additional historical arguments used to justify killing range from the illusory nature of our human existence, the fact that as humans we lack substance, we are no more than 'a trick of the senses', which in practice means that killing also is only an illusion, so it is better to kill another than to allow him to kill. The person who killed was expected always to act out of compassion, charity or even thoughtlessly so that the inner peace is not disturbed.[25]

Religious ambivalence towards violence is nowhere more marked than in the Hebrew Bible. On the one hand there is an unequivocal condemnation of killing in the Ten Commandments; on the other the sword and the bow are sanctioned as weapons that enable the Israelites to fulfil the divine plan to conquer their neighbouring tribes and to occupy their lands. The historical narratives record numerous battles in which thousands were slain. If Israel won, they believed that it was simply because God wanted their victory, and gave them the supremacy in war to achieve it. The belief in an interventionist God whose immanence empowers them is made explicit in a passage from the book of Joshua. In this narrative God recalls his own role in orchestrating their escape from Egypt and in helping them to conquer the land that provided them with a good living:

> When I brought your fathers out of Egypt, you came to the sea, and the Egyptians pursued them with chariots and horsemen as far as the Red Sea. But they cried to the Lord for help, and he put darkness between you and the Egyptians; he brought the sea over them and covered them. You saw with your own eyes what I did to the Egyptians. Then you lived in the desert for a long time; I brought you to the land of the Amorites who lived east of the Jordan. They fought against you, but I gave them into your hands. I destroyed them before you, and you took possession of their land . . . . Then you crossed the Jordan and came to Jericho. The citizens of Jericho fought against you, as did also the Amorites, Perizzites, Canaanites, Hittites, Girgashites, Hivites and Jebusities, but I gave them into your hands . . . You did not do it with your own sword and bow. (Joshua 24:6-8, 11-12)[26]

The book of Deuteronomy, which lays down the rules aimed at protecting the purity of the faith, is emphatic that none of the conquered should be spared nor treaties made with the native inhabitants of the newly conquered lands. The intention was to guard against the risk of the Israelites assimilating foreign beliefs and practices. They were to maintain their God-given distinctiveness and to protect their identity from alien traits, and so the normal code of behaviour did not apply (Deuteronomy 7:6-8). The conviction, though, that God was with them in battle and approved of what amounted to the ethnic cleansing of the land did not totally numb their moral sensitivities as to what was right and wrong. This fact is clearly illustrated in a passage from the first book of Chronicles in which the great warrior king David laments the fact that God does not want him to fulfil the ambition of his heart to build a temple to house the Ark, the symbol of God's presence. God told David, 'You are not to build a house for my Name, because you are a warrior and have shed blood' (1 Chronicles 28:2). Killing even when undertaken in the name of God was still considered as incompatible with the moral demands of the covenant, the Ten Commandments.

This belief is reflected in the rabbinic traditions that focus more on the importance of mercy and condemn all wanton destruction. The ideal, set by the Talmud, is 'Seek peace and pursue it.' The Jewish rabbis acknowledged the interconnectedness or essential unity of humanity and concluded from that fact that peace was God's original intent for all human beings. The obligation to promote peace was universal. Forgiveness was to take precedence over revenge. None the less, they did not rule out military service, as war was still accepted to be a regrettable necessity. They did, however, distinguish between 'optional' and 'obligatory' war. The obligation to fight was regarded as universal when God commanded it as in the conquering of the land, or when the nation was under attack from outsiders. To act to prevent a threat of attack or to expand territory was regarded as an optional war, which could only be undertaken if approved by the Sanhedrin, the appointed religious leaders. In an optional war people could be exempted from taking part on compassionate grounds. If, for example, they had just built a house that they had not yet lived in, or planted a vineyard and had not yet enjoyed the fruits of their labour, or were engaged to be married, they could be relieved of their duty to fight. The rabbis also laid down the acceptable rules of war, which called for the protection of women prisoners and respect for the environment.

Despite the rabbinic traditions that emphasized the essential unity of humanity, the obligation to work for peace, and the need for war to be authorized by a designated authority, their teachings did not deter the Maccabees, a group of Jewish warriors (166–29 BCE), from rising in violent revolt against the imposition of Greek religion and culture. When a Greek official tried to force a Jewish priest, named Mattathias, to make sacrifice to a pagan god, the priest murdered him. The priest and his five sons who began the war for Jewish independence were called Maccabees, the Hebrew name for 'hammer', because of their reputation of striking a hammer blow against their enemies. Even though the story of this war for religious independence recorded in the book of Maccabees is not recognized as part of the Hebrew Scriptures, their success in recapturing Jerusalem and the subsequent purification of the Temple is celebrated in the festival of Hanukkah. It was Pompey's arrival in 63 BCE that led to a renewed period of foreign domination and control, which in turn gave rise to a renewed struggle for independence and a new wave of terrorism in the name of God.

The Jewish-Roman historian, Josephus Flavius, recorded the activities of two Jewish terrorist movements, the Zealots and the Sicarii. Like many modern-day terrorist movements there were divided into several factions, with each trying to demonstrate their commitment to the cause by behaving even more daringly and outrageously than the other. Although Josephus emphasizes criminal intent as their prime motivation, religious and political concerns were undoubtedly high on their agenda. Their commitment to terror was guided more by their messianic hopes than greed. They were inspired by Jewish apocalyptic prophecies that spoke of massive catastrophes as the sign of the coming of the messiah.[27] Their goal was to speed up the process by causing a level of mayhem that would provoke an even more repressive response from the Romans, which they hoped would in turn lead to insurrection by the whole Jewish population. Their tactics were aimed at polarizing their society and preventing any kind of rapprochement between Jew and non-Jew. Their religious exemplar or role model was a high priest at the time of Moses by the name of Phinehas, who speared to death one of the tribal leaders as he was fornicating with a Midianite woman. By taking the law into his own hands in his effort to confront this kind of apostasy Phinehas won God's favour and as a consequence God intervened to stop the plague that had threatened to wipe out the whole of the community (Numbers 25:1-16). His action prepared the people to fight the 'holy war' that would give them the land God promised.

The Sicarii believed that it was their duty to prepare the Jewish people to wage a holy war against the alien occupiers whose presence threatened the very survival of their religion. They saw themselves as being engaged in a war that would end all wars. They regarded their enemy as being under the influence of Satan, so no rules applied.[28] They got their name from the dagger that they used to kill their unsuspecting victims. They targeted priests and others who were anxious to avoid revolt and who were willing to enter into collaboration with the Roman authorities or their Greek neighbours. Mingling with the crowds to avoid detection and to make good their escape, they attacked in public places, assassinating their victims in broad daylight. Their shock tactics had the maximum effect, according to Josephus. They succeeded in spreading terror among the public at large and created a climate of suspicion even among friends. They also openly engaged with the military, and as the normal rules did not apply they killed their prisoners, even when they surrendered.

The Zealots targeted non-Jews who had settled in their land. They wanted to attract maximum publicity for their crimes and frequently committed their atrocities on major religious feast days, making the point that not even a sacred occasion could stand in the way of their objective. The terrorist activities of both movements so outraged the Greek settlers that they rose up and massacred their Jewish neighbours, sparking off a further cycle of retaliation and violence. They succeeded in polarizing people according to their ethnic religious affiliations, and sustained those divisions by pressurising their own co-religionists through fear and manipulation to maintain the state of antagonism. They saw themselves as catalysts that through their outrageous acts of violence would usher in the new messianic age in which they would be delivered once and for all time from their oppressors. The insurrection that they hoped to provoke was only a means of securing God's intervention. They even burnt the food of their own besieged forces in Jerusalem to demonstrate to God their total trust that he would intervene to save them. God had no choice as he was bound to them by the Covenant. Even when it was obvious with the Temple burning that their twenty-five-year reign of terror was coming to an end, their fanatical belief in the immanent arrival of the messiah, who would liberate them from their oppressors, enabled them to enlist thousands of new recruits for their doomed cause.[29]

The Dead Sea Scrolls provide evidence that belief in a military-style messiah who would liberate them from alien domination and restore the theocracy in which there would be no division between the political and the religious, the Temple and the State, was rooted deep in the Jewish psyche around the second half of the first century BCE. An era of peace and prosperity, it was believed, would be ushered in only after a period of extreme violence in which the uncircumcised, their oppressors, would be 'swallowed up'. The Scrolls that are known as *Florilegium* contain eschatological commentaries on some of the references to the messiah in the Hebrew Scriptures. The verse from Psalms that reads, 'You will rule them with a rod of iron; you will dash them to pieces like pottery' (Psalm 2:9), is interpreted to mean that the messiah will act like a great warrior, who will struggle against the kings of the pagan nations, and who will be recognized as the messiah only after leading his people to victory in battle. The Dead Sea commentaries also show that at that time messianism had been linked with apocalypticism, the belief that the coming of the messiah would mark the end of time.[30]

The Christian Scriptures portray Jesus as a messiah who rejects the sword. 'Put your sword back in its place for all who draw the sword will die by the sword,' he told Peter, who tried to resist the group who had come to arrest Jesus (Matthew 26:52). Neither does he make claim to political power. 'My kingdom is not of this world. If it were, my servants would fight to prevent my arrest by the Jews,' he told Pilate, the Roman Governor (John 18:36). In the Sermon on the Mount Jesus is even more explicit on rejecting violence. 'You have heard that it was said to people long ago, "Do not murder, and anyone who murders will be subject to judgement." But I tell you that anyone who is angry with his brother will be subject to judgement' (Matthew 5:21).[31] The Letter to the Romans endorses Jesus' non-violent teaching, counselling against taking revenge and articulating the ideal that evil should be overcome by good (Romans 12:21). The founding texts are not, however, without ambiguity; the image of Jesus overturning the tables of the money-changers as he drove them from the Temple (Matthew 21:12), his words, 'I have not come to bring peace but a sword' (Matthew 10:34), and 'If you don't have a sword, sell your cloak and buy one' (Luke 22:36), and the violent images in the book of Revelation like that of the four angels who were released 'to kill a third of mankind' (9:15), have led some to question the non-violent credentials of the Christian Scriptures. It has even been suggested by some that it was Jesus' sympathy for the Zealots' cause that gave the Romans reason to execute him.[32]

Despite the apparent ambiguities in the texts there is clear evidence that for at least the first century and a half of their existence, Christians adopted a strongly pacifist approach, condemning the use of violence in any circumstances. War and military service were regarded as totally incompatible with Christian beliefs. When in the course of time soldiers were converted, they were allowed to become full members of the community only after they had left the army. In the meantime, as an aspiring Christian they were expected to refuse to be involved in any kind of killing, including public executions. Not everyone agreed with such compromises. Tertullian, the second-century theologian, condemned the presence of Christians in the imperial army, even if they were exempt from taking part in ritual sacrifices or punishment duties. He argued: 'For even if soldiers came to John and received advice on how to act, and even if a centurion became a believer, the Lord, in subsequently disarming Peter disarmed every soldier. No uniform is lawful among us if it is designated for an unlawful action.'[33] Tertullian's strictly non-violent interpretation of Jesus' teaching was shared by Origen. He also believed that Christians could never under any circumstances 'justify' the taking of human life. While they acknowledged that Cicero's ethical argument that war could be justified if it were fought for a just cause, declared by the legitimate authority and executed in a just manner, could apply to pagans, they argued that it did not apply to Christians as they were expected to live by a higher moral code. It was the acceptance, however, that pagans could take part in war under certain circumstances that John Ferguson believes 'opened the door for Ambrose and Augustine to apply this standard to the nominally Christian empire of their own day'.[34]

The conversion of the Roman Emperor, Constantine, marked the beginning of the merger between Church and State in the Roman-controlled world. It was also the defining moment in Christianity's moral legitimization of state-sanctioned violence. The early Christian historian and apologist, Eusebius of Caesarea, recorded the Emperor's own recollection of his conversion in his fourth-century work *Panegyric of Constantine*. He describes how Constantine on his way to battle recalled how previous emperors had placed their hopes in multiple gods and had been let down. Constantine, anxious for success, decided to turn to the supreme God for help. It was in this moment of prayer that 'he saw with his own eyes the trophy of the cross of light in the heavens, above the sun, and bearing the inscription CONQUER BY THIS.'[35] To commemorate this unexpected divine epiphany, which according to Eusebius his soldiers also witnessed, Constantine ordered that a likeness of the sign that he saw in the sky be made and carried on the banners that led them into battle to protect them against their enemies. In 313 CE Constantine issued the Edict of Milan, giving legal recognition to Christians and among other things granting them the right to own property. In response Christians felt that it was their duty to protect the well-being of the State. In an attempt to address this radical change in circumstances, Eusebius drew a distinction between the role of the clergy and that of the laity. The clergy were expected to devote their entire lives to the work of God and to live fully by the values of the gospel; the laity were expected to fulfil their civil obligations like any other citizens.[36] The foundation for an alliance of mutual self-interest and interdependence between State and Church, the sword and the cross, had been laid. To defend the empire was to defend the new-found freedoms granted to the Church.

It was within this new political social framework that a fourth-century bishop, Ambrose of Milan, began to set out the theological and moral justifications for the use of violence under certain conditions. Ambrose believed that the stories of the God-sanctioned wars of the Hebrew Scriptures provided the divine authorization that allowed him to bypass the predominantly pacifist message of the Gospels, and to justify the use of military force even to subdue those who challenged what they regarded as orthodox Christian beliefs. A combination of Cicero's just-war doctrines

and stories from the Hebrew Scriptures provided the basic moral foundation for Ambrose's teaching on the ethics of war. He argued that, just as it
was a Christian's obligation in love to intervene with limited force if necessary to protect a neighbour from being harmed by an unlawful attacker, so
too Christians had an obligation in love to protect society.[37] His fellow bishop
and one-time student, Augustine of Hippo, fine-tuned and developed the
Ambrosian doctrine on the use of force. He rejected outright violence for its
own sake or any kind of 'revengeful cruelty'. The use of violence could only
be justified, he taught, if it were used for the right motives and in proportion
to the threat posed by an unlawful perpetrator. Like his mentor in Milan,
Augustine was influenced by the war stories in the Hebrew Bible, and he
believed war was 'an instrument of divine judgement on wickedness'.[38]

In his letter to Boniface, a Roman general who was planning to abandon
the army to become a monk, Augustine tried to dissuade him on the
grounds that there was no incompatibility between his lofty vocation to be
a Christian and his engagement in active military service. Augustine told
Boniface that his army career was a worthy calling as he was fighting to
defend from the threat of the barbarians those who had dedicated their
lives to God. He wrote:

> Think, then, of this first of all, when arming for battle, that even your bodily
> strength is a gift of God ... Peace should be the object of your desire; war
> should be waged only as a necessity, and waged only that God may by it
> deliver men from the necessity and preserve them in peace. For peace is not
> sought in order to the kindling of war, but war is waged in order that peace
> may be obtained. Therefore in waging war cherish the spirit of a peacemaker,
> that by conquering those whom you attack, you may lead them back to the
> advantages of peace; for the Lord says: 'Blessed are the peacemakers; for they
> shall be called children of God.' ... Let necessity therefore, and not your will,
> slay the enemy who fights against you. As violence is used towards him who
> rebels and resists, so mercy is due to the vanquished or the captive, especially
> in the case in which future troubling of the peace is not to be feared.[39]

Augustine's positive spin on the morality of war, his seeing it as an
unavoidable necessity in checking evil in a fallen world and his sanctioning
of violence as a consequence, had a profound influence on shaping the
Christian attitude to the use of force in the post Constantine era. It did not,
though, totally eclipse the uncompromising gospel message of non-
violence. In the eighth century, for example, the Synod of Ratisbon
expressed an unequivocal condemnation of clergy participating in any kind
of warfare. Eusebius' concept of a two-track vocation, lay and clerical, with
higher expectations and moral code of conduct applying to the clergy, had

clearly become deep-rooted in the Christian psyche. It was a compromise that allowed the Church to function as an institution in the real world while at the same time maintaining some form of witness to the high ideals of the Sermon on the Mount. By the ninth century Pope John VIII was offering indulgences to those who died fighting the infidels and pagans that threatened a society in which Christianity had secured a place of privilege.

With the break-up of the Roman Empire, however, the limitations that Ambrose and Augustine had sought to impose on warfare were largely ignored as armed bands plundered the countryside and towns, setting their own standards of ruthlessness and cruelty. In the tenth century several French bishops tried to impose a moral code to regulate the lawless behaviour of these local militias or paramilitaries. They declared the 'peace of God' by threatening to excommunicate anyone who molested church officials, asylum seekers and other peaceful non-combatants. They also outlawed fighting on Sundays and holy days. Regional royal bureaucrats used their political and military authority to support the bishops' peace initiative, as it also helped to promote the interests of centralized authority. The idea spread to other regions of Europe but it did not become a universal practice.[40]

The eleventh century saw another church-based initiative aimed at limiting the impact violence was having on society. An idea first proposed by Pope John XV in 985 CE was endorsed by the Council of Elne in 1027, a period when Europe was facing an epidemic of private wars. The 'Truce of God', as it became known, forbade fighting from Saturday night to Monday morning; religious feast-days were also included. The imposed ban on violence was subsequently extended to include Thursday and Friday as well as the seasons of Advent and Lent, leaving only eighty days in the year on which fighting would be lawfully tolerated. The Truce, which began as a regional church initiative in France, spread to Germany, Italy, Flanders and Spain. A joint letter written in 1063 by Drogo, Bishop of Terouanne, and Count Baldwin of Hainault sets out the conditions of the Truce. From sunset on Wednesday to sunrise on Monday it declares,

> no man or woman shall assault, wound, or slay another, or attack, seize, or destroy a castle, burg, or villa by craft or by violence. If anyone violates this peace and disobeys these commands of ours, he shall be exiled for thirty years as a penance, and before he leaves the bishopric he shall make compensation for the injury, which he committed. Otherwise he shall be excommunicated by the Lord God and excluded from all Christian fellowship.[41]

It also required that merchants and travellers be allowed to pass through the territory in peace.

The Oxford historian H.E.J. Cowdrey makes the interesting observation that there is no evidence to suggest that the just-war teachings of Augustine had any influence on the Church's attitude towards violence and warfare in the latter part of the eleventh century. On the contrary the authors that he quotes would suggest that the pacifist mood of the pre-Constantine Church seemed to be reasserting itself. Canonists and papal courtiers alike were outspoken in their opposition to the sanctioning of violence and to the use of force for whatever reason. Cardinal Peter Damiani wrote that, 'In no circumstances is it licit to take up arms in the defence of the faith of the universal church; still less should men rage in battle for its earthly and transitory goods.' Cardinal Humbert condemned the use of force against heretics, claiming that Christians who used the sword in this way themselves became hardened in the ways of violence.[42] In the light of this clear reassertion of pacifism both in practice and thought it seems incongruous that Pope Urban II should have used the same occasion in which he officially promulgated the Truce of God as a law of the Church to launch the First Crusade, a holy war aimed ostensibly at regaining the holy places from infidel control. Urban II's sermon at the Council of Claremont in 1095 marked a turning point, a new era in papal-sanctioned brutality.

It was Urban II's predecessor Gregory VII who was the mastermind behind the radical shift in official church teaching on the use of violence. Driven by the desire to impose a Christian-dominated order on a fragmented world, Gregory sanctioned aggressive warfare, provided of course that it was waged under the banner of St Peter. He identified the spiritual combat against the flesh in which St Paul encouraged all Christians to engage with an earthly warfare that was undertaken for the sake of Christ. What had previously been regarded as sinful, even when prosecuted for noble reasons, became meritorious when men 'dedicated their swords to the service of Christ and of Saint Peter'.[43] Gregory himself had planned to lead a Christian army ostensibly to relieve Byzantine-rite Christians from the infidel threat. His real motive was probably to re-impose papal supremacy on the Christian world divided after the schism of 1054. Although he failed to mobilize adequate support to fulfil his personal ambition, his reformulation of traditional Christian thinking on warfare – the thought that the sword could be used to further the cause of Christ – gained sufficient hold on the Christian imagination to ensure a robust response to Urban II's call to arms to liberate the holy places a decade later. Certainly few in late eleventh-century Europe would have had any first-hand knowledge of Muslims or an awareness of the circumstances in which eastern Christians lived to warrant such a response. The Muslim world, in fact, was tolerant of other faiths provided that they accepted a lesser role in society and paid their taxes.

There were undoubtedly other factors that contributed to the popular response to Urban II's appeal. The late eleventh-century European society was experiencing demographic changes with all the internal social tensions that inevitably follow. Population growth, the development of the knight class looking for social mobility, and the increased enforcement of law and order meant that warriors and those wanting to climb the social ladder had to look elsewhere in their need for land and new outlets for their innate sense of aggression and the practice of their martial skills. These factors, however, would have been insufficient in themselves to persuade men to endure the sacrifices they would have had to undergo by embarking on a Crusade, had it not been for the religious mood, which Urban II identified and tapped into successfully. Cowdrey, in his article *The Genesis of the Crusades*, identifies that mood as eleventh-century Europe's preoccupation with sin and penance. At a time when the Church's penitential system was in a state of disorder and confusion, people were never sure whether or not their penance could gain them full remission for their sins.[44] The only two assured ways of receiving forgiveness until then were either to enter a monastery or to go on an unarmed pilgrimage. The Church was now offering a third way; warriors could gain remission for their sins by doing what they were good at: killing or being killed in God's name would assure them of a place in paradise.

Whatever high motives deluded them, by legitimizing the use of the sword in God's name, Gregory VII and Urban II unleashed a destructive energy that inflicted over the following three and a half centuries unspeakable human suffering on anyone who had the misfortune of being identified as an alien or infidel within or beyond the boundaries of western Christianity. Within a year of Urban's sermon at Claremont, Jews living in the Rhineland became victims of this new wave of religious fanaticism. In later years Byzantine-rite Christians were subjected to the same barbarities as their Muslim and Jewish neighbours. Sir Steven Runciman's description of the Crusaders' siege of Alexandria compares to what happened in the two other great centres of belief, culture and trade that the Crusaders plundered, Jerusalem and Constantinople:

> They spared no one. The native Christians and Jews suffered as much as the Moslems; and even the European merchants settled in the city saw their factories and storehouses ruthlessly looted. Mosques and tombs were raided and their ornaments stolen or destroyed; churches too were sacked . . . Houses were entered, and householders who did not immediately hand over all their possessions were slaughtered with their families.[45]

The Crusaders' record of barbarity could easily lead on to the question of whether these holy warriors were motivated more by a lust for violence and loot than any sense of religious idealism. Opportunistic behaviour and greed may well have overshadowed at times the religious intent of their mission. None the less, an analysis of the Crusaders' songs and writings demonstrates the religious mindset that at least initially motivated them and legitimized their cruel behaviour. An anonymous knight put on record his own motives for embarking on the First Crusade. He attributed his decision to fight to '. . . a great stirring of the heart throughout the Frankish lands, so that if any man really wanted to follow God and faithfully to bear the cross after him, he could make no delay in taking the road to the Holy Sepulchre as quickly as possible'.[46] The Crusader clearly saw himself as a pilgrim, albeit armed, who had undergone an inner conversion that led him

> to join the sacred army of God's saints. The foes he was to fight were internal foes, those perennial temptations and obstacles to the pure life. The battle, perhaps its most exciting part, might take place in France, at the time the crusader makes his agonized decision, as in the case of King Louis. The external foes, the Saracens, are merely extensions of the inner ones; they are not a real people, not a real enemy – at least for the observer in France.[47]

Slaughter for them had become a mystical virtue. Their war was holy and therefore total. Weapons that had been outlawed as too cruel or inhuman to be used in war against neighbours at home were sanctioned for use against the enemies of the faith.

The early thirteenth century witnessed the same crusading spirit being mobilized against Catharism, a heresy that had taken hold in Languedoc, south-western France. This new wave of religious enthusiasm that rejected materialism as evil was seen as a challenge to papal authority because its followers preached against the trappings of worldly power that had become so closely associated with the Church. The Crusade against the Cathars lasted for twenty years, partly because it could only be fought on the forty days that were sanctioned by the Peace and Truce of God. The restraints of piety, however, were compensated for by the sheer ruthlessness of what was done in God's name on the days that fighting was allowed. Whole towns were slaughtered and thousands were burnt at the stake in the effort to reassert papal authority. The record of atrocities began in the town of Beziers, which fell to the papal-sanctioned knights in July 1209. The Crusaders pillaged and slaughtered their way through the town until they reached the Church of the Madeleine, where, according to a contemporary record, they burnt over 7000 inhabitants that were locked inside. When the papal legate, the Abbot of Citeaux, was informed that Catholics as well as heretics had taken refuge in the church, he is said to have replied, 'Kill them all, God will know his own.'[48] The violent methods used to root out heresy in the course of this Crusade were in later years institutionalized by the Inquisition.

Not all western Christians endorsed the belief in divinely sanctioned violence. One notable exception was Francis of Assisi, who in 1219 succeeded in engaging al-Kamil, the Sultan of Egypt, in dialogue. Francis had hoped to bring to an end the senseless killing between Christians and Muslims, by persuading the Sultan to convert to Christianity. Although he failed in his immediate goal, Francis' presence and manner had such an influence on al-Kamil that he later sent a messenger proposing a truce, during which time he was prepared to explore with the Christian Crusaders the possibility of peace.[49] The Crusaders agreed to the truce but declined the Sultan's offer to discuss peace, presumably because they believed themselves to be engaged on a sacred mission that did not allow for such compromises. Later, in the same century that Francis embarked on his peace mission, the English Franciscan and scientist Roger Bacon expressed similar beliefs that the Crusades were 'cruel and useless' and that the infidel would be more open to conversion if Christians were less aggressive and predatory.[50] A couple of centuries later Erasmus, whilst not rejecting the principle of a just war, based his arguments in favour of pacifism on his understanding of the New Testament.

Far from participating in the Crusades Orthodox Christians found themselves as much the victims of this new surge of western religious militancy as their Muslim neighbours. Their own tradition none the less endorsed the use of violence when it was necessary to gain victory over evil. Christians were permitted to take up the sword in the defence of their neighbour, faith and homeland provided that they acted without malice and their intent was not just to humiliate or destroy the other. In 2000 the Council of Bishops of the Russian Orthodox Church published a document that provides the basis for their Church's teaching on war and peace. It records the story of when St Cyril, the ninth-century missionary, was sent by the Patriarch of Constantinople to preach the gospel among the Saracens and was challenged by Muslim scholars to explain the contradictions they saw between Christian belief and behaviour. 'Your God is Christ. He commanded you to pray for your enemies, to do good to those who hate and persecute you and to offer the other cheek to those who hit you, but what do you actually do? If anyone offends you you sharpen your sword and go into battle and kill. Why do you not obey your Christ?' they argued. Cyril began his defence with the question. 'If there are two commandments written in one law, who will be its best respecter – the one who obeys only one commandment or the one who obeys both?' Having elicited the answer that he wanted, he continued his argument.

> Christ our God who ordered us to pray for our offenders and to do good to them, also said that no one could show greater love in life than to give his life for his friends. For this reason we generously endure offences caused to us as individuals but in company we defend one another and give our lives in battle for our neighbours so that you cannot take them as prisoners and imprison their souls together with their bodies by forcing them to renounce their faith and to do godless deeds. Our Christ-loving soldiers protect our Holy Church with arms in their hands. They safeguard the sovereign in whose sacred person they respect the image of the rule of the Heavenly King. They safeguard their land because if it falls the home authority will inevitably fall too and the evangelical faith will be shaken. These are precious pledges for which soldiers should fight to the last. And if they give their lives in the battlefield the Church will include them in the community of the holy martyrs and call them intercessors before God.[51]

The leading Protestant Reformers of the sixteenth century Luther, Zwingli and Calvin also sanctioned the use of the sword. Luther believed that Church and State derived their authority from God and were ordained by God to operate independently, each in their own sphere of influence. He rejected the belief that the gospel should be defended by the use of violence and murder, but regarded 'the pacifism of Jesus as no more binding on his followers than his celibacy or his carpentry'.[52] The State, he believed, should not be engaged in religious warfare but it did have a right to fight infidels or others for its own political reasons. He also regarded the military as a worthy profession for a Christian. Zwingli and Calvin went much further in their approval of the use of violence. Zwingli, a Swiss priest, justified violence when used in the defence of the reformed faith. He believed that unresolved doctrinal issues should be settled on the battlefield.[53] He himself died fighting in 1531 and his death marked the beginning of the battles over belief and the atrocities in the name of God that plagued European society for the best part of the next century. Calvin also endorsed the belief in holy war. For him the State had the obligation to use force to support true religion. A century later Oliver Cromwell saw himself as a divine agent acting under the authority of God and therefore excused from adhering to the usual norms of morality.[54] He justified the massacre perpetrated by his troops at Drogheda in 1649 on the grounds that it 'is the righteous judgement of God upon these barbarous wretches, who have imbrued their hands in so much innocent blood'.[55]

The Reformers also had their pacifists. The Hussites, the Anabaptists, the

Quakers all rejected the use of violence as incompatible with the love of God. George Fox reflects the fundamental beliefs of these groups when he said, 'We love all men and women as they are God's workmanship, and so as brethren.' Conrad Grebel, one of the two Swiss founders of the Anabaptist–Mennonite tradition, was absolute in his commitment to non-violence in every aspect of life. He abhorred killing for any cause and admonished those who justified the use of the sword, on the grounds that the truth of the gospel did not need to be defended in this way and that being vulnerable is an important part of being a Christian.[56]

The introduction of the war-for-God belief that sanctioned the First Crusade marked also the beginning of the unsanctioned pogroms that marred the relationship between Christians and Jews for the next millennium. Until this new wave of religious zeal took hold in Europe, Jews had been protected from physical abuse and were allowed to practise their faith without interference. Far from reflecting a respect for pluralism this papal-sanctioned policy of non-interference was based on what would be recognized today as the perverse arguments of the fourth–fifth-century theologian Augustine of Hippo, who considered the presence of Jews, in their rejected and defeated state, as living witness to the triumph of Christianity. God, Augustine argued, wanted the Jews to be preserved with their Hebrew Scriptures, which foretold the coming of Christ, as these texts provided a ready answer to anyone who accused Christians of making up these prophecies. Jews would also give witness by converting at the second coming of Christ.[57]

Although there is no evidence to suggest a change of papal policy in respect to the position of the Jews at the launching of the First Crusade in 1095, the charismatic preachers, recruited to mobilize support for the papal war effort, laced their sermons with hate language for those that were not united in the one true faith. Jews became the focus of their venom and the scapegoat for what was wrong in western Christian society. The Crusaders' goal to liberate the Church of the Holy Sepulchre from infidel control drew attention to the historic role attributed to the Jews in the death of Christ. Individual Crusaders took it upon themselves to avenge his blood. Jews living in the Rhineland were forced to convert; if they refused they were killed by roaming bands of ill-disciplined Crusaders and local collaborators.[58] The erroneous belief that 'anyone who would kill a Jew would have his sins forgiven' seems to have so motivated these roaming bands of religious zealots that not even the local bishops could guarantee protection for Jews seeking sanctuary. Some Christians saw the slaughter of Jews in Worms and Mainz in 1096 as evidence that anti-Jewish violence had met with divine favour and used this murderous logic to justify further violence. A contemporary Jewish account of the Rhineland pogroms records the story of a Jewish woman named Minna who had been hidden by Christian friends during the assault on the Jews of Worms. Once the danger had passed they took the slaughter of her fellow Jews as a sign that God had abandoned her people and tried to persuade her to be baptized. When she refused, the same people who had protected her from the fury of the Crusaders had her put to death.[59]

The anti-Jewish violence that began in the Rhineland spread to France and England. Despite subsequent papal efforts to reinstate the policy of protection, the spirit of animosity generated by the initial preaching of the Crusades prevailed. In 1242 the Talmud was officially condemned and burnt in Paris. Its teachings, so judged a papal-appointed commission, did not qualify for protection under the Augustine doctrine and were considered to be the main reason why Jews had not converted.[60] By the late thirteenth and early fourteenth centuries Christian attitudes towards the Jews had so changed that Jews were expelled by royal decree from the kingdoms of Naples, England and France. When the Christian monarchs reconquered Granada in 1492, they expelled Jews before Muslims. Although the Jews were politically and militarily unimportant, and were looked upon as 'leaderless and downtrodden', they were perceived to be a greater threat to the unity of the newly formed Christian kingdom. The reason for this, according to Bernard Lewis, is that the survival of Judaism as a separate religion came to be seen by many Christians as impugning the central tenets of their faith. 'Jews, unlike Muslims, could not be accused of not knowing the Old Testament or of being unaware of the Choice and the Promise. Their unwillingness to accept the Christian interpretation of these books and of these doctrines thus challenged Christianity in a most sensitive area.'[61] The fact that Jews also believed that adherents of other faiths could find their own way to God was considered an insidious threat to ecclesiastical authority. In 1496 the Jews of Portugal suffered the same agonizing choice to convert or to leave the kingdom. Coerced into making such a choice many Jews on the Iberian Peninsula outwardly accepted Christianity whilst inwardly and secretly remaining committed to their Jewish beliefs and practices.[62]

A Muslim's world view is shaped entirely by his or her faith, as Islam draws no distinction between the secular and the sacred, between the believer's spiritual, social and political life. It is a comprehensive system of belief that imbues all aspects of life, individual as well as communal, creating compatibility and harmony between the spiritual and the material.[63] Islam's roots date back to 610 CE when at the age of forty the Prophet Muhammad underwent an intense spiritual experience that was to mark the first in a series of divine revelations that were to continue for the next twenty-two years. The revelations were written up in the Qur'an, the book Muslims believe to be the verbatim and literal word of God as conveyed to the Prophet by the Angel Gabriel.[64] Although God is acknowledged to be beyond human definition, the Qur'an describes God as 'Most Gracious, Ever Merciful', 'the Mighty, the Wise', 'the Self-Subsisting, All-Sustaining' (Qur'an 3:1-7). Belief in the Oneness of God is fundamental to the Islamic faith. It is also at the root of the Muslim belief in the essential unity of the human family, the fact that all human beings are to be honoured as 'children of Adam' whatever their race, origin or creed (Qur'an 17:70). Muslims also acknowledge Abraham, Moses and Jesus as prophets of the one and the same God, who chose Muhammad to be the final Messenger, the 'Seal of the Prophets' (Qur'an 33:41). The Qur'an expresses, therefore, the will of God for the whole of creation in its 'final and complete form'.[65] Its message is addressed to the whole human family as God has entrusted the care of creation to human beings who will be held responsible by God for their actions (Qur'an 33:73-4, 31:19-31). The human vocation is to be God's representative or 'vicegerent'[66] with the task of 'establishing and spreading Islamic order, that is God's rule on earth'.[67] To achieve this, human beings are called to strive to submit to the will of God as expressed in the Qur'an and in the *Sunnah*, which is a record of the life, words and example of the Prophet Muhammad. These two texts provide a sacred and immutable source for the sharia, the laws that govern every aspect of a Muslim's personal and social, individual and communal, spiritual and material way of life. In summary Muslims believe that the oneness of God reflected in the whole of creation calls for one law and one ruler.

The words *jihad* (striving) and *Islam* (submitting) express the true meaning of human life. It is by striving to submit totally to the will of God that people can attain peace with others and within themselves. The initiation into Islam is simple as all it requires is the declaration (*shahadah*), 'I bear witness there is no God but Allah and that Muhammad is his witness', made before two witnesses. This profession of faith binds one to live by the instructions and teachings of Muhammad. It commits the believer to practise a special form of ritual prayer (*salah*) five times a day: early morning, early afternoon, late afternoon, after sunset and after dark. Only the noon prayer on Fridays has to be performed in the company of others. With the words *Allahu Akbar* the believer is expected to turn from the world and to give God their full attention. Islam also requires its adherents to give as much money as they can in charity as well as to pay alms tax (*zakah*) which is approximately two and a half per cent of a believer's wealth after one has met one's own basic needs. This tax is passed on to the poor through various

Islamic institutions. Fasting (*sawm*) is also an obligation, especially in the month of *Ramadan* during which time the believer is expected to refrain from eating and drinking from dawn to sunset. The fast is only considered valid if one also avoids giving way to anger or misbehaving in any other way. The purpose of the fast is to help the believer to focus on his or her spiritual rather than material needs. In imitation of Abraham's faith-inspired journeys Muslims are also called upon to make a pilgrimage (*hajj*) at least once in their lifetime provided that their health will allow it and that they can afford to travel to Mecca. These are the five pillars of Islamic belief and practice that are aimed at moulding the true Muslim character. Islam is essentially a way of life that should be voluntarily embraced as the Qur'an rules out forced conversions: 'There is no compulsion in religion.'[69]

To understand how *Islam* and *jihad*, words that are essentially spiritual in meaning, came to be so closely associated with the use of the sword and engagement in war, we need to understand the social and political milieu in which Islam began, developed and expanded. Mecca at the time of Muhammad's revelations was a prosperous commercial centre that was surrounded by nomadic clans and tribes who sought payment to guarantee safe passage of the trade caravans through their territory. The tribes would also launch raiding parties to capture rival tribes' camels, goats and sometimes even women.[70] Driven by what he perceived to be a divine calling Muhammad began his prophetic ministry by challenging the religious, social and economic practices of the city. His rejection of polytheism and superstition, and his condemnation of the social injustices and questionable business practices attracted both followers and opponents. The rejection of his message and the strength of the opposition eventually led Muhammad and his followers to flee from Mecca in 622. They made their pilgrimage (*hajj*) to Yathrib where he had been invited to act as a mediator in a long-running feud that had divided the community.

It was in Yathrib, which was renamed Medina, where Muhammad set up his first Islamic community (*umma*). He was the new state's religious and political leader; all authority, civil and religious, rested in him. His role was defined by the Qur'anic injunction: 'Obey God and the Prophet' (Qur'an 3:32). Under his rule and guidance Islam developed as both 'a faith and a socio-political system'.[71] In the relatively short period of ten years Islam's supremacy was established over the tribes and urban communities of Central Arabia. Its extraordinary success was due in no small part to the military superiority that had been achieved over the surrounding tribes. Within six months of establishing his faith-based community at Medina, Muhammad authorized his followers to engage in intertribal raiding. Whether motivated by the community's need to survive economically or by a desire to disrupt the business interests, which he considered to be at the root of the social evils that were blocking religious reforms in Mecca, Muhammad himself fostered raids on the trade caravans.[72] In 630 Mecca succumbed to the continuous attrition and became part of the newly founded Islamic commonwealth. As Islam expanded intertribal raiding was banned within the boundaries of the *umma*, and the raiding expeditions moved further afield into new territories. It was in this indirect way, at least at first, that war came to play an increasing role in the spreading of Islam and came to be seen as part of the striving for the faith, the *jihad*, to which all Muslims were committed.[73] The only effective way to prevent harassment was to join the *umma*, the new faith-based federation.

Muhammad's death in 632 before he had designated his successor, combined with the fact that the *umma* had no system in place to select a new leader, caused a major crisis that led to political fragmentation and tribal rebellion. Some tribes felt that their alliance was no longer binding now that Muhammad had died, and they refused to recognize Abu Bakr, a close friend and colleague of the Prophet, as the newly acclaimed Caliph or leader. In a series of battles that later became known as the apostasy (*riddah*) wars, Khalid ibn al-Walid, the general whom Muhammad himself had labelled 'The Sword of Allah', restored political unity and consolidated Islam's hegemony over the entire Arabian Peninsula.[74] The appointment of Uthman ibn Affan as the successor of Abu Bakr in 644 caused further tribal factionalism. Some of Muhammad's close allies resented Uthman's succession to power because his family, who were natives of Mecca, had been among the leading opponents of the Prophet before their conversion to Islam.

The assassination of Uthman in 656 sparked off a series of further rebellions and feuds between members of the Prophet's family that led eventually to civil war. Aishah, a wife of the Prophet, tried to overthrow the new Caliph, Ali, himself the cousin and son-in-law of the Prophet, before she was defeated in battle. Soon after Muawiyah, the Governor of Syria, challenged Ali's rule. When it looked as if he too might be defeated in battle, he sought arbitration by ordering his forces to raise copies of the Qur'an on the tip of their spears and to cry out: 'Let God decide.' It was Ali's willingness to enter arbitration with Muawiyah that led to his downfall. A group of his supporters questioned his credentials as a true believer and rejected his leadership, claiming that he had failed in his duty to subdue the rebels, whom they regarded as grave sinners and no longer Muslims for challenging the Caliph's authority. The Kharijites, as they became known, murdered Ali in 661, providing the undefeated Muawiyah with the opportunity to seize power.[75]

The supporters of Ali remained loyal even after his death, forming their own religio-political group based on the doctrine that only male descendants of Ali had the right to act as religious and political leaders of the *umma*. They became known as the Shia or Shi'ites to distinguish them from the majority of Sunni Muslims who rejected their interpretation and claims regarding the leadership. The Kharijites also remained active but unlike the Shi'ites they believed that the leadership did not have to be restricted to the blood relatives of the Prophet. They focused their activities on eliminating those whom they considered to be apostates or heretics. They believed that, since the Prophet spent most of his time in war, the true followers of Islam should follow his example and be always ready to fight. They were ruthless in battle and unlike their Sunni brothers they killed prisoners and non-combatants. Muawiyah's succession ushered in a new style of leadership and a new era of expansion. Within the relatively short period of a hundred years, and despite continued internal strife and the doctrinal disputes that led to the sectarian split between Shi'ites and Sunni, the *umma* founded upon the revelations and leadership of Muhammad became 'an empire whose boundaries extended from Spain across North Africa and the Middle East to the borders of China'.[76] Driven by a mix of religious zeal to spread God's rule and a desire for greater wealth and power the Islamic armies advanced beyond the borders of Arabia into territories once ruled by the Byzantine and Persian empires. The inhabitants of these neighbouring lands were given the choice to convert, to accept Islamic rule and to pay their taxes as protected people, or to fight and to die by the sword. Conversion, especially of Christians and Jews, does not appear to have been the primary goal of these military expeditions. In fact, for a period at the beginning of the eighth century, conversion was prohibited because of the adverse effect it was having on the Islamic Empire's revenue through loss of taxes.[77] Those living in the *dar-al-Islam*, the territory under the political and military control of Islam, were allowed to practise their own religion provided that they acknowledged Islamic rule and paid their taxes for the protection they were afforded by their conquerors. Jews in Spain enjoyed greater toleration than they had under Christian rule, as did Buddhists who in India had previously suffered from Hindu persecution.[78]

The religious justification for fighting given in the Qur'an is rooted in the historical injustice that was done to Muhammad and his followers when they were driven out of their homes in Mecca and deprived of their livelihood because of their belief in God. In principle Muslims were only to fight to right an injustice, to defend themselves and to protect religion from destructive forces:

Permission to fight is granted to those against whom war is made, because they have been wronged, and Allah indeed has the power to help them. They are those who have been driven out of their homes unjustly only because they affirmed: Our Lord is Allah. If Allah did not repel the aggression of some people by means of others, cloisters and churches and synagogues and mosques, wherein the name of Allah is oft commemorated, would surely be destroyed.[79]

The reward for fighting unrelentingly against disbelieving neighbours was the assurance of paradise: 'Whoso fights in the cause of Allah, be he slain or be he victorious, we shall soon give him a great reward.'[80] In the real world of Arabia's inter-clan warfare, however, it would appear that attack was considered as the best form of defence, leading Muhammad and his followers to take the military initiative to ensure the survival of the *umma*, the community of believers.[81]

The concept of jihad was always considered to be broader than military action. This is well illustrated in the tradition that Muhammad himself emphasized the priority that should be given to the jihad of the heart, the struggle to purify oneself and to submit wholly to God alone, when on returning from battle he told his companions, 'This day we have returned from the minor jihad (war) to the major jihad (self-control and betterment).'[82] In the course of time Muslim jurists acknowledged the different nuances in the struggle to submit to God's will and that jihad could be performed with the heart, tongue, hands and sword. The jihad of the heart represented the individual's personal struggle with evil. The jihad of the tongue and the hands represented the struggle to promote what is right and to correct what is wrong. The jihad of the sword represented the struggle against the enemies of the faith, those unbelievers who reject the message and rule of Islam.[83] It was the duty of all Muslims to offer their wealth and if necessary their lives in this struggle. All Muslim men who were physically able to fight were expected to take part. The jihad of the sword, though, was regarded as a collective responsibility, and not one that should be undertaken by an individual believer acting alone. It could be an offensive or defensive action depending upon the particular circumstances and the nature of threat it was employed to counteract. It was justified within the *dar al-Islam* (the territory of peace) when embarked upon to punish wrong-doing or to eradicate the forces of disbelief, to defend the faith and to protect the unity and peace of the *umma* from the threat of apostasy, dissent, schism and rebellion: 'Fight those from among the people of the Book who believe not in Allah, nor in the Last Day, nor hold as unlawful that which Allah and His Messenger have declared as unlawful nor follow the true religion, and who have not yet made peace with you, until they pay the tax willingly and make their submission' (Qur'an 9:29). It was justified as a defensive measure against the endemic threat posed by the *dar al-harb* (the territory of war), those regions that were beyond the rule of Islam.[84]

Although it began as a non-violent means of achieving social and religious reform, the concept of jihad developed to sanction the use of the sword as the Muslim community grew to be a political power on the Arabian Peninsula. In the early days of the community at Mecca, Muslims accepted insult and rejection in their efforts to convert their fellow citizens to their new spiritual vision by their preaching and charity. It was after the *hajj*, the emigration to Medina, that Muslims were given permission to fight, essentially to right the injustice that had been done to them.[85] The order to fight in the 'cause of Allah' was given when it was felt that the survival of the community was under threat from hostile neighbours. The sanctioning of a more proactive use of the sword was justified when non-believers had dishonoured their pledges with Muslims.[86] It was at this stage that jihad became instrumental in the spreading of Islam and that the time-honoured aggressiveness of the Arabian tribes that now formed the Muslim community became focused on the world of the non-believer. The relationship between the *dar-al-Islam* and the *dar-al-harb*, the Muslim and non-Muslim worlds, was defined in terms of jihad, or a state of war that applied even when hostilities were suspended.[87]

As the practice of war developed to become for some at least a way of life, so the rules governing the conduct of war also developed. The jurists and scholars differed on the circumstances in which these rules applied, and to whom, but agreed that their prime aim was to limit violence and to avoid the risk of acting out of anger or revenge. As war was a collective responsibility it was to be declared only by the caliph or imam. No war was to be started, however, before the enemy was invited to convert to Islam or to enter into a peace agreement. Summary executions, the torturing of prisoners, mutilating the bodies of the dead, the use of poisoned weapons, the killing or molesting of non-combatants, rape and sexual molestation, ethnic cleansing, the devastation of crops and the destruction of religious, medical and cultural institutions were outlawed.[88]

From its earliest history the unity of Islam was threatened by a series of internal revolts and by those who believed they were justified in using violence to promote their self-proclaimed mission to purify their religion from the malpractices of leaders who had usurped power. Driven by the conviction that 'the subject's duty of obedience lapses where the command is sinful', and that 'there must be no obedience to a creature against his Creator'[89] these rebellious groups, led frequently by charismatic leaders, perceived themselves to be acting virtuously by killing the unrighteous. Tyrannicide was looked upon as a religious duty. In the long run, however, these extremist groups lacked the organization and popular support to withstand the military power and authority of the established leadership. A notable exception was the Assassins, whose terrorist activities spanned the best part of two centuries (1090–1275), and who only ceased to be a threat to the Sunni establishment when the Mongol invasion provided Baybars, the Mamluk Sultan of Egypt, with an opportunity to seize their network of mountain strongholds in Syria.[90]

Although it was not until around 1090 that the Assassins appeared first as an organized terror threat, their origins go back to the split between extremists and moderates that developed within the Shia tradition on the death of the sixth imam in 765. The imam's disinherited eldest son, Isma'il, and his followers became a secret sect known as the Ismailis. The sect was led by a hidden imam, chosen from the descendants of Ali and Fatima through Isma'il. The imam was believed to be 'divinely inspired and infallible' and demanded 'total and unquestioning obedience' from the sects.[91] By the second half of the ninth century the sect's radical practices so appealed to both the pious and the intellectuals that it grew to become 'a well-organised, wide-spread and powerful opposition movement' with the potential to overthrow the existing religious-political-social order. It was at the beginning of the tenth century that the hidden imam emerged and proclaimed himself the caliph in North Africa. For almost the next two centuries the Ismaili dominance triumphed in many parts of the Muslim world until their grip on power was weakened by internal dissent. At the same time the Sunni cause was strengthened by the conversion of Turkish invaders, who provided both the religious fervour and military strength to reassert their control.[92]

It was out of this failure by the Ismailis to reform and purify Islam that the Assassins, known also as the Ismailis-Nizari, emerged and continued to threaten the Sunni dynasty. They established their own state and operated out of a network of 'impregnable mountain fortresses'. Their violence, justified in their minds by the ancient religious duty of tyrannicide, ridding the world of unrighteous rulers, was directed at the pillars of the Sunni establishment, the princes and their religious and military minions, who for them represented a perversion of Islam. Their goal was to overthrow the bureaucracy by weakening it through the spread of fear and terror. Their tactics were to strike their prominent victims in the most public of places so their act of terror could be widely witnessed. Their weapon was always the dagger, which meant that the assassin was in effect on a suicide mission as he was almost always captured or killed. In fact, to survive one's mission was looked upon as shameful.[93] They were trained in monastic-type lifestyle and were taught to look upon themselves as martyrs for the greater cause of defending the purity of Islam. Like many modern-day terrorist groups they attracted sympathizers who formed support cells in urban centres. They used conversion, bribery and intimidation to recruit accomplices who provided access to the highest realms of power, thus creating an atmosphere of suspicion and mistrust at every level of the establishment. The fact that they sometimes developed a level of trust and friendship with the intended victims before executing them at an appropriate moment, added to the climate of fear and mistrust. While some may have admired their single-minded commitment and dedication, a majority of Muslims, it would seem, looked upon their activities as 'repulsive and inhuman'.[94]

Islam also has its pacifist traditions that have stressed the spiritual aims of jihad above all else. The eleventh-century writer, Thus al-Qushayri, emphasized the struggle with self that is acted out for ordinary people in the daily struggle to act rightly and for the elect in the striving to achieve a purity of mind and heart. A century later al-Jilani put the same emphasis on the struggle with self over and above all else as the true meaning of jihad. This tradition of a non-violent interpretation of jihad is central to the teachings of the Ahmadiyya sect, a contemporary Islamic movement with ten million followers founded in the Punjab at the end of the nineteenth century with the aim of revitalizing Islam in the face of the British Raj, Protestant missionary activity and resurgent Hinduism, and which is committed to a spiritual rather than a violent and bloody interpretation of jihad. Hazrat Mirza Ghulam Ahmad, the founder of the sect, declared, 'How could a religion be from God, whose teachings needed the flash of the sword to get an entrance into the human heart? The sword, far from revealing the beauties and excellence of truth, makes them dubious and throws them into the background.'[95] He believed that Islam could easily establish 'its truth and superiority by sound intellectual arguments, heavenly signs or other reliable testimony' and therefore it did not need 'the sword to threaten men and to force a confession of its truth from them'. The circumstances that necessitated the resort to arms in Islam's early history do not exist any more, he declared, and therefore all offensive wars are unholy. The true jihad, they believe, lies in the willingness to suffer, and not in the perpetration of violence. They do accept, though, the moral legitimacy of self-defence in the face of aggression.

A truly outstanding example of Islamic pacifism is the non-violent activities of Khudai Khidmatgars, the Servants or Army of God movement that was founded by Abdul Ghaffir Khan in 1929 to challenge the social and economic structures of British colonial rule in Northern India. Influenced by the example of Gandhi, Kahn persuaded the Pathans, a tribe renowned for its commitment to bloodletting and revenge, to follow the example of the Prophet Muhammad during the Mecca years when Muhammad and his followers endured abuse and persecution in their struggle to effect religious and social change. The Pathans' resolve to forego revenge and to adopt non-violence did not weaken despite years of imprisonment and executions.[96]

The fundamental belief of Sikhism, like Islam, upholds the essential unity of humanity under 'One God'. In Sikhism God can be acknowledged by many names. Consequently Sikhs are required to serve their fellow human beings without regard to religion, race or gender 'freely and disinterestedly'. Guru Nanak, its founder, was born in 1469 into a Hindu family in the Punjab. Disturbed by the hate and violent conflicts that existed between Hindus and Muslims, and determined to address the corruption and divisions that existed within his society, Guru Nanak set out to promote reconciliation between the different factions. His goal was peace but he was not a pacifist. 'To fight and accept death for a righteous cause is the privilege of the brave and truly religious,' he declared.[97] It was Guru Nanak's acknowledgement that the use of force is morally legitimate that prompted his later followers, when faced with active persecution, to take up arms in self-defence. It was Gobind Singh, the tenth Guru, who positively sanctioned the use of the sword when he established a Sikh army, known as the Khalsa, the Army of Salvation. In the belief that he was sent into the world 'to uproot evil and protect from tyranny the weak and oppressed' he actively pursued those whom he considered as enemies.[98] In his mystic writings he equated the sword with God in the sense that both subdue their enemies: 'I bow with love and devotion to the Holy Sword. Assist me that I may complete this work.'[99] By the time of his death he had established such an accomplished fighting force that the new commander of the armies, Banda Singh, was able to establish a power base that stretched from Lahore to Panipat.

Internal divisions, however, soon led to the collapse of Sikh autonomy and to a new wave of persecution. The price of being caught with long hair or a beard, the outward symbols of Sikhism, was death. To entertain a Sikh was a crime. These harsh laws drove the Sikhs into hiding and to embark upon a campaign of guerrilla warfare that eventually gained them limited recognition by the Hindu authorities. The truce, however, was short lived. In 1737 the Sikh leader was killed at a festival at the Golden Temple, an act of government treachery that led to a further cycle of persecution and revenge. The Sikh fighting spirit remained resilient despite suffering severe losses and the sacking of the Golden Temple at the hands of foreign mercenaries in 1762. They regained their autonomy which they held until their territories were annexed by the British in 1846. Their successful attempts at violent revolt against British rule led to a change in tactics. By the early twentieth century the Sikhs had adopted the practice of non-violent resistance to British intransigence. In their protests in 1922 hundreds were severely beaten 'without defending themselves or retaliating'.[100] The partition of India resulted in the wide dispersal of the Sikh community.

An historical overview of the world's mainstream religious traditions highlights how without exception each faith community has in the face of the threat of extinction or the opportunity to expand interpreted its fundamental teachings to accommodate the changing circumstances by sanctioning the use of violence to protect and secure its own sectarian interests. In each faith tradition one can find sufficient ambiguity in its founding texts and stories to justify killing for the glory of God. Each tradition has also its heroes who saw themselves as acting on divine authority as they plotted the destruction of those whom they perceived to be enemies of God. Today's religious extremists can find their rationale for inflicting terror in the name of their God in the ambivalence towards violence that is be found in each faith tradition.

4

Battles on Sacred Turf

The argument that religion matters and, as an actor in its own right, needs to be addressed, is well demonstrated in what is happening in Northern Ireland, Israel/Palestine and Sri Lanka. First, these conflicts provide contemporary examples of Christians, Muslims, Jews, Hindus and Buddhists as protagonists and perpetrators of violence. Second, they illustrate the complexity of conflicts involving competing truth claims, contradictory foundational myths and divergent aspirations linked to land designated by the warring factions as sacred. Third, the solution in all three cases requires an acknowledgement of the right of different faith and cultural traditions to cohabit the same land. Fourth, the peace processes initiated by the international community have deliberately ignored the religious component that has helped to shape and sustain these conflicts. Fifth, all three conflicts involve the problem of the 'double minority'. In each case the majority community suffers from a minority complex because of the close proximity of the larger communities of their opponents' co-religionists, which in these particular cases are Catholics in the Republic of Ireland, Muslims in the Middle East and Hindus in South India. Sixth, these conflicts have persisted over several decades, cost thousands of lives and are yet to be resolved.

The past thirty years has witnessed the publication of numerous interpretations and analyses of these conflicts. I have chosen to limit my observations to the religious dimension. I recognize, though, that religion is not the sole or prime cause. The communal violence in all three examples stems from a more complex interplay of colonial, economic, social and political factors as well. My goal is simply to illustrate that religion per se is a part of the problem and as such needs to be addressed if durable solutions are to be found. My recent journeys to Sri Lanka, Israel/Palestine and

Northern Ireland provided me with ample opportunity to meet with and interview many who are caught up at different levels of engagement in each of these conflicts. I very much welcomed the direct and honest responses that I received from all those with whom I met in each of these conflict situations. Some of my interviewees I have identified and not others. To attribute comments in certain circumstances could, I fear, inadvertently complicate certain individuals' positions or, worse still, put them at personal risk.

It could be said that the Irish 'Troubles' – a word that is used frequently to describe the communal conflict in Northern Ireland – stem from 1170 when Henry II of England gained control of Dublin and its surroundings, a first step in his attempted annexation of Ireland into his kingdom.[1] The surrender of Hugh O'Neil, the last of the Gaelic princes to resist English rule to Lord Mountjoy, the Lord Deputy of Ireland, in 1603 and his subsequent flight from Ulster to the Continent four years later with a hundred local chieftains were additional defining moments in Irish history that have helped to shape the current conflict. The English authorities saw the 'flight of the earls' as the opportunity to consolidate their rule in Ulster, a hitherto rebellious province. They confiscated the land abandoned by the Irish earls, and within three years began to colonize the province by encouraging English companies and individual settlers from the Scottish lowlands to migrate to Ulster. The majority of the English colonizers were Anglicans; the Scots were Presbyterians. This influx of these economic migrants from different ethnic and religious backgrounds created a 'radical transformation of the social structure'[2] that left the native Irish in Ulster totally marginalized – by 1703 they owned less than 5 per cent of the land.[3]

The differences between the colonizers and the colonized had become so entrenched by the early part of the twentieth century that Ulster Protestants threatened rebellion against the Crown to thwart the ambitions of the Irish nationals who were seeking an independent Irish state that would embrace the whole of the island. The London government conceded to their demands to remain within the Union, and in 1921 six counties in the northeast of the island were partitioned off to form a new state in which a Protestant majority would be ensured. The current phase of the 'Troubles' began in 1968 when the Catholic minority in Northern Ireland became more vociferous in their demands for equal rights. Their protests, marches and use of the media to publicize their grievances gave rise to such a level of civil disorder between the two communities that in 1969 British troops were ordered onto the streets, initially as 'peacekeepers'. The presence and perceived partiality of the army towards the majority community provoked a republican backlash that led to the rebirth of the IRA. In the intervening three decades of conflict 3600 people have died. More than half of these were civilians.

John Whyte's book *Interpreting Northern Ireland* provides an analysis of 500 alternative interpretations of the conflict. The former Irish Premier, Garret FitzGerald, wrote in the Foreword of the book, 'no one is likely to be able to write intelligently about the Northern Ireland conflict in future without having first taken account of John Whyte's last book.'[4] Whyte discovered that there were almost as many interpretations as books, as virtually every author differed in the details. None the less he found sufficient common ground to be able to group the range of interpretations into four main schools of thought. He did this by seeing how authors defined the different antagonists in the conflict. The four pairs he identified were: Britain versus Ireland, Southern Ireland versus Northern Ireland, capitalist versus worker, Protestant versus Catholic within Northern Ireland. Virtually every author according to Whyte recognized at least two and some even three of these different pairs of antagonists in their interpretations of the conflict. Whyte labelled these interpretations in the order listed above as traditional nationalist, traditional unionist, Marxist, and two-community or internal-conflict.[5] The traditional approach is to blame the source of the conflict on outsiders. An Irish nationalist sees Britain as the culprit; a unionist puts the blame at the door of the Irish Republic. Over the years, though, Whyte observed a shift in the interpretation of most nationalists who, he claims, without abandoning their aspirations for a united Ireland now see the core of the conflict to be between the two communities within Northern Ireland.

I find John Whyte's book on the Northern Ireland conflict a particularly helpful framework for my own observations as it relates well to my own past and present experiences of the problem. I lived in Leitrim, which is just south of the border with Northern Ireland, until my family moved to London in the late 1950s. I was educated in the local school that was run by the De La Salle Brothers, a religious teaching order which did not have a particularly pro-nationalist reputation. And yet I can recall that by the age of ten my own interpretation of 'the North', as it was referred to, would have fitted neatly under two of the headings identified by Whyte – traditional nationalist and two-community or internal-conflict. The British, so we were taught in school, were denying the lawful aspirations of the Irish for the unity and independence of Ireland, and therefore there would never be peace on the island until the 'English went home'. The 'black' Protestants, as they were usually labelled, were regarded as an alien presence in a land that was once a shining example of sanctity and knowledge; they were perceived to be the lackeys of British imperialism and persecutors of the Catholics in the North. There would never be peace, we were told, as long as Protestants remained in control at Stormont, the local seat of political power in Northern Ireland. Looking back I recognize how the demonizing of the other as the antagonist, combined with the teaching of a version of history that endorsed a victim mentality and glorified the use of the gun in Ireland's struggle for freedom, must have helped to provide, albeit inadvertently, a fertile recruiting ground for future republican activists. Given the strong nationalist mood that prevailed in Ireland in the 1950s and its endorsement, at least at the local level, by organizations with strong links to the Catholic Church, the support and the protection given to the IRA by the Catholic community especially in the early days of the 'Troubles' was hardly surprising.

My first real introduction to the alternative interpretations of the Northern Ireland conflict came in the early 1970s when I became actively involved in a programme that aimed at bringing together families from the most segregated neighbourhoods in Belfast by taking them on holiday in Britain and Southern Ireland. I recall many late-night discussions with traditionalist unionists who clearly believed the core of the problem lay in the Dublin government's aspirations for Irish unity and the untrustworthiness of their Catholic neighbours who shared those nationalist dreams. I also encountered Marxists on both sides of the divide who saw the 'Troubles' wholly in terms of a class struggle that had been complicated by religious labels and nationalist and imperialist ambitions. The experience of working together with Protestant and Catholic, unionist and nationalist families underlined for me the observation made by Whyte and numerous others that Northern Ireland is a 'deeply but not totally divided community'.[6] When given the opportunity to meet in a neutral setting and to work together in caring for their children and preparing meals, both groups discovered a commonality of language, humour, music and food as well as human concerns, fears and aspirations for themselves and their children.

The most notable areas of divergence of opinion, though, were on the questions of religion and politics, which clearly shaped their interpretations of the conflict. The realization of so much common ground on a human level, combined with the intensity of the encounters and an extraordinary level of neutral outside support, provided sufficient confidence among all of the participants in these holiday programmes to believe that by working together we could help to shape a different future. We were soon to discover that it was a naïve confidence as it failed to take sufficient account of the pervasiveness of the structural segregation of Northern Ireland society. Once the families returned to their segregated ghettos they found it impossible to maintain relationships with members of 'the other side' as to do so would call into question their own loyalties and trustworthiness. I recall being told by four Belfast ladies from the Shankill Road how on their first trip into the staunchly republican area of Ballymurphy to attend a Catholic mass at the invitation of those whom they met on holiday, they were told by a nationalist cab driver as they passed the cemetery that 'it was the only place one could find a good "prod" in this town'. They found the experience sufficiently threatening to break contact with their potential friends on the Catholic side of the divide.

Three of the main bulwarks of segregation identified by Whyte's analysis are residential, educational and marital. The history of the 'Troubles' outlined above shows that the roots of residential segregation stretch back to the early days of the 'plantation' of Ulster when the best agricultural land was allocated to the new settlers. The pattern of maintaining segregated areas continued with the growth of towns and cities during the period of the industrial revolution. By 1969, when street rioting began to take hold, Belfast was 'a highly segregated city'. The findings of one survey showed that '69 per cent of Protestants lived in streets which were 91 per cent or more Protestant, and 56 per cent of Catholics lived in streets which were 91 per cent or more Catholic.'[7] The 2001 census shows that the percentage of Catholics opting to live in segregated communities had risen to 66 per cent. Residential segregation along the lines of both religion and class has had a powerful impact on the shaping of Northern Ireland society. In support of this argument Whyte quotes the conclusions of the geographer Fredrick W. Boal who sees segregated areas as providing a base for self-defence, enabling the inhabitants to avoid 'embarrassing contacts with unfriendly outsiders', preserving a way of life and, for the more aggressive, 'a base from which they can attack their enemies'. A further effect of residential segregation, he claims, is that it 'can reinforce other forms of segregation'.[8]

In keeping with the rest of Britain Northern Ireland has a parallel school system funded by the State. In principle both systems should be open to children of all denominations but in practice the state-controlled schools are identified solely with a Protestant-unionist ethos, and the voluntary or maintained schools are regarded as predominately Catholic and nationalist in outlook. More recently a small number of integrated schools have been established but for the most part these provide for the children of the middle classes who are generally more mobile. The location of the schools many see as a major problem that helps to reinforce residential segregation. In the early days of the current conflict it was found that both at a primary and secondary level '71 per cent of schools were either totally Catholic or totally Protestant, and only 3 per cent of schools had more than 5 per cent of the pupils from the "wrong" religious group'.[9] Today, according to the Northern Ireland Council for Integrated Education, 90 per cent of all children go to schools that are totally either Protestant or Catholic in their make-up. The Catholic Church has staunchly defended the segregated school system, arguing that in principle it cannot be blamed for the conflict as there are too many other factors at work, and that the schools instil a moral discipline in their pupils which runs counter to 'the violence and intolerance' that fuel the conflict.[10]

Whyte, however, noted that several observers of the separate schools system drew attention to the fact that the differences in the schools' curricula are greater than just religious instruction. Catholic schools teach Irish history and encourage the use of the Irish language and the playing of Gaelic games. In contrast, the stress in the state or 'Protestant' schools is on the links with Britain.[11] Perhaps even more important, though, he notes that a study by Dominic Murray, which focused on staff room rather than classroom culture concluded that teachers were offering to their pupils two alternative sets of values, one pro State, the other suspicious of the State. Catholics, he found, were generally hostile to the British identity that was being pushed in state schools. The school one attends has long been a marker of identity in Northern Ireland, with anyone with local knowledge being well aware of the affiliations of the schools. I have always favoured a policy of integrated education as a major step towards bridging the divide but a recent visit to Northern Ireland helped me to realize that the desegregation of the schools must go hand in hand with other forms of institutional and societal desegregation. Today 5 per cent of Northern Ireland's children are attending integrated schools, the first of which began in 1981. The opposition to integrated education is strong on both sides of the community divide. Critics, both Catholic and Protestant, provided me with anecdotal evidence of pupils at one of these mixed schools arranging to throw stones at each other in out-of-school hours.

The lack of intermarriage between Catholics and Protestants is another notable feature of life in Northern Ireland. The custom in general is to marry within one's tribe. To begin with, residential and educational segregation limits the opportunities people have of more intimate encounters with members of the other community. Religious beliefs also play a significant role, and this is especially so because of the obligation a Catholic partner has to do everything within his or her power to baptize and educate the children of marriage in the Catholic faith. It was estimated at the end of the 1970s that couples from a religiously mixed background comprised less than 2 per cent of marriages. According to Whyte's analysis there is evidence that, even when intermarriage does happen, it has little impact on mending the divisions in society as frequently the consequences are that one or other of the partners is obliged to break his or her kinship ties.[12]

I recently witnessed first hand the impact systemic segregation can have on people's perceptions of those on the other side and, as a consequence, on their interpretations of the conflict when I took part in two separate conferences, one of which was held at Harvard and the other at the University of Ulster in Londonderry. These two week-long meetings were attended by politicians, academics and community activists from both sides of the community divide. Listening to the exchanges between the Northern Ireland participants confirmed the paradigm shift noted by Whyte: both sides clearly recognized that the core of their problem was internal and had stopped putting the blame exclusively at the door of the outsider, be it Britain or the Irish Republic. Since the signing of the Belfast/Good Friday Agreement, I also noticed a further shift had taken place among Protestants who were now talking of themselves as victims of the British as well as of the Dublin government and the nationalist/Catholic community. What also became clear was the high level of ignorance of the other community's history, cultural heritage and beliefs which still exists on both sides of the community divide. This lack of awareness undoubtedly feeds the susceptibility within both groups to prejudice and stereotyping. I was surprised at the extent and the depth of the divisions that I detected within the group of Protestant participants at each of these meetings. The division between liberal and fundamentalist Protestants was clearly reflected in their religious, class and political attitudes and, as Whyte previously observed, I too discovered that these were 'not trivial'. A number of the Protestant participants in both meetings shared their anxieties over the lack of understanding within their own community of what they refer to as their 'Scots Ulster' heritage. This lack of knowledge regarding their own identity and history, they felt, had put Protestants at a serious disadvantage in cross-community meetings on the Belfast/Good Friday Agreement. It was on these grounds that they argued strongly in favour of 'single identity development' programmes.

Northern Ireland Protestants are not alone in recognizing the need to consolidate their own community's sense of identity before engaging in cross-cultural/religious talks, nor is the concept of single identity development a new one. I recall, in the early days of *perestroika*, negotiating on behalf of the Jewish and Christian communities in Western Europe with the Russian Orthodox Church and the Soviet authorities on the question of setting up a Moscow-based Council of Christians and Jews. The initiative was being spearheaded by some prominent members of the Jewish community in the West who believed that this was the best way to support the Jews in Russia. The orthodox Chief Rabbi of Great Britain at the time, Lord Immanuel Jakobovits, thought differently. He told me privately his concern was that Russian Jews, having been isolated for so long from the wider Jewish community, were too insecure and fragmented to enter into inter-faith dialogue. He believed it to be more desirable for them to be given an opportunity to develop their own identity separately before embarking on a programme of inter-faith dialogue. In those particular circumstances I could understand his reasoning. Given the current situation in Northern Ireland, however, it could be argued that remaining isolated in order to develop a stronger group identity could be detrimental to the common good as it could lead to a further entrenchment of the sectarianism that is already so deeply rooted.

Recent research carried out by Peter Shirlow of the University of Ulster in neighbourhoods that are divided by so called 'peace lines' – these are physical barriers erected to keep neighbouring communities apart – indicates that since the current peace process began the gap between the two communities is growing wider, and especially among the younger generation. He found that prejudice was so ingrained on both sides that 68 per cent of the eighteen to twenty-five age group claimed that they had never had a meaningful conversation with anyone from the other community. His findings also revealed that 72 per cent of all age groups refuse to use health centres located in areas that are dominated by the other religion, and 62 per cent of unemployed people refuse to sign on in their local social security office if it is located in what is seen to be the other's territory.[13] When I met with Dr Shirlow to discuss his findings he told me that one of the main problems facing Northern Ireland is that everyone sees him or herself as a victim of the other side and is unable to recognize that self as a perpetrator of violence and intimidation. The challenge, he believes, is to help people on both sides to see that they are both victims and perpetrators in the current conflict.

The Irish School of Ecumenics published in 2001 the findings of their six-year research project that focused on the role of religion in sectarianism in Northern Ireland. The report, *Moving Beyond Sectarianism* by Joseph Liechty and Cecelia Clegg, uncovers the pervasiveness of sectarianism at every level of Northern Ireland society. It underlines the need to think about sectarianism as a systemic as well as a personal problem. 'Sectarianism', they write, 'has become a system so efficient that it can take our sane and rational responses to a situation which it has generated and use them to further deepen sectarianism.'[14] The example they provide is how people have responded to the violence over the past thirty years. The tendency has been to move from mixed residential areas to live 'exclusively among our own'. The authors recognize that this is a perfectly understandable and blameless response but the unfortunate effect, they claim, is to reinforce sectarianism still further. People, they found, approach sectarianism by drawing lines between themselves and others and, as they can always find people whose actions are worse than their own, they can point to them as the real problem. The consequences of the dynamics of systemic sectarianism, they claim, is that no one is ever responsible – 'the buck never stops passing'.[15] Sectarianism can also feed on what the authors call 'Christians' religiously motivated boundary maintenance'. People worship, educate and marry almost exclusively in their own communities with the intention not to be sectarian but to build strong communities. The result none the less is, according to the report, the 'strengthening of the sectarian divide'.[16]

Liechty and Clegg argue that understanding what sectarianism is and how it functions is a crucial first step in moving beyond it. The sectarian system, they found, works 'most smoothly and effectively' when it is largely hidden from view and accepted as normality, the way things have been and always will be done. Even to mention the word sectarianism in mixed gatherings of Protestants and Catholics in Northern Ireland can cause high emotions, they discovered. People, they noted, tend to discuss sectarianism only within their own group, and then it is always with reference to those 'others' and not themselves. As sectarianism, according to their definition, always involves religion in some way, they believe that the Churches in Northern Ireland face a particular challenge. They write,

> It is vital that the majority of people in Northern Ireland, especially the decent church-going people, recognize that there are subtle and polite forms of sectarianism, that there are attitudes and beliefs which they take for granted, which actually significantly underpin this phenomenon. The raw and obvious expressions of sectarianism are only the visible tip of a large iceberg. Only when people realize that, however benign they consider themselves and their communities to be, they are all tainted and shaped by sectarianism, and only when they start taking responsibility for this, will there be sufficient communal energy generated to dismantle the sectarian system.[17]

Based on the work of Brian Lambkin, Liechty and Clegg acknowledge that a 'religion-based interpretation' of the Northern Ireland conflict is gaining support, but they believe it would be premature to claim that this reflects the 'consensus' of opinion. Many scholars would still reject the religious component of this conflict as utterly insignificant. Notable among these are the political scientists John McGarry and Brendan O'Leary, who have attempted to offer a more updated version of John Whyte's comprehensive overview of interpretations of the conflict. They identify four 'generic types of religious explanation', which they summarize as follows:

religion matters equally to Protestants and Catholics, and is the cause of the antagonism; religion matters most to Protestants, and Protestantism is the root of the conflict; religion matters most to Catholics and Catholicism is at the source of the conflict; and religion matters in maintaining and reinforcing social boundaries between Catholics and Protestants, i.e. it matters equally socially rather than theologically.[18]

They acknowledge that 'the correlation between political partisanship and religion is very high' in the sense that nationalist parties and republican paramilitaries are supported almost exclusively by Catholics, while unionist parties and loyalist paramilitaries get their support overwhelmingly from Protestants. They also make the point that, when compared with other countries with populations that are similarly divided between Catholics and Protestants Northern Ireland scores extremely high in 'the index of religious voting', indicating that people vote along religious lines.[19] And yet, they maintain that it would be 'superficial' to conclude that 'the conflict must be religious if the groups engaged in electoral competition and para-military struggle are religiously defined'. They reject also the notion that the Churches are directly and indirectly responsible for maintaining the social boundary between the communities. Part of the problem, they argue, is the careless and interchangeable use of terms like Catholic/Protestant and nationalist/unionist that are used to define the conflict.

One of the major flaws for McGarry and O'Leary in explanations that emphasize the importance of religion is the fact that the conflict in Northern Ireland has escalated while religion has declined. Northern Ireland is becoming secular, albeit not at the same scale as elsewhere in Western Europe, they claim. They point to a marked increase in divorce and childbirth outside marriage as evidence. The increasing secularization of society has not affected the high level of support for the nationalist and unionist parties, which they see as evidence that political action and violence do not correlate to religious practice. Further evidence for them is that nationalist politicians 'propose secular not theological policies'. The fact that Sinn Fein believes an agreed or united Ireland would transcend sectarianism, rather than the construction of a Catholic state, they argue, provides support for their rejection of the importance of religion in this conflict. They consider it to be misleading to claim that unionist objections to a united Ireland are rooted in 'fear of the power of the Roman Catholic Church', arguing that there have always been 'economic as well as cultural reasons why Ulster Protestants resist incorporation'.[20]

They accept 'the salience of religion as an ethnic marker' but reject the notion that ethnic divisions can be 'reduced to religion, or church policy on education, or mixed marriages'. In conclusion, McGarry and O'Leary write, 'explanations, which accord primacy to religion, create blind alleys for policymakers and inhibit understanding'. They go on to argue that if the antagonisms are religious it would rule out the impact on the current conflict of 'colonial conquest, plantation and oppression ... economic discrimination against nationalists ... British mismanagement ... and the nature of the Republic's nationalism'. Finally they declare that when explanations that emphasize the primacy of religion are 'exposed to strong light ... they evaporate, leaving little residue'.[21] The main flaw I find with the arguments they put forward to arrive at such a conclusion is that these are based on an impoverished concept of religion.

If one were to work within what seems to be their limited definition of religion, it would require Ian Paisley and Gerry Adams to lead their followers into a pitch battle in the centre of Belfast over the doctrine of transubstantiation – the Catholic belief that the bread and wine used in the eucharist changes into the substance of the body and blood of Christ – before one could recognize a religious component in the Northern Ireland conflict. There is increasing evidence of a decline in the practice of religion at least in areas like Belfast. When I visited the city a few days before Christmas last year my attention was drawn to a sign in large red letters, wishing everyone a 'Happy Xmas'. It was hanging over the entrance of what was once a church but is now a Chinese restaurant. My conversations with Catholic priests stationed mainly in working-class areas of Belfast confirmed a notable drop off in church attendance. This superficial evidence, however, should not be used to rule out the potency of denominational beliefs in shaping people's world view and political judgements. McGarry and O'Leary appear not to factor in the 'believing without belonging' phenomenon observed elsewhere, and which I have referred to in a previous chapter. The impact of religion on a society cannot be assessed by a head count in the pews. Many of the politicians with whom I met during my research were explicit about the fact that their religion was more than just an 'identity marker'.

In support of their argument that religion does matter when trying to interpret the conflict in Northern Ireland Liechty and Clegg quote from the Opsahl Commission, which conducted a long and detailed enquiry, the findings of which were published in 1993. 'Religion may or may not be the prime cause of the conflict', the Commission report states. 'It is certainly a potent component of it ... It simply comes to this: the Northern Ireland conflict is in part economic and social, in part political and constitutional, and also in part religious, and damagingly so.'[22] These findings reflect the opinion of a number of academics that have recognized in the midst of social, historical, political, cultural and economic factors the salience of religion also. John Whyte summed up the significance of religion in the Northern Ireland context in two ways: '1. It can be a basis for segregating the population into two communities, largely ignorant of each other and susceptible therefore to prejudice and stereotyping. 2. It can be an actual cause of conflict, because of a clash of values and interests related to religion.'[23] He recognized, though, that this impact could vary from one place to another.

The Sinn Fein officials that I met on recent visits to Northern Ireland have always insisted that their motivation is purely secular driven, as McGarry and O'Leary have argued. To glance through their web site and official literature would seem to confirm this claim. I was told by a number of well-informed people that relationships between the republican movement and the leadership of the Catholic Church were in some places extremely tense because of the Church's public condemnation of violence. None the less it is equally well known that the republican movement and the IRA in particular have always found sympathetic support from some members of the clergy. In an earlier chapter I referred to the case of Father Jim Chesney who is suspected of having been directly involved in the bombing at Claudy, which killed nine people. I have also known personally priests that have been quite vocal in their justification of IRA violence, and who have applied the principles of the 'just war' theory to give their arguments a moral authority. Certainly, in the mind of many Protestants there is a strong suspicion that republican violence has at least the tacit blessing of the Catholic Church. In his book *Religion and the Northern Ireland Problem* John Hickey writes: 'This revival of Republicanism, coupled with the support it is given by Roman Catholic clergy, who condemn the activities of the IRA but bury its "heroes" with the full pomp and panoply of the Roman Catholic Church and therefore legitimate their actions, fuels Protestant fears and reinforces their suspicions of the intentions of their Roman Catholic fellow-citizens.'[24] Even though the number of republican funerals has greatly decreased in recent years, mainly because of the ceasefire in place, the perception that Hickey wrote about still lingers.

To gain insight into the mindset of loyalist paramilitaries I was advised to visit their web sites where I found a number of apologias for their actions. The most common defence for their activity is that they are soldiers in a conflict that they did not want but were compelled to engage in as Ulster people were being murdered because of their religion and their culture. One of the most ruthless loyalist killers whose activities are described on at least a couple of sites was Billy Wright, who was murdered in prison by presumed nationalist assassins in 1997. Having found God on his own,

Wright gave up his paramilitary activity to take up a career as a preacher and street evangelist which lasted for about three years. In 1985, fearing that the signing of the Anglo-Irish Agreement was an indication of Britain's imminent betrayal of Ulster, he returned to the gun. He is said to have had no regrets for the reign of terror he instigated and the people he executed.

Surfing loyalist paramilitary sites on the web one finds numerous links to fundamentalist Protestant groups. I recognize that web-links do not necessarily imply that these religious bodies either secretly condone or endorse the illegal activities of the paramilitaries. Nevertheless, reading through some of the material posted on these sites leaves one with little doubt that, for many of these fundamentalist religious groups, politics is an essential expression of their religious beliefs and values. The strong emphasis they put on loyalty, however, is conditioned by the belief that error has no rights. This Calvinist mindset is shaped by the 1647 Westminster Confession of Faith, which declares that 'God alone is Lord of conscience', and so to believe human doctrines and commandments that are not in keeping with his Word, is to betray 'true liberty of conscience'. It is therefore a religious duty to protest against error. On one of the official Orange lodge sites I read that: 'Papal powers and tyranny are children of one womb'; therefore, 'an Orangeman must be a Protestant'. Maintaining political and cultural links with mainland Britain, this site argues, is the only way to guarantee 'a pluralist society which can tolerate ethical and religious diversity'. It declared that 'whatever is false in church or state has none of our support'.

John Hickey believes that, while differences in the social structure between Protestants and Catholics are being slowly eliminated, the importance of other differences and especially religion are surfacing: 'the major differences between Protestants and Catholics in their view of Christianity are doctrinal statements which have, in themselves, enormous social and political repercussions ... the fact that they are not always explicit ... does not make such convictions less real.'[25] One person, who does make the differences explicit, Hickey acknowledges, is the Reverend Ian Paisley. The media in general seem to regard Paisley as a political opportunist who uses religion to mobilize support for his own ambitions for power. To misread 'the Paisley factor', I fear, would be seriously to misunderstand the undercurrent of influences that has shaped, and still continues to shape, the conflict in Northern Ireland. No matter how distasteful one may find Paisley's public brand of bigotry, his beliefs are widely shared and deeply rooted within not an insignificant sector of the Protestant community. Paisley, according to John Whyte, has an apocalyptic world view that aligns Catholicism with the forces of tyranny, a belief that 'necessarily involves perpetual conflict between Romanism and Protestantism' –

Catholicism represents the forces of evil, evangelical Protestantism the forces of good.[26] To compromise in any way with Catholicism would be the equivalent to surrendering to evil.

In 1951 Paisley founded the Free Presbyterian Church, which based its beliefs solely on 'the absolute authority and the divine verbal inspiration of the Old and New Testaments as the Word of God'. The mission of this new independent branch of Presbyterianism was to 'faithfully preach and defend the gospel of Christ in an age of growing compromise and apostasy'.[27] From its rural beginnings the Free Presbyterian Church has grown to embrace a worldwide membership, its success due to a combination of the energy of its leadership and the attraction of the style of fundamentalist Protestantism that it promotes. The Church also hosts the European Institute of Protestant Studies, which was founded by Paisley 'to promote, defend and maintain Bible Protestantism' and 'to expose the errors of Romanism'. Paisley's obsession with combating the influences of Roman Catholicism appears to be driven by the belief that Protestants in Northern Ireland are a people of destiny, a people chosen by God, a people with a divine mission that reaches beyond the borders of Ulster. His paper, the *Protestant Telegraph*, described this mission as follows:

> The Almighty does not make mistakes; He alone is infallible. Our presence in Ulster is no accident of history ... We have a historic and a Divine Commission. We are the defenders of Truth in this Province and in this island ... Ulster is the last bastion of Evangelical Protestantism in Western Europe; we must not drop the torch of Truth at this stage of the eternal conflict between Truth and Evil.[28]

Donald Akenson attributes Ulster Protestants' sense of being 'chosen' and being superior to others to their Calvinist roots. In his book *God's Peoples: Covenant and Land in South Africa, Israel and Ulster* he argues that Ulster Protestants, Afrikaners and Israeli Jews all share a world view that is framed by their understanding of the covenant with God described in the Old Testament. The basic concept of the covenant, Akenson claims, is neither ethereal nor intellectually demanding: anyone can grasp the fundamentals. God makes a deal with a people: they accept him as the only one God, and he provides for them the rules that give to the whole of life a purpose and sense of direction. In entering into the deal 'the Israelites in the scriptures assume a single corporate personality'.[29] The covenant offers what Akenson describes as a 'well-integrated conceptual grid' that can provide answers to life's problems. Post Reformation societies that adopted this 'scriptural grid' as a foundation for their societal life are, according to Akenson, apt to act like the ancient Israelites and are likely to have the following hallmarks in common: an emphasis on social law, a clear definition of enemies combined with an unforgiving spirit, a warlike image of the Almighty, an attachment to land designated as sacred, a sense of pilgrimage and a desire for group religious and racial purity.

Akenson claims that, 'although the Scots colonists did not delude themselves by believing that they were in fact *the* chosen people, the analogy was strong and they acted under the conviction that they were *a* chosen people'.[30] This scriptural mindset explains, he believes, their cohesiveness, their attachment to the land, their attitude towards the native Catholics, their opposition to intermarriage and their lack of concern for outside opinion. It also explains why they are not given to easy compromises: 'to keep the deal that is the covenant, a society must be uncompromising, adamantine, self-contained.'[31] It is an approach that outsiders may not like but it is not, Akenson claims, 'inchoate or crazy'.

On a recent visit to Northern Ireland I asked a number of Protestant academics, community workers and politicians if they considered 'covenantal' thinking to be prevalent today in the Protestant community. The consistent response I received was that a significant minority were still embedded in the mindset to which Ian Paisley so frequently gives voice. In conversation with a senior member of the Democratic Unionist Party, the party which Paisley founded in 1971 and which has grown in influence since the suspension of the Northern Ireland Assembly, he described to me the effect a biblical mindset can have on contemporary politics, and in particular within his own party. Those who believe in the Bible as the literal Word of God, and therefore as a truth that is unchangeable, he explained, frequently carry the same attitude into their political life. They find it difficult to understand how policies that were true yesterday can no longer be valid today. Belief in divine intervention also strongly influences their way of doing politics. If something is right, they believe that it is their duty to hold out, and eventually God will intervene to assure success. He explained also that opposition to the Belfast/Good Friday Agreement was driven not only by a concern that it was unfair to the unionist community but also by the fact that some of its terms, and in particular the amnesty granted to murderers, offended people's sense of biblical justice. If it went against some of the basic principles of the Bible, he explained to me, they reasoned it had to be flawed. If the British Government were to press ahead with implementing the Agreement without addressing the concerns of the unionist community, he feared that some, who hitherto have not been engaged in violence, would see it as a religious duty to resist. These are young intelligent people, he warned, who would be capable of making use of weapons far more lethal than the crude home-made bombs of the past.

The terrain, climate, culture and religious traditions of Sri Lanka stand in sharp contrast to those of Ireland, and yet there are some striking similarities between these two protracted conflicts. Colonialism, cultural chauvinism, economic and political grievances, competing truth claims on land rooted in religious texts, a sense of destiny as a chosen people, the demonizing of opponents, the double minority complex, collapsed peace agreements, and deep mistrust of the other all contribute to the complexity of the communal strife that has cost thousands of lives in this 'Venerable Place' – the meaning of Sri Lanka.[32] After several failed attempts to find a negotiated solution to this ongoing communal conflict between the Sinhala majority and the Tamil minority, the Sri Lanka government and the Liberation Tigers of Tamil Eelam (LTTE) responded to Norwegian overtures and agreed to a further ceasefire, a first step towards creating the positive atmosphere that would allow both sides to enter into a renewed peace process. The Norwegians for their part agreed to establish an international mission that would oversee on-site monitoring of the ceasefire agreement, and to act as facilitators in the talks between the government and the Tamil Tigers. The provisions of the ceasefire allowed government and Tamil forces to remain in the areas under their control. The Norwegians also agreed to invite the international community to contribute to a fund that would be used for the reconstruction of those areas affected most by the conflict, the North and East of the island. The first round of peace talks took place in Thailand in September 2002, and since then the two delegations have met regularly every four to eight weeks.

On my own fact-finding visit to Sri Lanka in November 2002 I found supporters, critics and sceptics of the peace process on all sides. At the Marga Institute in Colombo I met with a group of community activists who were organizing support for the process among the trade union movements. They were critical of the government's handling of the process, and expressed unease at the gap that existed between the government and civil society. They were troubled in particular over what they described as the 'Muslim factor' in the east of the island. They feared that the concerns and aspirations of the Muslim community were not being addressed and that this could lead to a new phase in the conflict, even if the government succeeded in reaching an accommodation with the Tamils. They considered Raoul Hakim, who is a member of the government delegation and a Muslim, to be unrepresentative of the marginalized Muslim community in the east of the island, many of whom had been 'ethnically cleansed' from the north by the Tamil Tigers and disenfranchised in recent local elections. The non-representation of Muslims in the peace process could put the whole process, they feared, in jeopardy.

Elsewhere in Colombo and also in the Tamil stronghold of Jaffna, I met with NGO leaders who were deeply sceptical about the government's motivations, which they judged to be driven more by economic interests than a genuine desire to address grievances. 'Businessmen are behind this process', one interviewee declared, 'as they see an opportunity to extend to the North the exploitation of the workforce that is taking place here in the South.'[33] Dr Sarath Amunugama, spokesman for the main opposition party, was also highly critical. He told me that the government was failing in the parliament to inform and to engage the opposition parties in the peace process. It seemed to him and others, who were observing the process from the outside, that the government representatives were conceding to the demands of the Tamil Tigers and the Norwegians, and failing to negotiate an agreement that reflects the concerns of the Sinhalese majority. 'At present', he claimed, 'no one knows where the bottom line is. We must have some idea where it must all end if we are to have confidence in the process.' This lack of cross-party political consensus, compounded further by the open hostility between the Sri Lanka President, Chandrika B. Kumaratunga, and the Prime Minister, Ranil Wickremesinghe, both of whom represent political parties that have been arch-rivals, gives rise to serious concerns over the durability of any final agreement that may be reached among the negotiators. In the current political climate in Sri Lanka party interests clearly trump the interests of the State.

The Tamils too have problems in reaching a political consensus. Muslim and non-Muslim Tamils have questioned LTTE's claim to be the 'sole representative' of their interests in the negotiating process. Even within the LTTE itself there are signs of internal tensions, partly due to the lack of institutional structures that are essential for internal debate and consensus building, and partly due to 'caste and socio-economic class issues'.[34] My visit to the Jaffna peninsula certainly confirmed a diversity of perceptions and concerns among the Tamil community. I detected a similar sense of detachment or 'disconnect' from the peace process to that I encountered among the Sinhalese in the south. There is an obvious and urgent need for the LTTE to create the institutional and political structures that will enable broader participation in the current negotiating process, especially by political opponents and minorities in the regions under their control.

As with Northern Ireland, interpretations differ as to the prime cause of the Sri Lanka conflict. Father Tissa Balasuriya from the Colombo-based Centre for Society and Religion rejects the view that ethnicity or religion is a prime cause of the current conflict. He points to the fact that, in the shanty towns where he works, Sinhalese and Tamils, Buddhists, Hindus, Christians and Muslims live and work cheek by jowl without tension, protecting each other's interests, united in their poverty and destitution. He claims that one can find a similar sense of unity among the business elites; there is no conflict in the ethnically and religiously mixed stock market and company boardrooms or among their children who attend Sri Lanka's elitist schools.

I met another Catholic priest who shared Father Balasuriya's analysis that the conflict was essentially an economic struggle. He too was working at a base community level where he found that the struggle against injustices had united people across the religious and ethnic divides. The government ambassador to the peace process, Bernard Goonethilleke, without fully endorsing Balasuriya's Marxist interpretation, pointed to 'economic mis-management' as one of the prime causes. Unfortunate economic policies from 1956, he claimed, had turned what was once a prosperous economy into a 'basket case'. If the economy had developed as it had done in Singapore, he argued, everyone would have had equal opportunity and there would have been less cause for conflict.

Unlike many of the other British colonies Sri Lanka (which used to be known as Ceylon) avoided a violent struggle and achieved its independence in 1947 after five years of negotiations that were led by the island's first Prime Minister, D.S. Senanayake. Through a skilful balance of reconciling the interests and concerns of the majority and minorities he succeeded in holding the country together in the years immediately following in-dependence.[35] The perception among the majority Sinhalese community that Tamils had gained unfair advantage in public life during British rule led to a level of political agitation that swept S.W.R.D. Bandaranaike to power on the promise that Sinhalese would be made the only official language of the country. The language policy was symbolic of a greater effort to restore Sinhalese Buddhism to what its followers considered to be its rightful position of superiority within the nation.[36] The controversial legislation led to 'bitter' riots in Colombo and the Eastern Province where Tamils and Sinhalese had intermingled, resulting in the death and injury of hun-dreds.[37] Relationships between the Sinhalese and Tamil communities rapidly deteriorated as the government pursued its language policy. In response the Federal party declared its intention to work non-violently for an 'autonomous Tamil linguistic state within a Federal union of Ceylon' in order to protect the cultural rights and identity of the Tamil-speaking people. The Prime Minister Bandaranaike reached an agreement with Chelvanayagam, the moderate Tamil leader, which may have gone some way to accommodate Tamil concerns, had he not capitulated to organized pressure orchestrated by the Buddhist monks who vehemently opposed what they saw as 'surrender' to Tamil demands.[38]

The main opposition party, the UNP, under the leadership of J.R. Jayawardene, joined forces with the Sinhalese extremists in declaring the pact a 'betrayal of the Sinhalese' thus redefining the conflict in ethnic terms. Joined by a group of chanting monks the UNP leaders set out to march on the Temple of the Tooth at Kandy as a combined act of worship and protest until the police prevented them.[39] The defacing of Sinhalese letters on the licence plates of national-owned buses sent to the north in March 1958 brought a swift reaction from Sinhalese gangs often led by Buddhist monks in the south, who combed the city obliterating the Tamil lettering. Two months later more serious violence erupted in different parts of the country. In Colombo roving gangs attacked Tamil homes and businesses, beating the occupants. When news of these attacks eventually reached the Tamil strongholds in the north and east of the island, groups set out to take revenge on their Sinhalese neighbours. Buddhist temples, police stations and other government buildings were also singled out for attack. The level of the violence was so great that some observers suspected that those whose business interests in the south were being threatened by Bandaranaike's government or whose criminal activities in the north were being menaced, had encouraged it.[40] Although in 1971 Sinhalese youth rose in opposition to the government, whom they accused of failing to meet their aspirations, the period between 1960 and 1977 was marked by the absence of anti-Tamil rioting. Stanley Tambiah attributes the relative calm to the fact that 'the aspirations and objectives of militant lay Buddhists and politically ardent Buddhist monks with regard to the restoration of Buddhism to a pre-eminent place had been largely addressed and fulfilled'.[41]

In the same period on the Tamil side, Tambiah points out, the sense of grievances began to increase greatly, and in particular over two issues. First, by the mid 1970s the places available to Tamils in universities were drastically reduced by the quota systems introduced by the government, leaving Tamils to fear that their higher educational opportunities were 'irretrievably eroding'. Second, the colonization and irrigation schemes, aimed at utilizing for agriculture the dry regions in the central, northern and eastern provinces of the island, resulted in mass Sinhalese migration which was seen by the Tamils as an intrusion into their traditional homelands. When Tamil protests were ignored the movement for a separate state of Eelam increased. The militants began their campaign of violence by targeting Tamil politicians and policemen who were condemned for collaborating. The response of the Colombo government was to send in the army, who were mainly Sinhalese. The 1979 Prevention of Terrorism Act gave the military sweeping powers that they used unremittingly to suppress the insurgence. By 1981 the level of violence against the 'occupying' soldiers had increased to the extent that the Sinhalese community elsewhere on the island were targeting Tamil neighbours in acts of revenge. In 1983, the killing and mutilation of thirteen soldiers, whose bodies were brought to Colombo and put on display before a military burial, is said to have triggered the worst riots of that year.[42]

Alarmed by the escalation in violence the Indian government put pressure on their Sri Lankan neighbours and in July 1987 the Indo-Sri Lanka Peace Accord was signed. The agreement acknowledged Sri Lanka to be a 'multi-ethnic and multi-lingual plural society' within which each group had its own 'cultural and linguistic' identity. It was agreed that Indian troops should help to restore order on the troubled island. The contents of the Accord and the presence of the foreign troops caused alarm among Sinhalese nationalists who feared that their previous victories for their language, culture and religion were under threat. The Tamil Tigers also rejected the Accord and engaged in bitter battle with the Indian troops until their departure in 1990.[43] Their departure led to a further escalation in the violence, with the LTTE supporting its campaign for independence with funds collected from local taxation and the large Tamil diaspora, many of whom it is said felt obliged to support the cause. The assassinations of Rajiv Gandhi in 1991 and the Sri Lankan President Ranasinghe Premadasa in 1993 have both been blamed on the Tamil Tigers.

Tamil traditional beliefs that their Dravidian language and religion are 'superior' over other traditions, and that a Tamil sovereign state existed in Sri Lanka from prehistoric times, some claim, are the inspiration behind aspirations for total autonomy from their Sinhalese neighbours. Tamil nationalist myths began to be more openly expressed after the riots of 1983, and became especially prevalent with some of the expatriate Tamil writers. These interpretations of their history may influence some of the present-day protagonists in the struggle for independence but, as David Little points out, such claims do not stand up to scrutiny. The more likely 'source of Sri Lankan separatism', he writes, 'is the special set of circumstances in Sri Lanka in which the Tamil community found itself'. He believes Tamil separatism to be primarily a 'reactive movement' fashioned more by local circumstances and traditions than external cultural influences. The evidence of the existence of a sovereign Tamil state from the thirteenth century till the Portuguese conquest, the systematic discrimination Tamils have suffered since Sri Lankan independence, and the fact that they have fought for and conquered the land, are, according to Little, the grounds for their present claims. The influence of South Indian nationalism on Sri Lankan Tamil consciousness in the 1950s and 1960s should not be overplayed, he claims, as during that period the Tamil political leaders were Christians. The interviews that I conducted in the Jaffna region recently would confirm David Little's evaluation. None of the LTTE fighters with whom I met referred to the founding myths of their race. The amount of Tamil blood that has already been spilt, however, seems to be a major motivation behind their struggle to see it through to the end.

The Sri Lankan constitution guarantees freedom and protection for all the religions on the island – roughly 70 per cent of the population is Buddhist, the remaining 30 per cent being Hindu, Christian and Muslim. In theory, the State is organized in accordance with a secular ideology; the constitution, however, grants Buddhism 'the foremost place' and this is reflected in the generous funding the State provides to 'foster' and 'protect' its position within Sri Lankan society. The constitution and the political mindset of the country take it for granted that 'religion and politics are intertwined' and that the State has 'a responsibility to foster religion'. In this respect Tessa Bartholomeusz writes, 'modern Sri Lanka has adjusted to a historical legacy in which, prior to the fall of the Kandyan Kingdom in 1815, "it was the monarch's unique role as defender and promoter of the Buddhist religion which in the final analysis confirmed his legitimacy".'[44] The relationship between 'religious authority and temporal power' is today solely 'symbiotic', and yet it is so important to keep this paradigm in mind in order to understand the phenomenon of the 'political' monk and the Buddhist lay-activists, who over the past century or more have exercised, and still are exercising, extraordinary influence in the shaping of Sri Lankan politics. A senior professor at Colombo University told me that, even though in private many politicians may regard the monks as 'rascals', they feel that in public they still need to seek their blessing.

While in Sri Lanka in November 2002 I was invited by the Venerable Sobitha, a senior Buddhist monk who has been most vocal in his criticisms of policy that risks weakening the link between Buddhism and the State, to attend a press conference that was given by five of the most senior and nationally respected hierarchs in the *sangha* – the order of monks. The meeting was held to coincide with the peace talks that were taking place between the government and the LTTE. Although they professed that it was not their intention to undermine the process, their clear warning to the government was that the current process was doomed to failure unless they were willing to pay more attention to the concerns of the Sinhala people. The monks claimed that the Sinhalese voice was not being heard and that the government representatives in the talks could not claim to represent their concerns and aspirations. Sri Lanka, they declared, should not sign agreements with terrorists who are still well armed and who discriminate against the Sinhala people. They demanded that those who had been forcibly evicted by the LTTE from the northern and eastern provinces be rehabilitated to their former homes, and be paid compensation for their losses. They also called for the immediate restoration of more than 250 Buddhist religious sites that have been damaged or destroyed by the LTTE. Finally, the monks reaffirmed their opposition to any settlement that would lead to 'carving out a separate state of the territory of Sri Lanka'.

There are numerous examples both in the lead-up to the country's independence and the subsequent years in the struggle for Sinhala Buddhist dominance where monks have taken their protest beyond words and have been actively involved in either agitating or perpetrating violence. Although the roots of contemporary political Buddhism stretch back to the revivalist movement of the nineteenth and early twentieth centuries, Stanley Tambiah singles out the writings and activities of Walpola Rahula, the first Buddhist monk to enter the Ceylon University College, as providing an ideological basis for the 'religio-nationalism' or 'religio-patriotism' that has been a mark of Sinhala Buddhism for the past fifty years or more. Rahula defined the monks' role as the 'custodians of freedom' as 'on every occasion of danger to both nation and religion, the monks came forward to save and protect them'. Based on this interpretation of history, he 'championed the monks' right and obligation to participate actively in the shaping of a better society'.[45]

The 1956 celebrations of the 2500th anniversary of the death of the Buddha, and the landing of Vijaya and his followers, the first Sinhalese, on the island of Sri Lanka, provided further incentive to assert the Sinhala Buddhist identity. The year marked the formation of the Eksath Bhikkhu Peramuna (United Front of Monks) who immediately became active in drawing up an independent manifesto for the national elections to be held in that same year. The monks 'listed ten points that Buddhists should take into account when voting' which included the proposal to make Sinhala the only official language.[46] They enlisted the support of a network of 'between three and four thousand monks' to promote their pro-Sinhala nationalist, anti-western, anti-Catholic manifesto, and to ensure the electoral success of the MEP party with Bandaranaike as Prime Minister. However, the political ambitions of the monks suffered a temporary 'setback' in September 1959 when a monk who had the support and help of the head of the famous Kelaniya Temple assassinated Bandaranaike, the Prime Minister whom they had helped to power.[47]

The close links that were formed in the 1970s and 1980s between many young monks and the JVP party – 'the egalitarian, populist, nationalist, anti-

Tamil' Sinhala Buddhist movement – have been well documented. When the party was banned after the 1983 riots, the young Buddhist monks provided a cover under which the movement could continue its activities.[48] When the JVP began a campaign of violence directed against Sinhala government officials and the opposition party UNP, some of the young monks are said to have been active participants in the violence, including violence directed at senior monks who disapproved of their activities. Government agents are said to have killed many JVP monks in an attempt to eradicate the threat posed by this militant movement.[49] The rationale behind the activities of these radical monks according to Tambiah was 'that the religion of the Buddha and the language and culture of the Sinhalese could not flourish without a sovereign territory, which was the motherland of Sri Lanka, and their uncompromising judgement pronounced on their elders was that they had been slothful in patriotic obligations and become trapped in worldly interests of property, rank and temple-building'.[50]

I heard similar criticisms of elders from a younger monk, the head of a temple in Colombo, to whom I was introduced as someone who had strong ties with Sinhala Urumaya, a movement that was formed in April 2000 to safeguard the sovereignty, territorial integrity and unitary state of Sri Lanka, and to reclaim the lost rights of the Sinhalese. This monk was also critical of Sri Lankan scholars, whom he claimed were too Marxist in their interpretation of the conflict and have failed to take account of the sociological, cultural and religious roots of the problem. He told me that in Sri Lanka you could not separate the social political milieu from the religious milieu – these overlap each other. It is true, he said, that the goal of Buddhism is to live without attachment to land or country, but this can only be achieved when one reaches a high level of spiritual awareness. Meanwhile, Buddhists like others have to live in the real world and to operate on a conventional level. The ideal way to resolve conflicts, he believed, was without arms but if your opponent lacks goodwill then you have no alternative but to deal with the problem in the 'conventional' way. 'Without Prabhakaran', he declared, 'things would be good in this country.' Prabhakaran is the leader of the Tamil Tigers, the LTTE. In response to my challenge as to how he as a Buddhist monk could desire the death of someone else, and as to how he could justify blessing the activities of the Buddhist soldiers caught up in the fighting, he replied: 'I know that as a monk it is wrong for me to think in this way, but I believe that the five precepts of Buddhism not to kill, steal, misbehave sexually, lie or drink alcohol work in normal circumstances: the situation in Sri Lanka is abnormal and therefore one has to suspend some of these principles.'

To support his apparently relativist approach to moral behaviour he appealed to history, claiming that one could find plenty of justification for Buddhists fighting to defend the integrity of their homeland today. He recalled for me the story of the famous Buddhist king, Dutthagamani, to which I referred in an earlier chapter. Although at heart he was a pacifist, Dutthagamani realized, the monk told me, that in certain circumstances war was unavoidable; he needed his armies to defend Buddhism and to free the island from foreign domination. Since the Sinhalese people had been charged by the Buddha himself to promote the *dharma* or teaching, he believed that therefore he had a spiritual duty to speak out when he saw that this sacred commission was under threat.

I encountered a similar line of argument in my interviews with the Venerable Sobitha and the Venerable Dr Bellanwila Wimalarathana Thero. Sobitha emphasized that the Sinhalese people were as much the victims as were the Tamils and the Muslims. He spoke of the atrocities committed by the LTTE against monks and the desecration of temples and holy objects. He feared that innocent Tamils were powerless to act independently of the LTTE, who in his opinion were holding the government to ransom despite the fact that they only represented maybe 10 per cent of the population. They were both adamant that a monk cannot forget politics as it has an impact on religious life. Bellanwila felt it was the duty of the monk to advise the government on how to rule well. A monk's main concern was the protection, sovereignty and integrity of the country. He feared that if the island were divided into two it would impact on their spiritual life because of the traditions, and furthermore it would not end the animosity. Buddha, he explained, was a Hindu before he achieved enlightenment and therefore Hindus and Buddhists can and do live in harmony, but to partition the island he feared would lead to real religious tensions between the two faith communities. 'Buddhism, which began in India had almost vanished until it reappeared in Sri Lanka, where it has undergone a revival. We have a religious duty therefore to defend the faith that we have inherited from our ancestors. We are not out to destroy other faiths, we are just anxious to protect our national heritage,' the Venerable Bellanwila explained. He admitted that the Tamils' grievances had not been properly addressed, but he feared that the root of the problem lay in the high expectations they were given by the government at the time of independence. Practising Buddhists, Bellanwila believes, should never kill or harm any living being, but if a person joins the army, they must think about what they are doing first, as once the choice is made, then, even as a practising Buddhist, they must carry out their duties; killing should always be a last resort.

Not all Sinhala Buddhists, monk and lay, agree with the role played by the political monks or indeed condone the use of violence under any circumstances. To understand what appear to be the un-Buddhist-like attitudes especially with regard to land and people that one can encounter among Sinhala Buddhists today, it is important to appreciate how Sri Lanka's colonial history and the interpretations of ancient myths and sacred Buddhist texts have contributed to contemporary Sinhala consciousness. At the beginning of the sixteenth century the Portuguese, in their search for spices and converts to Christianity, extended the foothold that they had established in Goa to colonize the coastline villages of Sri Lanka. The kingdom of Kandy in the foothills of the island was by the early seventeenth century the only part of Sri Lanka where the Sinhalese continued to rule in accordance with their ancient Buddhist traditions. Those Buddhists, Hindus and Muslims who came under Portuguese rule were subjected to discrimination and persecution as the colonizers pursued a mission of conversion.

By the mid seventeenth century, as Europe had begun to export its own internal religious conflicts to its expanded territories, the Dutch success-fully challenged the Portuguese dominance of the spice trade based in Sri Lanka, and as a consequence the Catholic colonizers' aggressive approach was replaced by Dutch Calvinism which was 'a bit less zealous' but equally militant.[51] The Dutch efforts to replace Catholicism with their own particu-lar brand of Protestantism met with little success despite the material and social incentives that were on offer for those who chose to convert; only those who were baptized Protestants were allowed to hold land or public office. Their policies towards the indigenous religions of the island were more tolerant, however, than their Portuguese predecessors. Although Hindus and Buddhists were forbidden to practise their beliefs openly in the urban areas, the Dutch did not interfere with such practices in the rural areas. The same level of tolerance was not extended to natives who had converted to Catholicism under the Portuguese rule. They were forbidden to practise their faith, and their properties were confiscated and replaced by Protestant chapels.

In 1796 the British replaced the Dutch colonizers after entering into a military alliance with the Kandyan kingdom that gave the British effective control of the coastal areas and the cinnamon trade. In 1815 the British extended their rule to Kandy when given the opportunity to intervene at the invitation of a group of local Buddhists who were in dispute with their king.[52] The new colonial power introduced its own brand of Christianity. Anglican and Methodist missionaries pursued what has been described as a 'full scale ideological attack on Hinduism, Buddhism and local folk traditions' through their 'preaching, education, and pamphletering'.[53] Their efforts to learn the local languages and customs were aimed solely at helping them to be more effective in challenging local beliefs and in pursuing their mission of 'aggressive evangelism'. Christian schools were given such privileges and advantages by the government that Christians, and Anglicans in particular, came to be looked upon as the elitist group.[54]

The contempt displayed by the new colonizers for Buddhism, combined with their failure to accept and to integrate fully the Sinhalese, who aspired through their English education system to join the ruling classes, were instrumental in provoking the Buddhist revival movement that began in the late nineteenth and the early twentieth centuries. George D. Bond claims that British efforts at marginalizing the influence of Buddhism left the religion in such a 'severely depressed and disorganized state' that it attracted the attention of 'the Anglicized elite' who 'although estranged from their Buddhist heritage, began to recognize it as the key to their identity'.[55] The first signs of a revival were noticeable by the mid 1860s when the demoralized monks began to accept the challenge of the missionaries to public debate in which they refuted Christianity's claims to superiority. The high point came, however, in 1873 when a two-day debate between a Methodist preacher and Mohottivatte Gunananda, a well-known monk, attracted ten thousand people. Gunananda's success in this debate was hailed as the turning point that sparked a renewed sense of confidence among Buddhists, both monk and lay.[56] Encouraged and supported by European and American Theosophists who came to help raise the Buddhists' consciousness of their heritage, the Anglicized elite who had felt rejected by the British establishment began to provide leadership for the renewal movement.[57] The new movement became known as 'Protestant' Buddhism. The reformers, without rejecting monasticism or rituals, emphasized the importance of 'lay responsibility' and adopted similar tactics to the Christian missionaries. They returned to the ancient texts and customs of Theravada Buddhism to find new meaning and purpose for their lives under British rule.

A key figure in the revivalist movement was Anagarika Dharmapala. He had been educated in Christian schools and had a good grasp of the Christian Scriptures and educational techniques. Inspired by the eloquence of Gunananda and his success in the debate with the Christian minister, and encouraged by the Theosophical Society, he devoted himself to the cause of Buddhism, describing himself as the 'homeless guardian of the Dharma', a new role as he saw himself as 'neither a monk nor a layman'. Through the newspaper *Sinhala Bauddhaya*, which he founded, he promoted the belief that the Sinhala are a special people, who were 'chosen' to administer 'the bright, beautiful island' of Sri Lanka, but who have been robbed of their destiny by 'barbaric vandals' like the British. His reasons for rejecting British imperialism were basically religious as he believed that Sri Lanka would only prosper when the influence of the 'religion of righteousness', Buddhism, was restored to its rightful place.[58] The rediscovery of their religious identity was for him the key to Sinhala success in dealing with the social, political and economic problems that confronted them.[59] He justified these claims by recalling the exploits of warrior kings like Dutthagamani who 'rescued' the religion and the nation from oblivion by freeing the island from the threat of Tamil domination. By resurrecting such stories found in the *Mahavamsa*, the traditional ethnic myths that had almost been forgotten about during the colonial times, Dharmapala succeeded in establishing the link between Buddhism and nationalism that would dominate Sri Lanka's political agenda in the years before and after independence.[60]

The accounts of Dutthagamani carrying the relic of the Buddha and being accompanied by fighting monks in his battles to unite the nation and to defend the *dharma* both challenge traditional Buddhist principles of non-violence and provide justification for demonizing those who stand in the way of Buddhism. As mentioned in the previous chapter, it is said that when Dutthagamani felt remorse over the millions that he had slain in his triumphant war against the Tamil king, Elara, a group of monks tried to comfort him by declaring that in fact he had killed only 'one-and-a-half human beings' – the one being a monk, the half being a novice. The others, he was assured, were unbelievers, evil and subhuman. The fact that the author of the *Mahavamsa* places these stories immediately after an account of the Buddha's first visit to Sri Lanka when he prepared the island for Buddhism by driving away its non-human inhabitants is interpreted as the Buddha's endorsement of the use of force when necessary to defend the *dharma*.[61] Sinhala Buddhists frequently refer to these traditional ethno-religious myths to justify their claim to the whole of Sri Lanka as their sacred turf, and to affirm their belief to be a chosen race, a people of destiny. The Tamils are looked upon by those who buy into these foundational stories 'as interlopers on their sacred Buddhist island'.[62] To them the claim for a separate Tamil state is non-negotiable; their beliefs provide 'a warrant for intolerance'.[63]

Some commentators on the conflict in Sri Lanka have argued that the Tamils also use their Hindu scriptures to justify their campaign of violence. The story most frequently quoted, some would say wrongly, by Tamils to legitimate the war, is from *The Bhagavad Gita*, a Hindu text that tells of two families fighting each other with religious justification. It is said that when Arjuna, the hero of the story, contemplated fleeing from the battlefield, the Lord Krishna advised him that 'it is a noble duty for a warrior to fight a just war', and that he should not waver in his resolve to protect righteousness and maintain law and order.[64] On my own fact-finding visit to Jaffna and its surrounds, I met with the regional leader of the LTTE, with professors from the University of Jaffna, medical officers, community workers and rank-and-file LTTE members, but none spoke to me of their struggle in religious terms. Likewise, when I met with LTTE prisoners at the Kalutara prison south of Colombo, none of them considered themselves as religious warriors. In fact the only Tamil I met in Sri Lanka, who offered a religio-moral analysis was a Catholic priest. He told me that, whilst not condoning everything they did, he considered LTTE's violence justified within the terms of the traditional just war theory as it was a last resort and their cause was just.

In my conversations with Professor Sivathamby, a highly respected Tamil scholar, he told me that religion was undoubtedly 'a conditioning factor' in the conflict. He drew an interesting comparison between the way in which Christian and Hindu Tamils have responded to the crisis since the early 1980s. In so doing he provided a helpful insight into how different religious formations can help either to initiate or to prolong a communal conflict. He pointed to how fundamental attitudes to conflict can be, and often are, shaped by such beliefs as resurrection, reincarnation, destiny, detachment and endurance. In the earlier days Catholic priests, he claimed, were more in the forefront of the conflict in Sri Lanka. The Catholic belief that you only have one experience of life on earth combined with a liberation theology that called for the active challenging of unjust structures, he believed, helped to shape their initial response. Because Christians do not believe in reincarnation, Sivathamby stated, they see their human life in much short-er terms than Hindus and Buddhists and are therefore less likely to accept destiny and indefinite suffering. The Hindu belief in rebirth and multiple life experiences had, he believed, an opposite effect on how they had initially responded. In the Tamil South Indian Hindu tradition, he explained, people are more willing to accept frugal living and suffering as part of life: 'the more you suffer, they believe, the better equipped you are for what is to come.' This outlook has conditioned them to be more accepting of the injustices they were forced to endure. It was the arrival of the Indian peace-keepers, he claimed, that changed people's perceptions and caused Hindu notions of destiny to become more prominent. The same long-suffering religious mindset is now helping to sustain the political struggle; people are able to accept a greater depth of suffering and agony, he explained, because they believe that one day they will be delivered from it. The religious factor also plays a part in the LTTE's ability to recruit fighters. Their recruits, he noted, come mostly from families in the lower social groups. Their religious formation, he believed, makes it easier for them to leave home as they would have been taught the spiritual importance of detachment; it also enables them to endure greater and prolonged hardships as they would have been taught the spiritual importance of resignation or acceptance of circumstances.

Professor Sivathamby felt that one of the greatest obstacles to achieving a negotiated settlement is the deep mutual mistrust that exists between Tamils and Buddhists. His own community, he claimed, were partly responsible for this, as they have failed to communicate to the Sinhalese monks, in particular, the real suffering that the Tamils have endured over the past half century. He sees the role of the Buddhist monks as crucial if there is to be a breakthrough in the impasse that exists between the two communities. The monks, he explained, play a key role in both rural and urban life in Sri Lanka. In the countryside the monk is looked up to as a family mentor. In the city he carries moral authority and influence as he is someone who has renounced the normal ways of living. The monks are looked up to by ordinary Sinhalese people as the political, social and moral guardians of the people. My contacts in Jaffna agreed with Sivathamby's assessment of the key communal role of the Buddhist monk, but some were more sceptical as to whether or not the monks would be interested in a meaningful dialogue with their Tamil neighbours. 'We have a saying,' a Tamil priest in Jaffna told me. 'If a man is asleep you can wake him up, but if he is pretending to sleep you can't wake him.' The General Secretary of the All Ceylon Hindu Congress told me that only a few Buddhists take part in the inter-faith group meetings that they arrange. They claim to show their support, he said, by the fact that they do not openly oppose such meetings.

I am very conscious that there are many other aspects – political, economic and cultural – to the communal conflict in Sri Lanka that have not been addressed in this chapter. I am especially aware that there are plenty of Sinhala and Tamil people in Sri Lanka for whom religion does not feature as a significant factor in their lives. I am equally conscious that within the Tamil and Sinhala communities there are internal tensions and different factions other than the two main protagonists that I have focused upon. Several interviewees referred to the plight of the descendants of the million or more Tamils that had been transplanted from South India by the British in the 1850s to work on the tea plantations. I have met Christians on both sides of the divide whose allegiance is clearly defined by their Sinhala or Tamil ethnic identity. I have met Tamil-speaking Muslims who feel that neither the government nor the LTTE is willing to acknowledge or to address their needs. I have spoken with a Muslim leader in Colombo who expressed the fear that the younger Muslims in the east of the island may resort to violence as they are claiming that it seems to be the only way to get the authorities to address their grievances. My aim was to illustrate that any attempt to understand the contemporary conflict in Sri Lanka requires an awareness of the religious factors that are to different degrees on each side, helping to define the nature of the conflict.

Ten years ago the Israeli author Amos Oz wrote a postscript to his previously published book *In the Land of Israel*. He uses the word 'tragedy' to describe the Israeli–Palestinian conflict as he explained he wanted to convey to outsiders that this was not some 'Wild West Show, containing good guys and bad guys' but 'a clash between one very powerful claim and another no less powerful'. Oz believed that 1993 offered an opportune moment to resolve this ongoing conflict as the leadership on each side was the most moderate and most willing to compromise there had ever been; the people too were feeling exhausted. 'Conflicts', he wrote, 'whether individual, intercommunal, or international, do not usually resolve themselves through a miraculous formula that sends rival parties falling into each other's arms like long lost brothers in a Dostoevski novel; rather most conflicts tend to gradually fade away, as a result, simply, of exhaustion on all sides. I think this blessed exhaustion is a syndrome recently observed among several Israelis and Arabs.'[65] He feared that, if the Israelis and Palestinians did not seize the moment, the whole tragedy that was being acted out on this small piece of territory could end like a Shakespearian tragedy with dead bodies strewn all around. The challenge, he wrote, is to 'work doubly hard' to ensure the end is more like a Chekhov tragedy – 'with everybody disillusioned, embittered, heartbroken, disappointed, absolutely shattered, but still alive'.

The hope that Oz and others wrote about ten years ago, and which I still sensed when I travelled around Israel and Palestine making programmes with the BBC in June 2000, has been totally shattered by the marked increase in violence that has claimed hundreds of lives over the past two-and-a-half years. My first visit to the region was as a student in 1971. I recall then being able to travel to Hebron on a local bus, and being able to wander freely around the Shrine of the Patriarchs and the local market without feeling any sense of fear or anxiety about my safety. When I returned to Hebron earlier this year to interview some Jewish settlers, I travelled in a bullet-proof car, having being strongly advised by both Israelis and Arabs not to risk the journey.

The hope generated in the lead-up to the Camp David summit in July 2000 I found had given way to anger, open hostility and bitter recriminations on both sides. The failure of Yasar Arafat and Ehud Barak at Camp David to reach agreement on the terms of a settlement regenerated such a deep sense of suspicion and mistrust within the two communities that the

visit of Ariel Sharon to the Temple Mount, accompanied by Israeli legisla-
tors and a large group of bodyguards and police, on 28 September 2000 was
seen by the Palestinians as sufficiently provocative to trigger the worst cycle
of violence in a decade.

Oz's description of the Israeli–Palestinian conflict as a clash between two
powerful claims highlights the core of the problem. The claims are for a
relatively small piece of land, which lacks both water and resources, but
which both sides believe to be essential to their existence as a people. Each
denies, of course, the validity of the other's claim, and as in Northern
Ireland and Sri Lanka, neither side is monolithic; ethnic, religious and class
tensions and differences on both sides of the conflict as well as external
interests complicate the search for a durable solution. The struggle for
sovereignty is complicated still further by the fact that the territory in dispute houses some of the holiest of sites for Judaism, Christianity and Islam.
Palestinians and Jews both claim to be descendants of Abraham. The Jews
trace their lineage to Isaac, the son of Sarah and Abraham; the Arabs to
Ishmael, the son of Abraham and Hagar, Sarah's servant.[66] In Hebron on the
West Bank a mosque and a synagogue stand side by side, marking the burial
site of Abraham. It was here in February 1994 that the American-born
Jewish settler, Baruch Goldstein, murdered twenty-nine Muslims as they
were prostrated in prayer. In Jerusalem the Temple Mount or Haram al-
Sharif, which means 'Noble Sanctuary', is for Jews the site of the two
temples that were destroyed by invaders; the first in 586 BCE by the armies
of Nebuchadnezzar, the second in 70 CE by the armies of Rome. The same
site for Muslims commemorates the Prophet Muhammad's trip from Mecca
to Jerusalem and his ascension to heaven. Immediately beneath the two
ancient mosques that dominate the Temple Mount plateau today are the
ancient remains of the Western Wall – a wall that circled the Temple Mount –
the holiest site of Jewish worship. In Nablus, also on the West Bank, there is
the tomb of Joseph, the great-grandson of Abraham, a site of pilgrimage for
Jews, which was attacked and badly damaged by Palestinians during rioting
in October 2000. In Bethlehem, the birthplace of Jesus, there is the Church
of the Nativity, a shrine that has been revered for several centuries, and
especially by Palestinian and other Arab Christians. It came under siege by
Israeli troops when Palestinian gunmen and security forces took sanctuary
in the shrine in April 2002.

As in the other conflicts outlined in this chapter, colonialism, ethnic,
political and economic interests as well as religion have all contributed to
the causes and complexities of the Palestinian–Israeli struggle. Even though
a majority of people on either side may not regard themselves as fully
observant in the strictly religious sense, religion is undoubtedly a focal

point in the conflict as it 'significantly shapes the attitudes of the protagonists towards each other'.[67] Neither Judaism nor Islam recognizes a
division between the secular and the sacred, the temporal and the spiritual.
The Torah and the Qur'an provide a world view that permeates relationships within society as well as with God. Both these sacred texts can be
interpreted to justify exclusive claims to truth and to provide the mandate
for violence in the face of what appears as a threat to the survival of the
tradition and its adherents. The alien or the other is accommodated for in
both traditions provided that they accept their inferior status in the social
and spiritual order that is determined by divine precepts and that are therefore unchallengeable. As in the conflicts in Northern Ireland and Sri Lanka
the salience of the religious factor in this conflict varies in accordance with
the circumstances and the religious mindset and commitment of
individuals engaged in the struggle. The role of the religious extremist on
both sides is highly significant in shaping the current phase of this conflict;
imams and rabbis have not only allowed the 'prejudices and negative
stereotypes' of the other as untrustworthy and cruel to go unchallenged but
they have also endorsed morally the violence that is being perpetrated
upon the other.[68]

In attempting to provide a brief historical outline of the conflict I am
acutely aware that one is dealing with highly contested accounts of relatively recent history that is perceived so differently by the protagonists and
apologists on either side. The Palestinians challenge in particular the Israeli
claims that when the Jewish resettlement of the region began in the late
nineteenth and early twentieth centuries Palestine had no defined borders,
and that the land had been more or less abandoned by the local inhabitants; they also dispute the claim that the earlier settlers had no choice but
to defend themselves with arms from relentless attacks of roving bands of
Bedouins. The Palestinian version describes an invasion of Zionist migrants
who were determined to cleanse the land of the inhabitants who had lived
on it for centuries, forcing them to defend themselves.[69]

What is known for fact is that until 1918 the region was part of the
Ottoman Empire and was administered partly from Damascus and partly
from Beirut. The Ottomans, according to Bickerton and Klausner, considered the region to be of little military or strategic importance and
neglected it until the second half of the nineteenth century when European
powers began to expand their interests in Palestine. Much of the land was
state owned, and was farmed by peasants without any formal legal title,
thus enabling the land to be bought and sold by absentee landlords without
the local farmers' consent or knowledge. At the beginning of the nineteenth
century the Jewish population of the region was estimated to be about

25,000, who lived mostly in cities like Jerusalem, Hebron, Safed and Tiberias – all sites sacred to their tradition. The Ottomans accepted their presence but in accordance with Muslim tradition regarded them as infidels or second-class citizens who were deprived of many civic rights.

The status of the Jews began to change around the middle of the century due greatly to the increased European interest in the region. Their numbers also began to swell with the arrival of new migrants from Europe, making them a more significant presence in Palestinian society.[70]

The birth of the Zionist movement and the declaration of its first congress at Basel in 1897 'to create for the Jewish people a home in Palestine secured by public law', and to further this cause by promoting 'systematically the settlement of Palestine' with Jewish artisans and farmers, changed the dynamics of the Arab–Jewish relationships in the region. Not all who believed in the principles of developing Jewish spiritual and cultural identity supported Basel. The Russian-Jewish intellectual Asher Ginsberg, writing under the penname Achad Ha-Am, rejected the position of those whom he regarded as 'mere' political Zionists that saw Palestine as 'a land without people for a people without land'. He believed it to be ethically wrong to ignore the Arab presence and openly warned against the consequence of such a policy.[71] The idea of a Jewish home in the land of Israel – 'Eretz Yisrael' – did gain the support of traditionalist Jews in Eastern Europe, who believed that the 'reestablishment of a religiously based Jewish culture located in the traditional Jewish homeland' was the sure way to preserve their traditions, and they began to plan actively to achieve this goal. Small groups began moving to Palestine to set up agricultural villages. Eventually with the financial backing of philanthropists like Edmond de Rothschild, who saw it more as an investment than a religious mission, they were able to acquire thousands of acres of land from the landowners but at the expense of the local farmers who were driven from their holdings.[72] By 1914 the Jewish population of Palestine was estimated to be 60,000 or 10 per cent of the total population. They were ethnically, religiously and linguistically separated from their Arab neighbours.

The German–Turkish alliance in 1914–18 led the British to court support from both Arabs and Jews for their war aims in the region. Ambiguous pledges were given to each community offering support for their claims while at the same time the allies were planning among themselves how they would divide the Ottoman Empire after victory. In November 1917 the British Foreign Secretary, Arthur J. Balfour, wrote to Lord Rothschild, the head of the British Zionist Organization, declaring the government's support for the establishment in Palestine of a national home for Jewish people, but stressing that this should be achieved without prejudicing the 'civil and religious rights of existing non-Jewish communities'. In the immediate post-war period the British, ignoring the views of the indigenous Arab populations, tried to reconcile the competing claims by encouraging unsuccessfully Jewish and Arab leaders to reach compromises. Given the growing strategic importance of the region, and especially the oil interests, neither France nor Britain was keen to relinquish their control. In 1922 the League of Nations agreed mandates that stipulated that the region should be divided into two zones and administered on its behalf by the French and the British until such time as it was judged to be ready for independence. The pre-war pledges were, under the 'mandates', put on hold.[73]

The mandates did allow for further Jewish immigration under 'suitable conditions' to be determined by the British. The Jews saw this as an opportunity to increase their numbers and to purchase more land; the Arabs were determined, however, to halt both immigration and land acquisitions. Tensions often erupted into violence, forcing the British to intervene. Splits also began to surface within the Jewish community, the socialists favouring better relationships with their Arab neighbours, others calling for a totally independent state with its own army and national way of life, and others still seeking the establishment of a bi-national state in which Jews and Arabs would have equal status.[74] The Arabs, determined to thwart Jewish ambitions, were more reluctant to co-operate with the British on the grounds that their co-operation could be misread as giving consent to the principles of the Balfour Declaration that had been incorporated into the League of Nations' mandate. Despite Arab hostility the Jewish population greatly increased between the years 1919 and 1938, with artisans, shopkeepers and intellectuals among the waves of new immigrants that were seeking protection from the growing anti-Semitism in Europe. In an attempt to address the growing Arab unrest, following a commission of enquiry a White Paper was issued in 1930 recommending a halt to immigration and the sale of government land only to landless Arabs. In the face of worldwide Jewish opposition the British backed away from the implementation of such a plan. By 1936 the Jewish population had increased to 400,000, or 30 per cent of the total population.[75]

In 1935 British plans for a Palestinian constitution and legislative council, comprising of Jews and Arabs, were rejected by both sides: the Arabs refusing to accept Jewish participation, and the Jews refusing on the grounds that they would be a minority. The relationship between the communities deteriorated still further, with the growing tensions leading to an Arab rebellion that lasted for three years. Civil disobedience and violence against the British in particular spread across the country.

In response to the violence the Peel Commission Report in 1937 recommended the partition of the territory into two separate states, a solution the Arabs found totally unacceptable. When the British reversed this proposal in yet another White Paper issued in 1939 both Jews and Arabs alike rejected it. The outbreak of war that same year brought a temporary lull in hostilities between the two communities and against the British as Jews and Arabs more or less united behind the British war effort.

By 1943 an awareness of the Holocaust prompted Jewish groups and their supporters to lobby Congress and the White House to support unrestricted immigration and a Jewish state in Palestine. Although the British and the Americans, for fear of alienating the Arabs upon whose support the Allies were relying, resisted the pressure initially, by mid 1946 the impact of the Holocaust on European consciousness assured that moves towards the establishment of a Jewish state would succeed.[76] The Arabs, meanwhile, were holding out for a unitary state in which they would be the 'permanent majority'. The British, unable to find agreement between the conflicting parties, referred the matter to the newly formed United Nations in January 1947 where by November the General Assembly voted in favour of partition – the Muslim countries voting against the resolution.[77] On 14 May 1948, as the British prepared to depart, David Ben-Gurion proclaimed the State of Israel, which was instantly recognized by the United States and the Soviet Union. The next day the Arab armies invaded Palestine and Israel's war of independence began – a war that created about three-quarters of a million Palestinian Arab refugees who fled from or were expelled by the Israeli forces.[78] The 150,000 Arabs who remained under Israeli control were allowed, under the Nationality Law of 1951, to vote and to run for office but not to join the army. In practice, however, they were forbidden under the emergency Defence Regulations to form their own political parties or to move freely outside their areas without permits.[79] Israel's alliance with the British and French in the Suez War of 1956 caused further strain in her relationship with the neighbouring Arab states. In the aftermath of war the Soviet Union extended its influence in the region providing military and economic support for nations with anti-western biases.

The inability to resolve the refugee problem, the perceived aggressiveness of the Israelis, Arab ambitions and desire for revenge, and the arms build-up in the region were, according to Bickerton and Klausner, some of the contributing factors that led to the war in 1967.[80] The shock defeat of the Arab forces and Israel's territorial expansion, and Egypt and Syria's subsequent defeat at the hands of Israel in 1973 brought a whole new set of dynamics into play on both sides of the conflict.

Working with Oz's allegory of a Shakespearean or Chekhovian tragedy to describe the Israeli–Palestinian conflict, it could be said that the above historical outline that takes us from the initial Jewish settlements to the 1967 and 1973 wars sets the scene for the most intriguing part of the plot – the role now played by the religious activists or peace wreckers on both sides of the conflict. Colonialism, internal divisions, external interests, superpower rivalry in the Cold War years, and the scarcity of land and water have all contributed to the complexity of the conflict. The missing factor on the list, which is at the very core of the contemporary struggle, is the unholy alliance between the Jewish secular and religious parties that was forced upon them out of the necessity to secure international recognition when the State of Israel was first declared.

In his recent book *What Shall I Do With This People?* Milton Viorst describes the tensions that surfaced between the secular and religious participants gathered to proclaim the creation of the state. In his analysis the root of the tensions was a clash between the Enlightenment values that the secular Zionists wanted written into the Declaration, values that would guarantee equality for all regardless of religion, race and sex, and the priorities of those who wanted a state based on the values of traditional Judaism. These competing aspirations gave rise to fundamental contra-dictions that have yet to be resolved, according to Viorst. The rift, he claims, was too wide for the writers of the Declaration to endorse common govern-ing principles. Consequently, important questions – such as, 'What would the relations of the Jews be with Muslims within its borders?' and 'Since God told Moses that Israel would be a "holy nation", could it then be "a nation like all nations"?'[81] – were left unanswered. The term *Zur Yisrael*, meaning 'Rock of Israel' – 'a biblical synonym for God' – was inserted as a last minute compromise to the religious lobby. Ben-Gurion, working under the con-straints of time to reach a compromise before they were deprived of the window of opportunity to declare independence, did not consider it neces-sary to try 'to resolve the problems of opinion and belief, over which we shall remain divided for a long time to come'.[82] Ben-Gurion avoided a confrontation because, according to Viorst, he was sure that in time religion would decline and that most Jews would follow the western trend towards 'secular liberalism'. He failed in Viorst's judgement to predict 'the tenacity' of the Ultra-Orthodox in rebuilding their community, devastated by the Holocaust. More understandably, he could not have predicted the impact that the Six-Day War would have on religious Zionism.

When it became clear that Ben-Gurion would not agree to the estab-lishment of a state 'according to the Torah', the Orthodoxy threatened to denounce the new state's establishment at the United Nations. The com-promise reached that secured Orthodox political, but not religious, recognition came with a price, according to Viorst. Ben-Gurion had to agree to certain stipulations: that the Sabbath and other holy days would in the new state be set aside as rest days; *yeshiva* students and Ultra-Orthodox women would be exempt from military service; kosher dietary laws would be observed in the army and in all state institutions; and marriage and divorce would be placed under rabbinic jurisdiction. The Ultra-Orthodox accepted Ben-Gurion's offer of a seat in the new cabinet, thus securing state funding for their own religious schools.[83]

Many Jews interpreted the astonishing victory over the numerically superior Arab forces in the 1967 war, and the reconquering of their ancestral biblical lands, as something more than just a military achievement. The scale of the conquest was attributed to divine intervention. Even hardened secularists like Moshe Dayan got caught up in the religious sentiment. 'We have returned to all that is holy in our land,' he declared. 'We have returned never to be parted again.'[84] The Land of Israel Movement was founded by a number of high profile intellectuals to ensure that the land – the Land of Israel – that God had given 'from the army's hands' would not be surrendered. Hebron, Beth-El, Jericho and Nablus, towns of great religious significance, were once again under Jewish control. The victory assumed 'a sacred meaning' and was interpreted by religious Zionists as a sign that the 'messianic process was reaching fruition'.[85] The Ben-Gurion doctrine that a 'state with modest borders was better that no state at all' looked 'timid' in the face of such a convincing victory.[86]

In the aftermath of victory new political alliances were formed bringing together groups that were ideologically opposed but united in the desire to retain Jewish control of the newly conquered lands. The religious Zionists who had sought to create a Jewish state in accordance with their religious beliefs were joined by the Revisionist Zionists, the group that had been founded in 1925 to work for a state that would cover both sides of the Jordan. The religious Zionists interpreted the Six-Day War as a war of redemption, and the victory as 'God's sign that every inch of the land was holy'. Inspired by a sense of 'territorial messianism' they became a significant force in determining the future course of Israeli politics.[87] They were driven by the eschatological belief that by reclaiming the land they would hasten the coming of the messiah. The 'land for peace policy' of the mainstream Zionists was for them anathema.

The religious teachings of Rabbi Abraham Isaac Kook, a Latvian Jew who had migrated to Palestine in 1904, became the driving force behind the movement to secure the land that Israel had conquered in the 1967 war. Kook was passionately committed to the resettlement of the biblical lands, believing it to be 'a duty' for Jews to return from exile.[88] Departing from the more traditional Orthodox interpretations of the process of repentance and redemption that tended to look upon Zionism as a heresy, Kook believed that Israel's return to Jerusalem was 'the very root of the coming of the Messiah'. He saw Theodor Herzl, the chief motivator of political Zionism, as 'an unknowing agent of a divine plan'.[89] The Jewish state, he believed, would be 'the pedestal of God's throne in this world'.[90] When Kook died in the mid 1930s his thinking had not had much of an impact on the political thinking of the time. His son, Rabbi Zvi Yehuda Kook, however, kept his legacy alive and was able to capitalize on his father's teachings in the immediate aftermath of Israel's 1967 victory. The son developed a new form of 'religious nationalism' that equated 'securing territory' with traditional piety. 'Not only must there be no retreat from a single kilometer of the Land of Israel, God forbid,' he declared to his followers in a sermon in 1975, 'but on the contrary, we shall conquer and liberate more and more, as much in the spiritual as in the physical sense . . . '[91] His followers, who spearheaded the early settlement movement in the occupied territories, were instructed to resist surrendering 'a single grain of holy soil, even if ordered by the Israeli army'.[92]

The losses suffered by Israel in the Yom Kippur war of 1973 proved a setback for mainstream Zionists who were blamed for the reversal of fortunes, even though the Israeli forces repelled the attack from her neighbours. The Ultra-Orthodox judged it to be a sign of God's punishment. The religious Zionists interpreted it differently. They saw it as a sign of 'God's impatience' at Israel's failure to expand to its 'full biblical borders' that stretched from the River Nile to the Euphrates. Kook, the younger, declared that 'Jews had to be ready to give up their lives to repossess the land.'[93] His call inspired a new organization Gush Emunim – the Bloc of the Faithful – who were committed to achieving the territorial ambitions of religious Zionism. This group believed that they had a divine mandate to work beyond the legal confinements of the secular state. Although numerically it was a relatively small organization, its motivation and intensity, according to Milton Viorst, gave it a political power that was disproportionate to its size.[94] Gush Emunim vehemently rejected any moves towards peace that would involve withdrawal from any land under Israeli control. They were also openly hostile and at times violent towards their Arab neighbours. In 1979 they demonstrated their readiness to turn their violence towards their fellow Jews in a stand-off with Israeli troops in the Sinai.[95]

Even though the Ultra-Orthodox did not share the zealousness of the religious Zionists who were ready to sacrifice Jewish lives to hold on to the land, they did for their own internal reasons share their opposition to peace. In 1988 they opted to join the alliance that already existed between the religious Zionists and the Likud party to create a formidable opposition bloc to the secular Zionists who favoured trading land for peace.[96] Yitzhak Rabin's willingness to make peace with the PLO by signing the Oslo Accords in September 1993 was seen by many Ultra-Orthodox and religious Zionists as an act of treachery. A coalition of settlers and Ultra-Orthodox students launched an open campaign aimed at vilifying Rabin. It was in this atmosphere of open hostility towards the peace process and Rabin in particular that Baruch Goldstein, a doctor from the Kiryat Arba settlement, entered the mosque in Hebron and murdered twenty-nine Muslims while at prayer. His friends claimed that he believed that to preserve their hope of redemption, the Jews had to stop the peace process.[97] Rabin attempted to divert Arab anger at this massacre by removing a small group of settlers from an enclave in the centre of Hebron. The settlers enlisted the support of a council of West Bank rabbis who declared that Rabin's decision ran contrary to religious law and therefore could be ignored. The rabbis also called upon the army to refuse orders to evacuate these families. Rabin felt obliged to back down rather than to risk civil war.[98]

The hate campaign against Rabin continued. In a letter, circulated worldwide by three prominent rabbis claiming to be motivated solely by scholarly interests, Rabin and his government were warned that if they were to continue to implement the Oslo agreement, they could be judged under ancient Jewish laws as those 'who surrender the life and property of Jews to the Gentiles'.[99] Another West Bank rabbi publicly accused Rabin of sin by trading land for peace. When Yitzhak Rabin was murdered in November 1995, the assassin, Yigal Amir, a young religious Zionist from an Ultra-Orthodox background, claimed that his action had been sanctioned by the judgements of two nationalists rabbis who accused Rabin of violating laws that warranted death.

Since Ariel Sharon's provocative visit to the Temple Mount/Haram al-Sharif in September 2000, and the subsequent breakdown in the peace process, there has been a marked increase in 'wildcat takeovers' of Palestinian land in the West Bank. Radical young Israelis with no mind for compromise, most of whom were born in settlements, have set up about seventy encampments on hilltops to act as outposts for surrounding settlements. 'The messianic passion that drove their parents to the West Bank,' writes Samantha Shapiro, 'is only stronger in this generation, the first to pass through a religious Zionist school system that teaches that both personal and global redemption can be hastened by Jewish settlement throughout the biblical land of Israel.'[100] While negotiating in 1998 as Foreign Minister with the Palestinian Authority the implementation of the Wye River Accords that called for the dismantling of some settlements, Sharon publicly encouraged settlers to 'grab as many hill tops as they can', as everything they fail to grab will go to the Palestinians. The Shas rabbis who traditionally were in favour of the land for peace process, believing that Jewish lives matter more than territory, now appear like other Ultra-Orthodox parties to be more supportive of the settlements and holding on to the West Bank and Gaza Strip.[101] The Israeli army are also said to be reluctant to see the dismantling of the settlements as many were chosen because of their strategic positions overlooking Palestinian communities. The relinquishing of territory is further complicated by the fact that nearly one-third of the water consumed in Israel comes from aquifers – underground natural rainwater storages – that are in the occupied territories.[102]

The settlers, with whom I met during my visit to Beth-El, a settlement of about 6000 inhabitants that overlooks Ramallah, confirmed that both security and water were important factors, but more important to them was the belief that God wanted them to be there. 'This is the birthplace of the nation of Israel, the place where Jacob had his dream – the name Beth-El means House of God,' explained one of the founder members of the settlement, an army rabbi. He told me that he was born in America, and that on the day after he graduated he bought a one-way ticket to Israel. 'I had no reason to leave,' he assured me. 'It was a spiritual option. Jews have been praying for the opportunity to return to the land since the time of the exile.' Beth-El is officially a religiously observant community where the Torah law is observed. A small percentage of settlers are Russian economic migrants who were not religious when they arrived in Beth-El, but I was told that 90 per cent of them chose to become observers within two years of their arrival. I asked the rabbi why he chose to live under the daily threat of being attacked by his Palestinian neighbours. 'Leaving is not an option,' he replied. He did not hold much hope in the peace process. 'When you are disputing holy soil, there is no middle ground,' he warned. That message, he feared, has not been understood by those involved in the process. 'Nor do they understand', he claimed, 'that violence is deeply rooted in the Arab mind and culture.' When asked how he as an observant Jew could justify killing, he and the others present quoted a law which they attributed to the Torah and which they claim sanctions pre-emptive actions as a means of self-defence – 'If someone rises up to kill you, you should kill them first.' They would have no objection to non-Jews living in Jewish biblical lands, they told me, provided that they were willing to live in a society governed by the law of the Torah. When I pressed them on whether they would resist with force any attempt by the army to dismantle Beth-El, they insisted that such a confrontation was inconceivable as they were convinced that no soldier would carry out such orders. 'We are part of the army. We know that our colleagues would not act against us; many soldiers have already asked not to take part in these forced deportations,' he assured me. 'The government could not deport us from Beth-El. Even the formation of the mountains here, when looked at from space, spells the name of God.'

In Kiryat Arba I spent an evening in the home of a young couple and their four children. The wife had been born and brought up in North London, the husband was Israeli born and was a student of the Torah at a *yeshiva*, a religious school in Hebron. Their house was situated close to the settlement fence, and there were armed guards in a lookout less than twenty yards from their door. I asked them how they could justify putting their children at such risk by living in Kiryat Arba. 'It is our religious calling,' they both replied. 'We believe that by being here, even though the majority are non-religious in this settlement, we are helping to build up the community of Israel in a land that belongs to us.' Their fear was that Palestinians do not want peace. Some of their Arab neighbours were friendly, they told me, and so they tried to introduce their children to them to help them to understand that Arabs can be good people. 'Hamas had warned their neighbours not to engage,' they claimed. 'So we have had to cut off all contact so as not to put our neighbours at risk.' Unlike the settlers that I interviewed in Beth-El, they told me that they would be willing to move if asked to do so by the government or the army. Towards the end of my visit two armed neighbours arrived at the door. It was time for the husband to join the vigilantes who were setting off on their nightly foot patrol. 'It is our religious duty to defend ourselves if our lives are under threat.'

Rabbi Arik Aschermann, the Executive Director of Rabbis for Human Rights, offered a personal analysis of the current crisis. 'My feeling is that even if a solution were proposed that would address the needs of both the Palestinians and the Jews it would be rejected by both because people today are reacting emotionally and not rationally,' he claimed. In the Jewish religious psyche, he explained, the connection between the nation and the land is fundamental. The Torah testifies that this is the basis of the covenant between God and Israel. 'One of the reasons why Jews survived in the Diaspora is that they lived in the hope that they would be given another chance to return to the land and to prove their fidelity. The problem we now face is that the actions required to hold on to this land are the very actions that should deny us the land.' He believes that the majority of settlers would be willing to move if they were offered alternatives, and that what he called 'the religious fanatic gun toters' who would resist with violence were at the most only 3 to 5 per cent of the settler population. Quoting the Ultra-Orthodox rabbi, Ovadia Jusef, Aschermann declared, 'As holy as the land of

Israel is, human life is more sacred. If by giving up territory, you can save human life, then it is a good reason to do so.'

Rabbi Henri Kahn, the editor of the Orthodox monthly magazine *Kountrass*, affirmed that even though the connection with the land was crucial to Jewish self-understanding, most Jews, he believed, would consider it wrong to kill for the sake of the land. 'Secular politicians have failed to grasp the religious significance for both sides in the current conflict,' he claimed. 'They are dealing with the situation as if it were purely a humanitarian issue whereas it is essentially an eschatological problem. There is a relationship between the Text (Scriptures) and what is happening today.' Israel, he believes, is in 'a reaction mode' and the real fear in his opinion is Islamic domination. 'We are living through a moment of the rebirth of Islam which prevents them from getting into any kind of dialogue. Islam has a very imperialist vision of its presence in the world. They desire to dominate Israel. You can only make peace with people who want peace. Oslo has opened up a veritable Pandora's box of Islamic domination,' he declared.

Internal tensions between secular and religious aspirations also exist among the chief protagonists on the other side of this conflict, the Oz tragedy. But before focusing on those tensions in more detail, I want to map out some of the significant events in the past three decades that helped to shape the dynamics of the conflict within the Palestinian camp. In 1964 the Arab governments, attempting to control the growth of 'unorganized guerrilla groups' among the Palestinians, formed two movements, the Palestine Liberation Organization and the Palestine Liberation Army.[103] Both these organizations denied Israel's right of existence and were committed to its armed overthrow. After Israel's victory in 1967 the PLO reformed and became more independent of official Arab control. In 1969 Yasar Arafat, a founder member of the al-Fatah guerrilla group, became the leader of the PLO. Arafat's Fatah movement did not have a strong ideological base other than its opposition to Zionism and its goal to liberate Palestine, and so it appealed to a wide constituency. Muslim activists could identify their religious motives with Fatah's secular goals.[104] The PLO embraced as well some more radical Marxist groups, some of which were led by Palestinians of Christian background. The new PLO structure had become so entrenched in Jordan that by 1970 its presence was seen as a threat to the stability of the country. After open warfare in which a few thousand Palestinian 'fedayeen' were killed, the PLO was expelled and in July 1971 it moved its operations to Lebanon. The following year a splinter group, known as Black September, was responsible for the atrocities at the Munich Olympics where eleven Israeli athletes were murdered.

In October 1974 the Arab League summit recognized the PLO as the sole and legitimate representative of the Palestinian people. In 1975 the UN Security Council allowed the PLO to participate in the debate on the Arab-Israeli question. Although in 1978 Egypt made peace with Israel, relationships with the surrounding Arab nations remained hostile. In 1982 Israel invaded Lebanon, an action that forced the PLO to withdraw from Beirut. It was while Beirut was under the control of the Israeli forces that the Christian Phalangists were allowed to enter the refugee camps of Sabra and Shatila where they massacred hundreds of Palestinians. The PLO's dislodgement from Beirut caused new factions within the organization, with the more radical elements wanting to intensify the armed struggle against Israel. The failure of Arafat's attempts to make progress through diplomacy was evident by the end of the 1980s when violence erupted on the streets of the West Bank and Gaza. Palestinians, frustrated by their living conditions under two decades of Israeli occupation, took to the streets; the *Intifada* – their effort to shake off Israeli control – had begun.

The year 1987 was a key turning point in the Palestinian–Israeli tragedy. New religious actors began to fill the space created by a weakened PLO, who found it difficult to control what was happening on the streets from their exile base in Tunis. Prominent among the newcomers was Hamas, an offshoot of the Muslim Brotherhood. Hamas is an acronym for the Islamic Resistance Movement, but it also means 'zeal' in Arabic. The Muslim Brotherhood, founded in Egypt in 1928, had long associated itself with the Palestinian cause. With the financial support it received from the Saudis and other Gulf States from the early 1970s the Brotherhood began to develop an institutional network in Gaza and the West Bank that provided for the welfare and religious and educational needs of the poor. Their network of schools attached to mosques enabled them to influence a whole generation of Palestinians that had grown up under occupation. Sheikh Ahmad Yassin, the spiritual head of the Brotherhood in Gaza, launched Hamas as a 'religious' alternative to the 'secular' PLO. Yassin sanctioned the struggle against Israel as the first stage in a 'holy war' to create a pan-Islamic state.

Article 6 of the Hamas charter states: 'The land of Palestine is an Islamic *Waaf* (holy possession) consecrated for future Muslim generations until Judgement Day. No one can renounce it or any part of it, or abandon it or any part of it.'[105] Hamas began to pursue its goals by continuing to operate at the community level providing welfare for the needy while at the same time its armed wing, the al-Qassem Brigades, carried out executions of suspected collaborators and raids against Israelis. Even though Hamas saw no room for compromise in this struggle against Israel, it did not completely distance itself from the Palestinian authority.

By the mid 1990s suicide attacks became one of Hamas' most deadly weapons of terror. Although this type of martyrdom is unusual within the Sunni tradition (as in general suicide is condemned as sinful), it was justified as one of the most effective ways of achieving their overall goal, the demise of Israel. Most of the suicide attackers work from deeply religious motives. They 'clean' themselves before carrying out their attack so that they are prepared to meet God with a pure conscience and body.[106] Their actions are reinterpreted in a way that they are seen to be martyrs, people who have chosen to die in battle with the infidel and who are, therefore, assured of a place in paradise. To die in this way is seen as a prolongation of life. It will also bring economic benefit and social recognition to the family. The title 'martyr', *Shahid*, is also given to anyone killed or wounded in the *Intifada*.[107] For Palestinians at the grassroots, Hamas has succeeded, through its active engagement, in redefining the conflict in religious terms.

Palestine Islamic Jihad is another religiously motivated movement that has taken a more major role in the violence of recent years. Fathi Shaqaqi, a medical student from Gaza, was emboldened by the Islamic revolution in Iran. For him and others it served as a role model of how a western-supported regime in the Islamic world can be overthrown. They formed themselves into a movement that dedicated itself to the pursuit of armed conflict with Israel. The *Intifada* provided the group with the ideal opportunity to recruit from a wider circle. It operates in a decentralized and highly secretive way, sometimes co-ordinating its attacks with Hamas and Hizb'allah. The PIJ also make use of suicide attacks as a weapon of terror.[108] Both Hamas and the PIJ are said to have been tutored in the art of guerrilla warfare by Hizb'allah, the Party of God, a militant Shi'ite movement that was created in response to the Israeli invasion of the Lebanon in 1982. Although its prime goal is the liberation of the Lebanon from foreign influence, its stated aims also include the liberation of Jerusalem and the establishment of an Islamic *umma*. Shi'ite religious leaders play an important role in the movement's internal structures.[109] The leadership of all three movements is 'highly educated with an advanced knowledge of western culture and politics'.[110]

The current ongoing *Intifada*, triggered by Ariel Sharon's visit to the Temple Mount/Haram al-Sharif in September 2000, has given birth to the Al-Aqsa Martyrs' Brigades, a 'secular' rival to Hamas and Islamic Jihad. This group was formed by activists with allegedly close ties to Yasar Arafat, though he is careful to disassociate himself from the Brigades' activities. The Al-Aqsa Martyrs were the first to enlist women as suicide bombers. The mood that I encountered on the streets of East Jerusalem and Bethany in January 2003, and in conversations with both Arab Christians and Muslims, had changed from the mild optimism, tainted with suspicion and mistrust, which prevailed in early 2000, to one of anger and rage at what the Israelis had done with American compliance in the intervening period. There was a clear reluctance to condemn the actions of the suicide bombers whose tactics, if not explicitly endorsed, were understood to be a symptom of frustration, given the asymmetric power relationship between the Palestinians and Israelis.

In my meetings with senior officials of the Palestinian Authority I encountered a similar mood of anger and bewilderment, and especially over the blame that has been placed upon them by both the Israelis and the Americans for the failure of the Camp David summit in July 2000. 'What we have witnessed since the Oslo Agreement is an accelerated expansion of the settlements, encouraged by the Israeli government,' I was told. 'Arafat could not have signed up to what was being offered by Barak and Clinton as the territory the Israelis wanted to keep we need if we are to be politically, strategically and economically viable as a state.' The exclusion of the right of Palestinian refugees to return to their land and the claim to Jewish sovereignty over Haram al-Sharif (the Temple Mount), one of the holiest shrines in the Muslim world, were additional major obstacles that made it impossible for the Palestinians to accept the terms of the Barak deal. The sovereignty claim on Haram al-Sharif came, I was told, as a particular shock to the Palestinians as no such claim had been made in previous negotiations. Concern was also expressed at the influence of the American 'religious right' with the Bush administration. Christian millennialists who are opposed to the land for peace policy are supporting, they maintained, the religious Zionists' campaign to retain the occupied Palestinian lands.

The Palestinian academic and conflict specialist, Nadim N. Rouhana, fears that in the present political context 'the obstacles for reconciliation seem insurmountable'. 'The question of whether parties whose relationship involves historical injustice and vast power asymmetries, such as in the Israeli–Palestinian conflict, can resolve their conflict without reconciliation is still open,' he writes.[111] The plight of Palestinian refugees has to be faced, he argues, to allow for reconciliation. The controversy about whether they were expelled or left under duress of war is 'irrelevant' to their basic moral right to return to their homeland, he claims. He accuses Israel of developing 'a massive and sophisticated system of denial mechanisms and multilevel justifications' in order to avoid the fundamental moral issue and to come to terms with its own history.[112] While acknowledging that in the process towards reconciliation Palestinians will have to address their use of 'extreme rhetoric and terrorism', however that may be defined, the difficult truth they have to face is the historical reality that a large part of their homeland has become a state belonging to another nation. Recognizing the right of the Israeli state to exist, he argues, is different from recognizing the moral and legal right of the Jewish people to establish a homeland in Palestine in the first place. 'Asking Palestinians or even expecting them to recognize such a right is morally questionable,' he declares, 'at least because it embraces a request for self-negation.'[113]

The refusal of the Arab nations to negotiate, the Cold War divisions within the international community and the failure of Israel to contain the religious and secular euphoria that led to the settlement movement in the immediate aftermath of the 1967 war have all contributed to the complexity of the Israeli–Palestinian conflict. The presence of the religious actors who rode on to centre stage on the back of the Israeli military successes and the Palestinian secular leadership's failure to make progress, for whatever reasons, have not only heightened the sense of enmity between the conflicting parties, but have also created divisions within their own respective communities that will undoubtedly complicate still further the search for a durable solution to a tragedy that has already claimed thousands of lives.

My purpose in addressing the Northern Ireland, Sri Lanka and Israeli–Palestine conflicts was simply to illustrate the role that religion has and still plays in shaping or redefining the dynamics of these conflicts, all of which have yet to be resolved. In all three situations there are religious people on both sides who are working to promote understanding and reconciliation between the conflicting parties. But the efforts of the reconcilers, I discovered, are for the most part either ignored or at times even violently opposed by the extremists. The efforts of the international political community have failed, as yet, to produce durable solutions. The talks that have led to interim agreements have so far produced only faltering peace processes. Religion in each case has been a missing factor on the agenda. The presence of the old proverbial elephant in the room has not been recognized, presumably out of a fear that any discussion about the role of religion may distract the participants from focusing on the 'real' issues. The reality is that religious concerns are preventing strategically significant, if not numerically strong, groups within these warring communities from buying into the peace processes reached at the purely political level, a fact that seems to have gone unnoticed by the international peacemakers. Allegedly, none of these conflicts could be defined as religious in the sense that the protagonists are battling over the wording of theological statements. All three, however, fit a religious definition to the extent that competing world views, shaped by a narrow interpretation of foundational texts, have made it difficult, if indeed not impossible, for the different religious and ethnic communities to cohabit the same piece of turf. The battle as perceived by the protagonists themselves is for the national soul.

5

Poverty, Tolerance, Leadership

In the immediate aftermath of the attacks on the World Trade Center and the Pentagon poverty and illiteracy were singled out as root causes of this new wave of global terrorism. President George W. Bush was among the first to articulate this supposed causal link between poverty and terrorism when he declared, 'We fight against poverty because hope is an answer to terror.'[1] The South African President, Thabo Mbeki, captured, it is said, the broad consensus of opinion among the delegates at the General Assembly of the United Nations two months after 9/11 when he stated that 'the fundamental conflict in the world today is the deprivation of millions coexisting side-by-side with islands of enormous wealth and prosperity. This necessarily breeds a deep sense of injustice, social alienation, despair and a willingness to sacrifice their lives among those who feel they have nothing to lose and everything to gain.'[2] The British Prime Minister, Tony Blair, offered a similar analysis in his speech to the Labour Party conference in October 2001. He declared,

> I believe this is a fight for freedom ... not only in the narrow sense of personal liberty but in the broader sense of each individual having the economic and social freedom to develop their potential to the full ... The starving, the wretched, the dispossessed, the ignorant, those living in want and squalor from the deserts of Northern Africa to the slums of Gaza to the mountain ranges of Afghanistan: they too are our cause.[3]

Influential political figures like Senator Joseph Biden and former US Secretary of State Madeleine Albright added their weight to the argument by urging people to stop thinking of foreign aid as a 'handout' or 'welfare' and to consider it instead as 'strategic investment in America's security'.[4]

The belief that poverty fuels terrorism was strongly endorsed by many world leaders at the development summit in Mexico in March 2002. Several leaders spoke of the need to defeat poverty in order to put a stop to a major driving force behind international terrorism. The UN Secretary-General, Kofi Annan, said that it was in the interests of the rich states to help the poorer as 'no-one in this world can feel comfortable, or safe, while so many are suffering and deprived'.[5] Mark Juergensmeyer's book *Terror in the Mind of God* supports the widely held view that poverty and terrorism are linked. His profile of the religious terrorist, regardless of faith or denomination, is that of a young, jobless, unmarried, socially marginalized male who sees no hope of escaping the daily feeling of humiliation that he experiences at the hands of what he sees to be a feckless or indifferent government. Juergensmeyer discovered that in such circumstances normal youthful concerns over 'careers, social location, and sexual relationships' become exacerbated. 'In Palestine, for example,' he writes, 'where the unemployment rate among young men in their late teens and early twenties has hovered around 50 percent, economic frustration has led to sexual frustration. Without jobs, which is usually a prerequisite to searching for a wife in traditional societies, they cannot marry. Without marriage, in strict religious cultures such as that of Palestinian Arabs, they cannot have sex.'[6] Violence endorsed by religious authority, Juergensmeyer argues, provides the sense of empowerment that these marginal young men lack.

Not every religious terrorist, though, fits the profile that links terrorism and violence to poverty and illiteracy. Nasra Hassan, a United Nations relief worker, who interviewed nearly two hundred and fifty Palestinian militants as well as some of the families of deceased suicide bombers, discovered the biggest problem facing the leaders of Hamas, Islamic Jihad and the al-Qassam Brigade was not how to recruit but how to select candidates from the large numbers who were volunteering as suicide bombers. A high level of education, he was told, was the criterion used to judge the level of commitment and the ability of a potential suicide bomber to succeed in his mission. Far from being 'uneducated, desperately poor, simple minded or depressed', Hassan observed, many were 'middle class and, unless they were fugitives, held paying jobs'. The most commonly expressed motive, he claims, was the sense of being humiliated by the Israelis who 'occupy our land and deny our history'.[7]

The commonly presumed link between poverty and terrorism was further called into question by the fact that Osama bin Laden is a multi-millionaire and most of the 9/11 hijackers were middle-class Saudis and Egyptians. Jerrold Post, a political psychologist at George Washington University, claims that American support for authoritarian regimes like Saudi Arabia and Egypt is one of the main causes for the Arab anger and the violence currently directed at the United States.[8] Hungry people, others argue, are far too concerned with conserving energy to find their next meal to throw rocks or to plant bombs. The real poor, they claim, are too politically passive and unimportant in their own eyes to revolt. As a journalist friend recently asked me: 'Name a single riot that has been caused by Africa's famines?'

Poverty is undoubtedly a factor but in itself it is not the prime cause for the rise in religious fundamentalism and the indiscriminate use of violence in the name of religion. Faith-based terrorism stems mainly from how the advocates of such violence interpret their foundational texts, sacred scriptures and own religious traditions and history. None the less, if we fail to acknowledge at least an indirect causal link with poverty and illiteracy, we risk misjudging the complexity of dealing with religiously justified or inspired violence. The Crawford and Lipschutz study, *The Myth of "Ethnic Conflict" Politics, Economics and "Cultural" Violence*, concluded that religious and cultural differences can lead to violent conflict when one group is targeted for privilege or discrimination and when economic factors, no matter how impersonal, lead to disproportionate hardships. 'Economic strength', Crawford claims, 'contributes to the institutional strength that mutes the political identity of culturally defined groups or channels identity politics to peaceful conflict resolution.'[9] Inequality does matter and needs, therefore, to be addressed to avoid the danger of communal strife in multi-faith/multicultural societies as well as to lessen the risk of global terrorism. Extreme poverty, social injustice, unemployment, illiteracy all contribute to the milieu that can provide both a trigger and a fertile recruiting ground for high-minded and idealistic young religious entrepreneurs who believe that it is their sacred or religious duty to act on behalf of the downtrodden and to spearhead social and economic change.

Religious activists reject what they see to be western hypocrisy demonstrated both in its willingness to support repressive regimes that deny millions their right to freedom, and in its failure to work to implement the ideals it proclaims to be universal. A good example is the fact that in 1948 the United Nations Universal Declaration of Human Rights proclaimed that 'everyone has the right to a standard of living adequate for the health and well being of himself and his family'. Access to food was recognized as a human right. And yet today according to Kofi Annan, 'well over a billion people go to bed hungry every night'.[10] Even though there is enough food in the world for 6 billion mouths, Robert F. Drinan, the Georgetown University Law Professor, writes that the sad fact 'is that the fundamental right above all human rights – the right to food – has not been given the attention it deserves as a part of international law'.[11] The gap between the rich and the poor, even in the industrialized countries, has in fact grown wider in recent years.[12] The 'trickle down' wealth creation theories have failed to deliver for the millions who die each year prematurely. Consequently, in countries like Egypt, according to the journalist Geneive Abdo, Islamic activists are more interested in achieving social reform than 'establishing economic equilibrium between the rich minority and the impoverished majority'. 'All you had to do was to look at the feet of the faithful on Ahmed Hishmat Street', she writes, to appreciate that the Islamic revival movement was 'broad-based, touching Egyptians in every social class and all walks of life'.[13]

In the face of poverty and their own powerlessness to effect change under their corrupt and ineffective governments religious entrepreneurs world-wide seek faith-based alternatives to the present economic and political world order that is clearly failing to provide either hope or dignity for billions of impoverished people. Without the basic necessities of life or the hope of acquiring them, desperation makes people more vulnerable to the message of the extremists. Even if people are reluctant to adopt or to endorse their violent methods they are equally reluctant to disown their co-religionists whom, even if misguidedly, they see as espousing their cause. I found this especially true among the Catholic and Protestant communities in Northern Ireland at the height of the 'Troubles', and more recently among the Tamil community in Sri Lanka.

At the Millennium Summit the world's political leaders declared their intent to devote the first fifteen years of the twenty-first century to a major onslaught on poverty, illiteracy and disease. To date the world has wit-nessed little evidence of any serious efforts on the part of the international political community to implement the realization of that hope they offered to the impoverished billions, the passive victims of our global economic and social structural imbalances. The universal right to food places upon all governments a legal and moral obligation to eradicate hunger. Sadly, it was the fear of the legal implications of failing to act on this obligation that prompted the United States to question the validity of this basic right at the 1996 World Food Summit.[14] Even non-governmental organizations who campaign against the violation of civil and political rights have tended to ignore the blatant violation of social and economic rights around the world. During the Cold War period capitalists and socialist countries used, on the one hand, the violation of political and civil rights and, on the other, the indifference towards economic and social rights as tools to criticize each other's systems. With the end of the Cold War stand-off there is less excuse for the apparent continued western indifference towards the plight of the billions worldwide who still lack such basic human needs as food, housing, health and education.

Madeleine Albright is right to claim that the West has 'the intellectual resources, experience and, yes, money to do something meaningful ... we just need the will to do the work'.[15] The West should no longer use the corruption and ineffectiveness of the governments in poorer countries as an excuse for minimal or no action on behalf of the world poor. Tighter controls on aid and more realistic approaches to sustainable development can help to eliminate these human obstacles. Sadly, it may take an en-lightened sense of self-interest, a concern for national security in a post 9/11 world rather than a sense of human compassion or moral and legal obligation to motivate the leaders of the G8 countries to act decisively on behalf of the world's poor. Meanwhile, in a world where the rights of billions remain no more than empty platitudes some religious fundamentalists will continue to believe that the hypocritical values of western civilization as they perceive them justify their resort to violence in their effort to challenge a world order that has failed and is continuing to fail to deliver the basic fundamental needs for their own peoples. In the mind of the religious ter-rorist the 'fault line' between good and evil is clear. Poverty and inequality act both as trigger and fuel for the fervour of the religious terrorist and need therefore to be addressed if the growth of a terrorism that seeks divine authority to justify its atrocities is to be curtailed.

The International Covenants on Civil and Political and Economic, Social and Cultural Rights that were proclaimed by the United Nations in the 1960s will indeed be costly to implement on a global scale. Their imple-mentation, however, may in the long run prove less costly than the global impact of terrorism that is fuelled by images of a cosmic battle between good and evil. Mark Juergensmeyer warns that when 'a struggle is seen as hopeless in human terms, it is likely that it may be reconceived on a sacred plane, where the possibilities of victory are in God's hands'. To illustrate this point Juergensmeyer uses among others the example of Shoko Asahara, the leader of the Japanese Buddhist sect, who, as we saw in chapter two, released nerve gas on the subway in an effort to 'elevate the struggle to the level of cosmic war'.[16] The faith-inspired terrorist is capable of inflicting unimaginable human suffering in the struggle to achieve what he perceives in his perverse sense of logic to be a righteous cause. Biden and Albright are right when they argue that development aid should be looked upon as 'national security support'. Regrettably, as already mentioned, it may take enlightened self-interest rather than moral conviction to motivate the world's political elites to act more decisively on behalf of the world's hungry.

Philip Alston, a world expert on human rights, has said that 'the right to food has been endorsed more often and with greater unanimity and urgency than most other human rights while at the same time being violated more comprehensively and systematically than probably any other right.'[17] Article 18 of the Universal Declaration on Human Rights, which upholds the right of everyone 'to freedom of thought, conscience and religion' including 'freedom to change his religion or belief, and freedom, either alone or in community with others and in public or private, to manifest his religion or belief in teaching, practice, worship and observance', would be, I suspect, a close runner-up in a list of rights most systematically ignored or violated. States as diverse in culture, ideology and religion as Singapore, Iran, Saudi Arabia, India, Pakistan, China, North Korea and many of the tribal societies of Africa question what they claim is the western emphasis on individualism that dominates the human rights debate.

In the Bangkok Declaration a number of Asian-Pacific countries formulated this concern. While reaffirming their belief in 'the interdependence and indivisibility of economic, social, cultural and political rights' they stressed the necessity to bear in mind 'the significance of national and regional particularities and various historical, cultural and religious backgrounds'.[18] Their message was that 'culture matters'. Individualism they see as a historic intervention, a product of liberal European thought, emanating from the period of the Enlightenment, and as such has little relevance for their religious and cultural traditions where allegiance to community is considered more important than the rights of individuals. To impose western norms universally is, they claim, a form of neo-imperialism and is unacceptable. The application of human rights, they argue, must vary according to cultural differences. The argument that the contemporary human rights discourse has been shaped by the philosophies of the Enlightenment is true but not the whole truth. The horror of the Holocaust was the catalyst that led to the Universal Declaration in 1948. The widespread moral revulsion that was felt at what had been done in the name of Fascism and at the defence of the perpetrators at Nuremberg that they were 'following orders' demanded a set of universal norms to govern human relationships and to allow people to say 'no' when asked to do what was civilly 'legal' but morally 'wrong'. The Declaration was an attempt to find a higher law that would empower individuals and enable them in particular to resist immoral orders. Given, though, the diversity in beliefs and ideologies in the newly formed world assembly religion could not be appealed to as the source of this higher law. It is said that when Eleanor Roosevelt first convened the drafting committee, the disagreement over 'the philosophical and metaphysical bases of rights' was so sharp that it was agreed to disagree and to take these rights as 'givens'.[19] The thoughts of John Locke, the seventeenth-century political philosopher, and those eighteenth- and nineteenth-century European philosophers who promoted the idea that rights belong to a person by the nature of being human and not by virtue of citizenship, religion or ethnic origins are clearly reflected in the Declaration.

In 1689, while in exile in Holland, Locke published anonymously the first of four letters on the subject of toleration.[20] Against the background of a religiously polarized society Locke takes the pragmatic view that a policy of toleration is in the public interests. He considered it irrational for the State to force people into believing. His argument was rooted in the conviction that people cannot change their beliefs at will and therefore the use of force was counter-productive. He writes, 'true and saving Religion consists only in the inward persuasion of the Mind, without which nothing can be acceptable to God. And such is the nature of the Understanding that it cannot be compell'd to the belief of anything by outward force.'[21] Locke's solution is the disestablishment of Church and State. These two institutions, he believed, should not meddle in each other's affairs as 'they occupy different spheres of life'.[22] It was the State's role to advance civil interests, the Church's to save souls. The authority of the Church, therefore, should not extend beyond its members, and the State should only intervene in religious matters if a religious sect were to teach 'opinions contrary to human society'.

Jews, Muslims and religious pagans all fitted under Locke's umbrella of tolerance, but not Catholics and atheists. These exclusions underline the pragmatic nature of Locke's arguments. He ruled out Catholics, as they owed political allegiance to a 'foreign prince' – the pope – and atheists, as they had no basis for acting morally since they had no fear of divine punishment. Whilst prepared to set limits on tolerance in the interests of a state's security and well-being, Locke felt no such restraint in promoting pluralism in beliefs within churches. He based his arguments on the number of people who profess the creed without fully understanding what it means. He writes,

> If ever you were acquainted with a country parish, you must needs have a strange opinion of them, if you think all the ploughmen and milkmaids at church understood all the propositions in Athanasius's creed; it is more, truly, than I should be apt to think of any one of them; and yet I cannot hence believe myself authorized to judge or pronounce them all damned; it is too bold an intrenching on the prerogative of the Almighty; to their own Master they stand or fall.[23]

The seventeenth-century French Protestant philosopher Pierre Bayle used an entirely different argument to Locke in presenting a case for the toleration of competing religious beliefs. Bayle, born the son of a Protestant minister, in his search for truth briefly converted to Catholicism before returning again to his Protestant faith. In an attempt to curb the wars between Protestants and Catholics that had marred life in France for most of the second half of the sixteenth century, the Edict of Nantes in 1598 decreed that the State should not prescribe religious belief or practice. The decree permitted French Calvinists, otherwise known as Huguenots, to worship freely in many, but not all, parts of France. It was the revocation of this Edict in 1685 that provoked Bayle to launch a vigorous crusade of the pen against religious intolerance. Unlike Locke, Bayle defended the rights of atheists arguing that people did not need to be religious to be moral. He challenged the popular perception that people chose to be atheists so that they could indulge in 'uncontrolled sensuality' without feeling that they would be ultimately accountable by pointing to the example of the Crusaders, who though not atheists committed what he describes as 'unspeakable crimes'.[24] Conscience and not religion, Bayle argued, made people virtuous and therefore the inviolable rights of an individual's conscience had to be respected.

In defence of this position Bayle challenged the received interpretation of the words attributed to Jesus in the Gospel, 'compel them to come in', that had been used since the time of Augustine of Hippo to justify forced conversions. 'Any literal interpretation', he wrote, 'which carries an obligation to commit iniquity is false.'[25] This being so, he concluded that Christ meant that unbelievers should be persuaded to convert by rational argument. Persecution he believed to be both immoral and irrational because it discourages the discovery of truth. No one, Bayle maintained, had 'a right to claim such complete possession of truth as not to need to compare his ideas with those of others'.[26] Atheists, therefore, who fail to listen to reason, he argued, should be allowed without interference to pursue their mistaken path. Beliefs, which do not require people to act immorally, he maintained, should be tolerated. Bayle's defence of the rights of the erring conscience proved too much for many of his fellow Protestants who dismissed what he wrote as a 'eulogy of religious disbelief'.

In the following century François Marie Arouet, who is better known by his pen name Voltaire, championed the Locke–Bayle campaign for the rights of the individual and religious tolerance. During his three-year period of exile in England Voltaire became acquainted with the philosophy of John Locke. It was the execution of Jean Calas, a 68-year-old Protestant merchant in Toulouse, having been wrongly accused of killing his son who supposedly wanted to convert to Catholicism, that outraged Voltaire and inspired his *Treatise on Tolerance*. Voltaire protested against the popular anti-Protestant bigotry that created a climate in which 'rumour' became 'certainty' and was responsible for the death of a 'feeble' old man whom he believed to be innocent.[27] Voltaire saw the Calas affair as 'a case of vital interest to the human race' not because he had any particular fondness for Huguenots. His greatest concern was for the 'physical and moral well-being of society'.[28]

Voltaire was sceptical of all organized religion, and in particular Protestantism and Catholicism, as he believed that religion had stifled the voice of nature. No one religion he felt had a right to claim an exclusive hold on the truth. Human weakness and the tendency to err, he believed, should inspire humility and forbearance towards one another.[29] He argued that an individual should 'be permitted to believe only in what his reason tells him, to think only what his reason, be it enlightened or misguided, may dictate ... provided always that he threatens no disturbance to public order'.[30] On this last point Voltaire agreed with Locke, but he disagreed with him on the relationship between Church and State.

Voltaire believed that religion had an important role to play in society but what he rejected was the bigotry and superstition to which religion had so often given birth and which had in his opinion 'held the entire world in subjection'.[31] The Church should be subordinate to the State, he argued, to curb bigotry and to guarantee a tolerant society. He also argued that the civil rights denied to Protestants by the revocation of the Edict of Nantes should be reinstated and that Protestants should be less demonstrative in their display of religious fervour at least in public so as to promote a greater sense of civic harmony. He challenged his contemporaries to broaden their outlook and to learn from the example of others:

> Let us reach out of our narrow little sphere for a moment, and examine what goes on in the rest of the globe. The Turkish prince, for example, rules peacefully over twenty races of different religious convictions; two hundred thousand Greeks live in Constantinople in perfect safety ... this empire is stuffed with Jacobites, Nestorians, Coptics, Christians of St John, Jews, Gebers and Banians. The annals of Turkey bear no record of a revolt raised by any of these religious communities.[32]

Tolerance, Voltaire maintained, should reach beyond the boundaries of one's own culture and religion to be universal in its embrace. It should be rooted in an awareness of the interconnectedness that exists between human beings despite the diversity of ethnicity, culture and religion. 'I tell you,' Voltaire writes, 'we ought to regard every man as our brother. What? The Turk, my brother? The Chinaman, my brother? The Jew and the Siamese as well? Yes, assuredly, for are we not all children of the same Father and creatures of the same God?'[33]

The seventeenth- and eighteenth-century writings of Locke, Bayle and Voltaire among others undoubtedly helped shape a level of political thinking that prepared the twentieth century world to respond to the horror of the Holocaust with a set of rights that transcend boundaries and are aimed at protecting the individual from state tyranny and empowering him or her. It would be wrong, however, to attribute the claim to 'rights' talk exclusively to a group of European thinkers. We find similar arguments against coercion in religion and supporting the right of the individuals to appeal to conscience and to follow their own beliefs in the writings of the second-century author and moralist, Tertullian. Born into a pagan family in Carthage, which is in modern-day Tunisia but was then part of Roman Africa, Tertullian was educated in the Greco-Roman tradition. In middle age he converted to Christianity at a time when it was still at least officially looked upon as an illegal sect. He soon became one of its renowned polemicists.

In 197 CE Tertullian wrote to the provincial Roman governor protesting against the persecution of Christians and the violation of their rights. Their treatment, he complained, was inconsistent with the normal judicial procedural practices of the Roman Empire. The policy towards them, he maintained, was driven by ignorance, fear and misrepresentation. The right to religious liberty, he argued, is rooted in the nature of both the human person and religion itself. The concept of 'freedom' is essential to the understanding of both. He wrote:

> By both human nature and natural law, each one is free to adore whom he wants; the religion of the individual neither harms nor profits anybody else. It is against the nature of religion to force religion; it must be accepted spontaneously and not by force; the offerings demanded, indeed, must be made willingly. That is why if you force us to sacrifice, you give, in fact, nothing to your gods: they have no need of unwilling sacrifices.[34]

The inviolability of the right of an individual's conscience and the essential importance of freedom of choice in matters of religion were discovered as much in the interaction of culture, learning and religion – the second-century clash between Greco-Roman thought and practice and Middle Eastern beliefs – as in the polemics of seventeenth- and eighteenth-century European philosophers. Tertullian like Locke set limits on what should and what should not be tolerated. Whilst he appealed to conscience and freedom to support his argument that one could be a loyal citizen and yet a dissenter in religious matters, he did not reflect Voltaire's openness to other traditions and beliefs or indeed Locke's conviction that people come to God through God-given powers of reason. In his *Prescriptions against Heretics* Tertullian asks, 'What does Jerusalem have to do with Athens, the Church with the Academy, the Christian with the heretic?' His answer was without nuance; 'I have no use for a Stoic or a Platonic or a dialectic [i.e., Aristotelian] Christianity.' Tertullian was so convinced of the truth of the Christian message that he felt no need of what he referred to as 'research' or 'speculation', fearing that the 'fruitless questionings' of the philosophers could prove a distraction to believers.[35]

In the introduction to *Religious Human Rights in Global Perspective* the editor, John Witte Jr writes with reference to Judaism, Christianity and Islam, 'To be sure, none of these religious traditions speaks unequivocally about human rights, and none has amassed an exemplary human rights record over the centuries. Their sacred texts and canons say much more about condemnations and obligations than about liberties and rights.'[36] The concept of 'individualism' that lies at the core of Locke, Bayle and Voltaire's 'rights' talk may seem more like 'a manifestation of pride' and a threat to communal responsibilities than the exercise of any God-given right to many of the world's main religious traditions. Tolerance certainly has not been the hallmark of relationships either within or between different faith communities. Exclusive claims on truth have given rise either to high boundaries that have marginalized outsiders or to aggressive attempts to impose those beliefs on unwilling neighbours. None the less, within the foundational texts and teachings of these competing traditions there is an implicit recognition of the dignity and the right of others to live differently and in peace.

Hinduism believes in a world that has a common ancestry and sees the whole of nature as 'the symbol of a higher reality'.[37] Buddhism teaches that it is possible for others to discover the moral and spiritual laws, 'the one truth' that governs life.[38] The Judaic texts speak of the human person being created in 'the image of God' (Genesis 1:27). The golden rule of Christianity is, 'Do to others what you would have them to do to you' (Luke 6:31). Again the New Testament letter addressed to the Romans proclaims that 'God does not show favouritism' (2:11). The Qur'an too acknowledges the one-ness of humanity before it was divided by human rebelliousness and teaches respect for People of the Book – Jews and Christians. In practice, however, these spiritual insights into the essential unity or interconnected-ness of humanity have never been fully developed. The distressing consequence of this failure is, as chapter three records, that 'the blood of thousands' of innocent and vulnerable people stains the doorsteps of churches, synagogues, mosques and temples. Christianity's record of cruelty and intolerance is particularly disturbing.

As members of an outlawed sect within a militarized colonial empire, Christians frequently found themselves victims of coercion and persecution. The use of force or violence within their own ranks, however, was strictly forbidden. Internal dissent and moral lapses were dealt with through dialogue and compassion. The Edict of Milan in 313, however, proved to be a defining moment that changed the Church's social status and along with it some of its core values. The high ideals of Tertullian and others were now overshadowed by a new sense of self-understanding, prompted by their redefined role within an empire that needed a new ideology to maintain its unity.[39] The alliance between 'throne and altar' that was established through the Emperor Constantine's conversion to Christianity had a profound influence on Christian attitudes towards others. A Church that had argued for its own liberty of faith and practice on the grounds of conscience and the nature of religious belief found itself a century later morally sanctioning the death penalty for pagans and religious dissenters. Jews also were singled out for their failure to conform. In 388, a mob led by the bishop attacked and completely destroyed a synagogue in Callinicus, a small city on the Euphrates. Their prejudiced act of vandalism was judged to be 'a righteous act' by the saintly bishop Ambrose of Milan, who described a synagogue as 'a haunt of infidels, a home of the impious, a hiding place of madmen, under the damnation of God himself'.[40]

Under the throne and altar alliance Jews found themselves 'utterly dependent upon the goodwill of the Christian majority'.[41] Always the victims of discrimination and periodic acts of violence, they were afforded some level of tolerance and protection through the arguments of the medieval theologians who upheld the paramount importance of conscience and freedom in the realms of faith. These same principles were not extended to heretics, religious dissenters who were judged to have lost their right to appeal to conscience once they had freely embraced the Christian faith. Thomas Aquinas so believed in the sacredness of conscience that he held to act against conscience, whether correct or mistaken, is always wrong, even to the degree that if a person believed 'abstinence from fornication to be sinful', abstinence for that person would be sinful.[42] And yet Aquinas justified the use of physical force to persuade lapsed Catholics and doctrinal heretics to recant and to resume the practice of their faith on the grounds that they were obliged to honour the promises made at baptism. In the case of persistent defiance he had no problem with the death penalty being applied, except in cases where the individual had a substantial following. In such cases Aquinas taught that prudence was required in order to avoid the risk of a schism.[43] The voices in the following centuries that called for greater toleration and understanding sowed seeds that would eventually find fruition in the teachings of the Second Vatican Council.

The perception of 'Christendom' as a society based on unity of a faith that believed in its own exclusive and universal mission to bring salvation to all was a major factor in helping to create the milieu of intolerance towards dissent that has been the hallmark of Catholicism since the conversion of Constantine to the present age. These doctrinal beliefs made it difficult to see how heresy or internal dissent could be tolerated. The Catholic Church's attitude to the diversity of beliefs that existed in the outer world and its relationship with the State was shaped by what became known as the 'thesis/hypothesis' theory that has its roots in medieval theology. The 'thesis' was that it is not good that worship, based on erroneous beliefs, should be allowed. The 'hypothesis' was that it could be tolerated, none the less, in the hope that some greater good may evolve or some greater evil be avoided.[44]

In practice, the 'thesis/hypothesis' doctrine served as a paradigm for the Church's relationship with the outer world. The thesis led to the belief that in countries where the majority of the population were Catholic the State should recognize in law that the Catholic Church was the only religious body that had the God-given right to exist and to function in public. In principle, this meant that other religions had no legal right to practise in public and should, therefore, be repressed by the State for fear that their mistaken and erroneous beliefs and practices could harm society.[45] People, it was claimed, had a right to be protected from the dangers of error that may drive them away from the truth. The hypothesis argued that in states where Catholics were not a majority the Church could forego its claim to exclusivity and therefore tolerate the public presence of other faiths. People rightfully subjected the inherent ambiguity in a doctrine that demanded tolerance for your beliefs when you were in a minority and allowed you to deny tolerance when you were in a majority to scornful criticism.[46]

The double fear that error leads to loss of salvation and tolerance to indifferentism or relativism in matters of religion – the thinking that all religions are either of none or of equal value – was undoubtedly a root cause of the Catholic Church's refusal to engage in any level of meaningful dialogue with a post-Reformation, post-Enlightenment world. In 1864 Pius IX published his *Syllabus of Errors* in which he condemned the proposition: 'Every man is free to embrace and to profess the religion which, by light of reason, he believes to be true.'[47] A hundred years later John XXIII published his encyclical letter *Peace on Earth* in which he declared the belief that, 'Every human being has the right to honour God according to the dictates of an upright conscience, and therefore the right to profess his religion in private and in public.' His argument in the letter is based solely on the nature of the human person and his or her right to seek truth by free enquiry. To obey conscience, he maintains, is to obey God.[48] In 1965 the

Second Vatican Council overwhelmingly approved the new direction which John XXIII had given to church teaching on matters of freedom and conscience. The Council's declaration on *Religious Liberty* argues that people are endowed with 'reason' and 'free will' and are therefore morally obliged to 'seek the truth'. It would be impossible, however, to do this unless, the document states, they 'enjoy both psychological freedom and immunity from external control'. The protection and promotion of these inviolable human rights is, the Council declared, 'an essential duty of every civil authority'.[49] The Council, whilst upholding the traditional Catholic belief that only in the Catholic Church could one find the fullness of truth, recognized that other faith traditions may contain 'some truth' and therefore recommended all forms of dialogue as a means of seeking moral and spiritual enrichment.

A number of factors contributed to this fundamental change of attitude in the Catholic psyche that led to the abandonment of the traditional doctrine of intolerance towards what was perceived to be 'error'. The horrors of two world wars and the emergence of Fascism and totalitarianism obliged the Church's authorities to reflect on issues of human dignity and freedom. The signs of a shift in official thinking became apparent in 1943 when Pius XII condemned the use of force or coercion on people.[50] In the intervening years Catholic writers like John Courtney Murray prepared the way for further development when they argued pragmatically that the Church should avoid promulgating policies that were likely to lead to social conflict.[51] Another significant factor was that by the time of the Vatican Council over 60 million Catholics were living under communist rule and many were victims of severe repression. The vacant seats reserved in the Council chamber for those who were not allowed to attend by their totalitarian governments provided a constant reminder of this fact throughout the debates.[52] I suspect that it was the consciousness of being 'victim' once again after enjoying in general over sixteen hundred years of privilege that prompted more than anything else a return to the Tertullian emphasis on conscience and freedom, those fundamental principles that had been almost completely overshadowed by internal doctrinal concerns. The cycle from being victim to perpetrator to victim once again helped Catholicism to rediscover the precious truth of the sacredness of the human conscience in the search for truth. The language used by the Vatican more recently, however, to impose a two-year silence on the Belgian Jesuit theologian, Jacques Dupuis, for his book *Toward a Christian Theology of Religious Pluralism*, which was judged to contain 'ambiguities' that could lead readers to 'erroneous or harmful positions', would seem to indicate that forty years on from the Council the old mentality still prevails at least in the Vatican.[53]

Most of the Reformers were not advocates of toleration or freedom on matters of religion. In 1553 Calvin instigated the condemnation and execution of Servetus and in the following year wrote a treatise justifying his actions and advocating death for all heretics. The French Protestant intellectual, a professional colleague of Calvin, Sebastian Castellio, thought differently. He condemned the killing of people over differences in doctrine and sought to promote the idea of freedom of conscience in matters of belief. He argued that if the ultimate goal of Christianity is to be a blessing to humankind, persecution must be its 'extreme antithesis'. If persecution therefore becomes an essential element of a religion, that religion becomes 'a curse to mankind'.[54] The Pilgrim Fathers who fled England in order to be able to practise freely their own beliefs were accused of denying the same liberty to others when they settled in the new world. Their defence was that they viewed themselves more as a Church than a State.[55] In England and elsewhere attempts were made to impose the reformed faith on the whole nation. In the face of such intolerance Milton among others pleaded for religious toleration. He believed that persecution hindered the discovery of truth and advocated toleration for all forms of Protestantism but, like Locke, he did not extend his principles to embrace Roman Catholics.[56] The seventeenth-century English theologian, William Chillingworth, who like Bayle had a brief encounter with Catholicism before returning to his Protestant roots, believed it to be a great sin to force on others one's own interpretation of Scripture. This, he argued, was the cause of all the 'schisms and disorders of Christianity'.[57]

The writings of John Hick, a philosopher of religion and Church of England minister, reflect the more liberal approach to pluralism within contemporary Protestantism. He argues that Christians need to take a more God-centred and less Christ-focused view of life. For him God is the sun, 'the originative source of light and life, whom all the religions reflect in their own different ways'. The experience of living and working in a multi-faith society like modern-day Britain led him to conclude that 'the great world traditions constitute different conceptions and perceptions of, and responses to, the Real from within the different cultural ways of being human'.[58] Conscious of the fact that his theist-centred approach may be unacceptable to Buddhists, for example, Hicks speaks of God in terms of 'the Real', meaning that 'infinite reality' people can encounter through various religious experiences. The more conservative and fundamentalist trends in the Protestant tradition reject the pluralistic approach to faith, fearing that it leads to relativism that gives equal value to all religions or deconstructionism that challenges any attempt to establish an ultimate and secure meaning in a text or religious tradition. The Lutheran pastor, David

Benke, was accused of heresy and idolatry by a group of his colleagues because he worshipped publicly in the company of non-believers. The event was the national prayer service held at Yankee Stadium twelve days after the 9/11 terrorist attacks.[59]

The Orthodox Church's belief that they alone have maintained 'unbroken continuity' with the early Church strongly influences Orthodox attitudes towards other faith traditions. In practice, however, these attitudes vary according to local customs and traditions as each church within the Orthodox family is autocephalous or self-governing. In the twenty-five years that I was engaged in regular dialogue with members of the Russian Orthodox Church I was always received with respect and fraternal friendship. Although we never shared in a common eucharist as Catholics were officially considered to be schismatics, we frequently prayed together and attended the eucharistic celebrations of the other. When I was invited by the BBC, however, to present an act of worship from the Greek Orthodox monastery, built on the site of the cave in which John is believed to have received his 'apocalyptic' visions on the island of Patmos, I had to conceal the fact that I was Catholic as the monks would have found my presence in their monastery church unacceptable. The recent headlines declaring that more than 100 reclusive monks living on Mount Athos were determined to wage a 'spiritual war' against the Ecumenical Patriarch Bartholomew, the spiritual leader of the world's Orthodox Christians, because of his efforts to improve relationships with the Roman Catholic Church is further evidence of the deep suspicion that many Orthodox believers have regarding other denominations and inter-religious dialogue.[60]

The Greek Orthodox historian, Demetrios J. Constantelos, explains that the Orthodox reluctance to engage in dialogue stems from the fear that such encounters can cause 'the gradual weakening of the Orthodox conviction' that their Church 'is the one, holy, catholic, apostolic Church of Christ'. The danger that they may come to be viewed 'as equal to heretical, schismatic or even sectarian groups' and that through these exchanges their own dogmas may be reduced to 'human-made teachings' and even 'changed' adds to their reasons for shunning ecumenical contacts.[61] None the less, as Constantelos points out, frequently 'historical realities belie theoretical positions'. The fact that Orthodox Christians have co-existed with Jews and Muslims for many centuries is evidence of this. The beliefs that truth emanates from one source, the Creator, and that the divinity is 'present in all places and filling all things' enable Orthodox believers to acknowledge the divine presence outside of Christianity. The Spirit of God 'is not confined to the frontiers of the Church' but 'meets people everywhere'. Whilst they acknowledge, however, that 'a Brahman, or a

Buddhist, or a Muslim' can receive grace and enlightenment through reading their own scriptures, they believe it is the task of the Orthodox believer 'to reveal to the world of the religions the God there hidden'.[62] The ultimate goal of dialogue in the Orthodox mind is to evangelize, which put simply is to show 'how humanity can be brought back into God's presence'. In so far as other religions share this goal they are perceived by the Orthodox as 'instruments of God in God's world'.[63]

Judaism more than any other religion has had the longest exposure to pluralism and diversity. For the best part of two millennia Jews have had to live in the shadow of other beliefs, learning to retain their own distinctive identity in what were all too frequently sectarian and hostile environments. Basic to their faith and identity is the belief in one God to whom they owe loyalty and obedience. Through the Sinai covenant God had entered into a special relationship with the Jewish people but in their understanding that relationship does not exclude the possibility that others too could have different levels of relationship with the same God. Their belief in the universal nature of God's love is recorded in the book of Genesis, which tells of the covenant that God made with Noah. The 'rainbow' God declared 'is the sign of the covenant I have established between me and all life on earth'.[64] The Jewish Rabbinic tradition has endeavoured to maintain an awareness of the importance of others through non-exclusive interpretations of the Sinai experience. What became known as the 'Noahide Laws' decreed every non-Jew to be 'a son of the covenant of Noah'.[65] It was acceptable for pagans, therefore, to worship in their traditional way provided that they understood the objects of their devotion to be purely symbolic and not ends in themselves. Some emphasized that 'revelation occurred simultaneously in all the seventy languages of humankind'; others, the fact that the 'event took place not in the land of the Jews, which would thus make it pertinent to them alone, but in the wilderness – no man's land, or more properly, every man's land'. The sand, wind and sky of the wilderness, they taught, 'belong to no one and to every one, so too is the Torah the possession of all human beings'. Others dispute this, believing that the Torah was received in their language for their exclusive use.[66]

The defeat the Jews suffered in 586 BCE and their subsequent exile to Babylon had a formative influence on Jewish attitudes towards outsiders. It was interpreted as a sign that God was using the Babylonians to punish them for their infidelity and failure to observe their part of the covenant agreement.[67] The soul searching in exile led to a more 'exclusivist approach' towards others and their beliefs. On their return they drew up a new 'binding agreement' between themselves, restricting relationships with neighbours and prohibiting marriage with outsiders.[68] The spirit of sectarianism that permeated their post-exile relationships failed, however, to eclipse totally the more global outlook that allowed space for others in God's overall plan for creation. The stories of Ruth and Jonah in the Jewish Scriptures were reminders that God's gaze extended far beyond their tribal borders.

The tension between the conflicting demands of an exclusive and a universal interpretation of the Sinai experience is reflected in the intervening centuries of Jewish thought and practice. The first-century Jewish philosopher, Philo of Alexandria, wrote of a God whom he believed completely transcends the human boundaries of time and space. For him it was the same God who spoke through Greek philosophers as through his Jewish faith, and the different religions were diverse manifestations of the one divine 'Logos' – the word.[69] The twelfth-century thinker, Moses Maimonides, who in general had a reputation for an openness to cross-cultural enquiry, took an entirely contrary view, condemning Christians, but not Muslims, for being polytheists and idolaters.[70] He believed that Judaism alone was revealed by God and that Jesus and Muhammad were false prophets, their only merit being that they helped to pave the way for the spread of Judaism and the coming of the messiah. By the eighteenth century the influences of the Enlightenment can be seen in the writings of Moses Mendelssohn. For him the truth of religion is immanent in human reason and is available to all. Diversity he believed to be part of God's overall plan. 'Providence', he writes, 'made wise men arise in every nation and bestowed upon them the gift to look with a clear eye into themselves as well as around themselves, to contemplate God's works and to communicate their insights to others.'[71]

Centuries of institutionalized anti-Semitism has helped to reinforce a sense of Jewish exclusivism, which in the twentieth century gave birth to messianic-style movements like Gush Emunim that seek to establish a Torah-governed state and to enforce separatism between Jews and non-Jews even by the use of coercion and violence.[72] The extreme separatists are very much a minority voice within modern-day Judaism. In addressing increasing concerns over globalization the Chief Rabbi of the United Hebrew Congregations, Jonathan Sacks, asks: 'Can we make space for differences?'[73] 'Can I as a Jew hear echoes of God's voice in that of a Hindu or Sikh or Christian or Muslim or in the words of an Eskimo from Greenland speaking about a melting glacier? Can I do so and feel not diminished but enlarged?'[74] Sacks, who describes himself as orthodox and not liberal in matters of faith, declares his belief in the sanctity of human life and the inalienable freedoms of a just society as religious absolutes. 'They flow directly from the proposition', he argues, 'that it was not we who created God in our image but God who made us in his.'[75]

The challenge he sees facing what he calls the 'religions of revelation' – Judaism, Christianity and Islam – is to return to the sources of their faith and to listen afresh, to find 'in that word, as it speaks to us now, a narrative of hope' that will enable them to deal with extremism within their own faith. Sacks also challenges the received paradigm that looks upon 'particularities' as the source of error, parochialism and prejudice, and upon 'truth' as abstract, timeless, universal, 'the same everywhere for everyone'. He sees this way of thinking, what he describes as the 'ghost of Plato', to be a prime cause of conflict. If all truth, he argues, is the same for everyone at all times, then, if I am right, I must convert you to my point of view. 'Universalism', he concludes, 'must be balanced with a new respect for the local, the particular, the unique.' The moral universals he recognizes are those of the 'covenant of Noah', which as a basis for human rights, he maintains, 'create space for cultural and religious difference, the sanctity of human life, the dignity of the human person, and the freedom we need to be true to ourselves while being a blessing to others'.[76] The glory of the created world is for Sacks its 'astonishing multiplicity'. The challenge facing everyone, he believes, is to discover in the variety of languages, faiths and cultures 'the voice of God telling us something we need to know'. That, he says, is what he means by the 'dignity of difference'.[77]

The Qur'an describes Muslims as 'the best community ever brought forth by God for the benefit of humanity'. This self-image, combined with the belief that the message of the Qur'an is God's complete and final revelation to humankind, inspired the Muslim poet and philosopher Muhammad Iqbal, the advocate of Pakistani independence, to see the Muslim community as a 'model for the final unification of mankind'.[78] He believed that the Qur'an contains foundational principles essential for a coherent system of life, giving perfect harmony, balance and stability to society while at the same time providing the individual with freedom of choice and opportunity for personal development. Iqbal's dream was that an independent Pakistan would become a living embodiment of these Qur'anic principles, a shining example of a message that had universal application and that the world greatly needed to hear.[79]

Muhammad Iqbal's conviction that Islam alone can bring a durable peace to the world is widely shared and in great part prescribes the relationship between Muslims and non-Muslims. Their early political and military triumphs convinced Muslims that 'Islam and political power go together'. 'Almighty God', writes Khalid Duran, 'came to be seen as rewarding the believers with supremacy over others.' This ingrained belief leads many Muslims to the conclusion that their loss of political supremacy is the result of a lack of commitment to faith, and that the remedy lies in stricter observance. A return to their former glory requires motivation and avoiding 'foreign' influences that can dilute the purity of the faith. Muslims, according to Duran, are burdened with a triumphalist past legacy 'that makes it difficult for them to integrate into a pluralist society where all are equal partners and no single community rules supreme'.[80] Many believe that Islam cannot be fully implemented if the government is not in the hands of Muslims and sharia law enforced.[81]

The key to understanding the Muslim psyche is, according to the Muslim scholar Khalid Duran, the migration of the Prophet Muhammad and his companions from Mecca where they had met with opposition to Medina where they set up the first Muslim polity. This migration, or *hijra* as it is called in Arabic, was entirely religiously motivated; they chose to be 'refugees in the path of God, not migrants for worldly gains'. It was the beginning of Islamic history, thus setting the example for all 'oppressed Muslims' to follow. It is every Muslim's religious obligation to seek a safe place to practise their faith without restriction. This belief, Duran claims, enforces separatism. A devout Muslim is expected to move from the *dar al-harb* – the abode of war, areas outside Muslim control – to *dar al-islam* – the abode of peace, areas where Muslims have control and can practise their faith freely.[82] It is the inability to fulfil this obligation, Duran believes, that has led many economic migrants to set up their own islands of *dar al-islam*, that is self-imposed, self-sufficient 'ghettos', in the midst of what they perceive to be hostile western environments.[83]

Whether it is true or not that these particular beliefs influence present-day Muslim attitudes to outsiders, Islam in thought and practice has a long record of tolerance. The Qur'an itself is unequivocal in its condemnation of forcible conversion: 'Let there be no compulsion in religion,'[84] it declares, and again 'if the Lord had pleased, all who are in the world would have believed together. Will you then compel men to become believers? No soul can believe without the permission of God.'[85] It singles out Jews and Christians for special treatment as they believe in the same God as Muslims, and the relationship with these faith communities should, therefore, be friendly: 'God is your Lord and our Lord; we have our works and you have your works; between us and you let there be no strife: God will make us all one.'[86] It also prescribes that those of other faiths seeking to know more about 'the word of God' should be given that opportunity and granted asylum. The prophet Muhammad observed these injunctions in his own dealings with peoples of other faiths. He wrote to the bishops, priests and monks of Najran promising them the protection of God and his apostle for their churches, religious services and monastic institutions. He guaranteed them their rights and freedom from interference as long as they were faithful to their obligations. Muhammad also allowed the Jews of Medina to practise undisturbed. It was only when they became openly hostile to his leadership that they were expelled.[87]

As the Muslim empire expanded efforts were made to find accommodation with the diversity of faiths and practices they encountered. Although the Qur'an condemns idolatry there is evidence that idol, fire and stone worshippers were tolerated if they were willing to pay a special tax. T.W. Arnold records the account of a ninth-century Muslim general who ordered an *imam* and a *mu'adhdhin* to be flogged for destroying a fire-temple in Sughd and building a mosque in its place.[88] Hindus were also protected provided that they too paid the tax which guaranteed non-Muslims immunity for life, property and religion. In practice it appears that each protected community was allowed to manage its own affairs. Christian sects like the Nestorians, it would seem, enjoyed greater toleration and freedom under Muslims than they had for centuries previously under Byzantine rule. A seventh-century Nestorian patriarch wrote: 'The Arabs to whom God at this time had given the empire of the world . . . attack not the Christian faith, but, on the contrary, they favour our religion, do honour to our priests and the saints of the Lord and confer benefits on churches and monastries.'[89] The Nestorians used their new opportunities under Muslim rule to expand its missionary activity to Persia, China, India and Egypt.

The tenth-century Saxon nun, Hroswitha, described the most celebrated example of Islamic colonizing as 'the brilliant ornament of the world'.[90] She was writing about the caliphate based in Cordoba, which had become renowned for its wealth, culture, learning and religious tolerance. Under this enlightened leadership, Muslims, Jews and Christians had moved beyond mere co-existence to engage in a new level of cross-culture interaction. Jews and Christians 'embraced nearly every aspect of Arabic style' from philosophy to architecture.[91] Synagogues and churches reflected the architectural style of Muslims and often had Arabic writing adorning their walls.[93] Christians and Jews had been assimilated into different levels of government acting as ambassadors and ministers as the Cordoba caliphate reached out diplomatically to their more hostile Christian neighbours. Its eventual downfall was not due so much to outside aggression as to a challenge from their North African Muslim neighbours, the Almoravids, who viewed the cultural openness of the 'Andalusian Muslims' as a threat to traditional Muslim identity.

Tolerance was not always, however, the hallmark of relationships between Muslim rulers and their non-Muslim subjects. The same fanatical streak that destroyed the milieu of tolerance and cross-cultural co-operation created in Andalusia was operative in the destruction of Hindu and Buddhist temples and the mistreatment of Jews and Christians at various times and in different places.[94] Periods of persecution under certain rulers were such that at times Jews and Christians felt forced to convert. But even in these darker moments it seems that the prescriptions guaranteeing that non-Muslims be treated 'kindly and sympathetically' were never fully lost sight of. This is well illustrated in a story, which it must be said some dispute, about the Jewish philosopher Moses Maimonides, who under the fanatical rule of the Almoravids is said to have feigned conversion and recanted when he fled to the safety of Egypt. Later on in his life, a Muslim jurist accused Maimonides of apostasy and demanded the death penalty. It is said that the case was dismissed by an eminent judge and Prime Minister of Saladin, who declared that a man forced to convert 'could not be rightly considered a Muslim'. A similar story is told of Buddhist monks who in the thirteenth century converted to Islam when their temples were destroyed but were later allowed to return to Tibet and to practise their own faith.[95]

Within Islam there have always been differences in interpretation and practice, and consequently many schools of theology and law. The Qur'an sees this diversity as positive: 'a manifestation of divine mercy'. These differences have, at times, erupted in violence, the prime example being the split between Sunnis and Shia Muslims that happened over the question of who was to be the lawful successor to the Prophet Muhammad. Sunni Muslims have almost always been the ruling faction and the Shia an oppressed minority. 'Shia historical memory', writes Islamic scholar John L. Esposito, 'emphasizes the suffering and oppression of the righteous, the need to protest against injustice, and the requirements that Muslims be willing to sacrifice everything, including their lives, in the struggle with the overwhelming forces of evil (Satan) in order to restore God's righteous rule.'[96] Disputes have risen also over whether or not it was lawful to depose leaders whose behaviour was judged to be sinful.

The eighteenth-century scholar Muhammad Ibn Abd al-Wahhab, who became disillusioned by the lack of commitment among his contemporaries, called for a rejection of past scholarship that determined misguided practices and a return to the strict principles of the Qur'an and the *Sunnah*. In partnership with a local Arabian tribal chief, Muhammad Ibn Saud, he formed 'a religious–political movement' to spearhead reform. Their world view was divided by what they saw as good and bad, belief and unbelief, Muslim and non-Muslim. Those who did not share their vision, Muslim or non-Muslim, were to be subdued, and killed if necessary, in the name of Islam.[97] In their quest for religious purity they destroyed many venerated sites, giving rise to further tensions and resentments within the Muslim family. This 'ultraconservative version of Wahhabi Islam' has been exported by the Saudis and was the mentality behind the recent destruction of the ancient Buddhist statues in Afghanistan.[98]

Despite the fact that the majority of scholars and clergy are products of a more conservative and inward-looking education, there are a small number of Muslim scholars who recognize the need for reform and to rethink Islam's role in the modern world. In chapter one I referred to the work of Abdullah Ahmed An-Na'im, the Sudanese scholar who sees no incompatibility between Islam and modern-day human rights claims. Nurcholish Madjid, the prominent Indonesian scholar, is another example of someone who seeks to promote a more inclusive form of Islam. He believes that religion should remain in the realm of the transcendent. World religions for him have more in common than not as 'we all come from the same fountain of wisdom, God'. The idea of an Islamic state, he believes, is contrary to the teachings of the Qur'an.[99]

Hinduism differs from the monotheistic traditions that have developed around a common scripture, creed and ritual. It resembles more 'a multitude of religions of the Indian sub-continent', which are based upon 'divergent scriptures' but hold sufficient beliefs in common to justify the use of a collective name.[100] Hindu attitudes towards outsiders and other faiths have been shaped by the belief that there is 'one divine reality that manifests itself in many forms'.[101] In theory this would mean that other religions can help their followers to attain release from *karma-samsara* – the endless cycle of rebirth by which one's social status next time around is determined by one's present behaviour – and to achieve *samadhi* – the ultimate state of true being and freedom.[102] In practice, however, the effectiveness of other faiths achieving this goal, according to Hindu beliefs, depends on how much the message of these non-Hindu revelations harmonizes with the Vedas – the revealed wisdom that was given to them alone. The value of the Qur'an and the Jewish and Christian Scriptures rests only in so far as it can be verified against Hindu revelation.[103]

It was only in the twentieth century that Hinduism began to develop a universal missionary sense. Prior to this one had to be of Indian ancestry to be accepted as Hindu.[104] The Hindu scholar, Sarvepalli Radhakrishnan, who was the Spalding Chair of Eastern Religions and Ethics at Oxford in the 1930s, was convinced that western society needed some wisdom from the 'East' to deal with the difficulties that it was encountering. Hinduism and the Vedas he believed to be the ultimate truth but their message had a universal appeal. The Hindu emphasis on 'individual experience' and understanding of religion as 'not so much a revelation to be attained by us in faith as an effort to unveil the deepest layers of man's being and get into enduring contact with them', were especially relevant for modern western society.

'Creeds and dogmas, words and symbols have only instrumental value', he wrote. 'The name by which we call God and the rite by which we approach Him do not matter much.'[105] To impose one's faith on others, Radhakrishnan maintained, is to rob religion of the 'richness of the diversity of the various paths to God'. Individuals need to have the freedom to choose the path that is best suited to their nature and cultural background. Religions and cultures can develop through dialogue with each other. Hinduism had recognized this in its long history and therefore could be the 'guru' and example for other religions, encouraging enquiry and devotion to truth that reaches beyond individual traditions. His vision of what religious life should be was that of 'cooperative enterprise binding together different traditions and perspectives to the end of obtaining clearer vision of the perfect reality'.[106]

The example and contribution of Mahatma Gandhi in promoting tolerance between different faith traditions and ethnic groups has been well documented. Less well known today, perhaps, is the thought of a nine-teenth-century illiterate Hindu mystic, Ramakrishna Paramahamsa and his western-educated disciple Vivekananda. In his search for truth Ramakrishna embraced the different forms of Hinduism as well as Islam and Christianity. His experiences taught him that all religions could be considered true as no matter what name God is given those who seek earnestly will come to what he calls a 'God realization'.[107] His faith journey also taught him that all religions have their limitations and imperfections. As I mentioned briefly in chapter three, his disciple, Vivekananda, brought this message to the Parliament of Religions in Chicago in 1893 where he was an outspoken advocate of pluralism in religion. Whilst remaining firmly committed to his Hindu beliefs and traditions he encouraged the need for unity and mutual enrichment in diversity.[108]

Vivekananda declared himself proud to belong to a religion whose sacred language, Sanskrit, had no translation for the word 'exclusion'. And yet, he was aware that in practice Hindus excluded from their social contacts not only those who belong to a different caste but also Muslims and other outsiders. The reason for this, Kana Mitra explains, is that from the Ramakrishna–Vivekananda perspective they lack a level of 'spiritual maturity' that is necessary to overcome the tendency to deny other ways as valid.[109] The rise to power of the PJP, the Hindu Nationalist Party, was seen by the more militant elements as an opportunity to rid the country of other religions and Christian missionaries in particular. For the untouchables Christianity can provide a quick escape from caste oppression.[110]

Buddhism has been described as 'the very absolute antithesis of all religion' as the foundation, on which the entire teachings of Buddha rest, excludes belief in a creator God, a devil and a human soul or concept of self.[111] With no revelation, dogmas, prayers, commandments, or sense of accountability to a superior being that controls the destiny of humanity, Buddha Dhamma, the teachings of the Buddha, offer a totally different 'alternative' understanding of life from the other faith traditions. Born of royal parentage Siddhartha Gotama, the Buddha to be, abandoned his family and luxurious lifestyle as he set off in search of more intelligible answers to the reasons for the inequalities, suffering and death that he witnessed in life. Determined to find the truth about life without the help of others, the Buddha's internal journey of reasoning led him to an understanding of human existence in terms of an interplay between three ultimate realities – matter, mental factors and consciousness – the human being is a combination of a mental phenomenon and a material phenomenon supported by consciousness 'with no self or soul behind'.[112] Through the use of reason and the power of his own intelligence Buddha discovered the natural laws that govern human existence. His teachings are an invitation to people to examine and to discover for themselves these 'noble truths' that are independent of time. The Buddha's discovery of these laws taught him that 'man is his own absolute and total master in the sense that no external being has control over him'.[113] He also learnt that even though human beings are free from the fear of being accountable to someone superior and they do have control over their own destiny, they are subject to influences of greed, hate and delusion. These are the 'roots of all the unwholesome mental factors that defile the mind'. They are the reason for the repeated cycles of birth and death. The practice of meditation, non-attachment and compassion lead to Nirvana, escape from the cycle, the ultimate goal of which is the realization of the non-existence of a self or soul.[114]

The idea that Buddha discovered truth through his own reasoning and not by revelation from a higher power means it is also possible for others to discover truth for themselves. The realization of this predisposes Buddhism to be open and tolerant to other ways of discovering the same causal laws of the universe.[115] Buddhism is 'a path of life' and does not make claim to be the only way to Truth. Belief in a creator God to whom humanity is accountable many would see as a delusion that can easily get in the way of true enlightenment. Internally, differences are tolerated on the under-standing that diversity can be a way of achieving the same goal.[116] The Buddha himself taught that not even his word should be taken without putting it to the test. Each individual is responsible for his or her own enlightenment.

Although Buddha did send out his disciples to make his teachings available to others, Buddhists do not perceive themselves to be missionary in the way in which Christians and Muslims do. They make their teaching available, leaving it to the individual to respond as he or she wishes: 'Religion is a matter of a committed heart which cannot be brought about by force.'[117] Mahayana Buddhism, however, has a strong commitment to promote good and to prevent problems in the world. They use a wider selection of scriptural texts than the teachings of the Buddha and believe that it is possible to achieve Nirvana while still in society. In theory Buddhists who follow faithfully the teachings should not have a sense of superiority over others but in reality this does not seem to be the case. Theravada Buddhists in particular are said to regard their religion as 'best'.[118] The Theravada school draws its scriptural inspiration from what is known as the Pali Canon that is said to contain the earliest surviving records of the Buddha's teachings. It is prominent in South-east Asia and Sri Lanka. Their sense of religious superiority does not overrule laws of politeness and compassion that for the most part remain a hallmark of their spiritual life. Tibetan Buddhism emphasizes the importance of humility in order 'to be able to serve other sentient beings'.

The risk in attempting to provide synopses of the thought and practice of the diverse religious traditions on tolerance and attitudes to pluralism is the lack of nuance, the result being that I may appear to be oversimplifying the complexity and contradictions that so often exist at the core of religious teachings. None the less, these sketches enable us to identify important resemblances in belief that exist between the mainstream world religions despite an obvious diversity of thought and practice. In each faith tradition we see an affirmation of life that extends beyond the physical boundaries of their own communities. We recognize also an inherent respect for individual choices and the acknowledgement that there should be no coercion in matters of religion, a precept based on the belief that faith rests essentially in the freedom of the individual to say yes or no to what is proposed as truth. In each tradition, crossing boundaries of culture and ethnicity, there is clearly a seminal presence of the right of the individual both to seek truth and to dissent – principles that lie at the very heart of the Universal Declaration of Human Rights. In the application of these beliefs, however, competing claims on the exclusivity or superiority of one interpretation of truth over the other have frequently led to abandonment or outright violation of these principles. The important point to note is that the right to think and to act differently in the quest for truth was not, as is sometimes suggested, achieved as the result of the intervention of a group of seventeenth- and eighteenth-century European philosophers. It is also implicit in the teachings of world faiths that represent a diversity of cultures, East and West. Locke, Bayle, Voltaire and others undoubtedly contributed to the development of these concepts and perhaps even more importantly helped to lift them out of a 'sectarian milieu' that had failed to practise what it preached.

Modernity may have challenged and in many places even threatened the very existence of a sectarian milieu but a sectarian mindset remains pervasive even at the highest level of religious leadership. Commenting on the meeting of more than 2,000 religious leaders that was held in the United Nations building in New York in August 2000, Jonathan Sacks found it easy to understand 'why religion is as often a cause of conflict as it is of conciliation'. He criticized his fellow participants for their failure to rise above 'the narrow loyalties of faith'. The peace spoken of was too often 'peace on our terms'. The general message, he writes, was: 'Our faith speaks of peace; our holy texts praise peace; therefore, if only the world shared our faith and our texts there would be peace.'[119] John Stuart Mill's arguments that diversity should be nurtured and not merely endured on the ground of it leading to truth and human progress[120] appear to have been overshadowed by the climate of theological particularism – the belief that one group has exclusive possession of truth, knowledge and goodness that are universally applicable – that still shapes the outlook of many of today's religious leaders.

The word 'tolerance' for many today defines a positive attitude towards diversity, calling for respect and acceptance of people who think and act differently from oneself. The Latin roots of the word meaning 'to endure or to put up with the objectionable' indicate that tolerance as it was originally defined had more negative overtones. Far from embracing diversity and pluralism Aquinas and others saw it as the lesser of two evils: the willingness to permit or to concede the practice of a religion judged to be false as to act otherwise could possibly involve a greater evil.[121] Even Locke endorsed 'toleration' only because he considered the 'consequences of intolerance are a greater evil than the evil that is tolerated'.[122] The original concept of tolerance prevails today and especially in religious circles. The 2003 edition of the *New Catholic Encyclopaedia* distinguishes between 'personal' tolerance – 'permitting others to hold and to put into practice views that diverge from one's own' – which it endorses, and 'doctrinal' tolerance – 'permitting error to spread unopposed' – which it judges to be 'reprehensible'.[123]

The caution, particularly in Christian circles, towards diversity and pluralism is driven not only by the climate of theological particularism that Christians share in common with others and to which I refer above, but also by a fear of relativism, the belief that every religion in some way uncovers a different aspect of the truth, and is, therefore, necessary if truth is to be discovered in its fullness. The modern-day philosophical definition of a 'tolerant' person as someone who affirms the truth of his or her own views but refrains from making a value judgement on the truth claims of others, thus leaving open the possibility that they too may be right,[124] would find little resonance in most of today's religious circles. In his study of American community life, Robert Putnam discovered that the more religious a community is, the less tolerant it is also likely to be. Communities that are closely knit around creed, code and cult, he found, tend to shun those who do not fit in. New denominations, he claimed, were less engaged in the wider community, focusing their own community-building efforts inward rather than outward. Education is the key factor, according to Putnam, in answer to the question, can religion play a part in building up a civic community, combining social capital with tolerance, in other words creating 'a Salem without witches'?[125]

The traditional concept of tolerance, even with its negative connotations, that allows for would-be warring communities to co-exist side by side without violence should not be undervalued. The achievement of 'mere co-existence', as it is sometimes disparagingly referred to, is no mean achievement, especially in communities that have been marred by inter-ethnic or inter-religious strife. The real threat to human existence, presented by the face of intolerance today, underscores the urgent need for religious communities in particular to re-evaluate their own attitudes towards diversity and pluralism. The French Catholic existentialist philosopher, Gabriel Marcel, believed that far from embattling people with negative attitudes towards others, a genuine religious experience or conviction mandates a person to be proactive in defending the right of others to believe differently. He maintained that the 'intense conviction' a religious person experiences and which is so much part of who he or she is, should enable that person to empathize with another's convictions that are different but equally intense. This ability to identify or empathize should enable believers to move beyond that state of passive acceptance that is usually referred to as tolerance.[126]

To uphold and to defend actively the right of others to make truth claims, different from our own, and to act upon them, provided that these are not detrimental to the rights and well-being of others, would be an important first step that takes people beyond 'the sectarian milieu' in which their own convictions have been formed. Robert Putnam judged education to be the key to counterbalance the drift towards intolerance that he found in American communities that were more religious in their make-up. I would agree that education could help to dispel the myths that allow others to be looked upon as outcasts or 'demons', but it is equally true that indoctrination in a form of religious dogmatism based on absolute claims can reinforce separatism and an intolerance of what is judged to be false. Respect for others and their conscientious beliefs and opinions is the framework for dialogue that allows for an honest exchange of conflicting ideas. High on the agenda of such exchanges should be a willingness to test truth claims that authorize a sense of exclusiveness or superiority over others.

Equally high on that agenda should be the willingness to consider the reordering of that hierarchy or canon of beliefs that determines the faith and practice of each tradition. The affirmation of human life as a sacred experience or gift should take priority over what name we give to God or how we define our understanding of the divine. For the first time in our history human beings have it within their power to extinguish the whole of life, and in the process to cause grotesque disfigurement to the face of the globe. This awesome fact places a special responsibility upon those religious traditions that regard the whole of creation as a sacred gift that needs to be cherished and that believe that humans will be held accountable for their stewardship of the earth. The present is undoubtedly a defining moment in human history that calls for an exceptional and imaginative response from the world faiths. Whether the world's religions will be capable of responding to that challenge depends on the quality of religious leadership within the diverse traditions.

The past decade has seen the publication of numerous books that offer guidance to business leaders and other authority figures on how to respond more effectively to the changes and challenges that can threaten the whole future of their organizations and enterprises. A helpful insight that I consider to be particularly relevant to the challenges facing religious leaders is the distinctions that some of the literature makes between authority and leadership and 'adaptive' and 'technical' challenges.[127] Leadership and authority, Don Laurie maintains, perform two different functions within an organization. People are given positions and the authority that goes with them to enable them to perform a particular function. In the normal run of affairs this arrangement works and those in positions of authority are able to address and solve problems that arise. This is what people expect of them. Where leadership and authority must part company, he argues, is when there are no quick-fix solutions to the problems because the answers require a re-evaluation of the overall strategies or values of the organization. 'The real work of the leader', Laurie concludes, 'is not to provide pat solutions but to mobilize the group to work on the problem.'[128]

Ron Heifetz and Marty Linsky from the Center for Public Leadership at

Harvard's Kennedy School of Government claim that in their experience 'the single most common source of leadership failure' in politics, community life and business 'is that people, especially those in positions of authority, treat adaptive challenges like technical problems.' For them technical problems are those that can be solved by the 'know-how and procedures' already to hand. They define problems that are not amenable to such solutions and that cannot be solved by 'someone who provides answers from on high' as 'adaptive challenges'. These require adjustment at every level within an organization or community.[129] When facing these challenges, they claim, leaders do not need to know all the answers but they do need to ask the right questions. The problem, they identify, is that in times of distress people don't want questions: they want answers, and in particular they want to be told that they will be protected 'from the pains of change'.[130] Leaders who respond to these expectations inevitably fail.

To mobilize and inspire people to take greater responsibility for their destiny, to be part of the solution when confronted with systemic problems, they discovered, has to begin with a willingness to address people's unrealistic expectations and their 'exaggerated dependency' on authority to solve problems. The risk of instability, conflict and resentment cannot be avoided, they argue, as the adaptive work necessary may involve 'upending deep and entrenched' norms, values and beliefs that can be so much part of people's identity. People can feel that their personal, family and tribal loyalties are being challenged as they are asked to abandon what has been handed down from parents and grandparents.[131] The leadership demands in addressing adaptive challenges also require a willingness to promote people's 'resourcefulness', and to recognize the possibility of leadership being exercised from multiple positions within an organization or community. When faced with adaptive challenges everyone should have the opportunity to exercise leadership whatever his or her role.[132] The 'balcony perspective' is also essential. This involves leaders removing themselves at least momentarily from the fray in order to gain both a clearer view of reality and overall vision of what is happening in the bigger picture.[133] Adaptive challenges often mean 'going beyond the boundaries of your constituency and creating common ground with other factions, divisions and stakeholders'. Leaders who are prepared to do this can appear as 'a traitor' to their own who expect them to champion their cause and not to challenge their perspectives.[134]

To act in accordance with these insights would require a major paradigm shift for many leaders who are more accustomed to the old authoritarian style of leadership that is expected to provide answers to the problems presented by subordinates. This is especially true in religious circles, and in particular in the Catholic Church. The Second Vatican Council offered two equally valid, but competing models or images of what the Church should be. One is a hierarchical structure governed by the pope and his appointees, the bishops. The other is a pilgrim people, a community in which each member has equal standing as they gather around the eucharistic table.[135] The first model provides a style of leadership that is accustomed to acting as if all the problems encountered are of a 'technical' nature and therefore within the competence of those appointed to positions of leadership to deal with in accordance with the established procedures as outlined in the Church's own legal system. The second model is more suited to dealing with 'adaptive challenges' as it implicitly recognizes the distinction between leadership and authority and acknowledges and endorses the concept of multiple sources of leadership within a community.

In the immediate aftermath of the Council there was a creative tension between these competing models. People were encouraged to participate actively in the 'adaptive work' that was required as the Church attempted to change the cultural and legal structures of previous centuries that were hindering it from communicating more effectively with contemporary society. The uncertainty created, though, by the simple acknowledgement that the Church hierarchy did not have all the answers to the moral, ethical and spiritual problems that people were encountering, and the essential questioning of traditional norms and values that the quest for answers required, were perceived by some as a threat to the very existence of the Church. The papacy of John Paul II responded to this perceived crisis by trying to re-impose its authority through Vatican efforts to micromanage the life of the local churches. The Pope replaced bishops who had spear-headed the kind of reforms that required 'adaptive work' with men who felt more comfortable operating within an exclusively hierarchical model of leadership and authority. The shift in favour of a more centralized system of church governance concurred with a rebirth of clericalism.

The term 'clericalism' first came to be used in the nineteenth century in France and Italy to describe those who defended the power of the Church and especially the pope's claims as a temporal sovereign. The original goal of clericalism to make civil authorities subservient to the clergy,[136] failed but the mindset remained. Today clericalism aims to protect the personal authority of the individual priest or bishop by focusing on outward appearances and micromanaging the affairs of the parish community or diocese. Dress, title and privilege are each important as these are seen to be symbols of authority. Public image matters greatly as it enhances the authority of the Church, its hierarchy and the individual cleric. Excessive concern over public image creates the culture of denial that was exposed in the recent scandal over the manner in which church authorities failed to deal with the problem of child sex abuse by members of the clergy. Clericalism deals with adaptive challenges as if they were technical problems. It functions in a manner that favours high boundaries between communities as the most effective way of maintaining its own influence and control. It perceives leadership that is exercised without authorization as a threat that has to be marginalized.

Clericalism is not exclusive to the Catholic Church. Thirty years of active involvement in ecumenical and inter-faith dialogue have taught me to recognize the signs of a similar mindset within other faith communities. Although Islam does not have an ordained clergy or a hierarchical structure like Christianity, and in theory at least any Muslim can lead prayers or preside over weddings and funerals, the men who perform these functions have developed over the years their own distinctive dress code and clergy-like authority over their communities. Many of the scholars that form the *ulama,* or 'the learned' group, who are responsible for the interpretation of the Qur'an and Islamic law, can be distinguished by their dress and titles.[137] In Sri Lanka I learnt that the Buddhist monks, with their distinctive dress and titles, have considerable moral authority within their communities. The moral authority of rabbis also can be equally pervasive within the synagogue community.

Clericalism is not the only mentality that can hinder a commitment to the adaptive work that is necessary to ensure greater understanding and co-operation among the diverse religious traditions. I recall a conversation I had with a Reformed Church bishop in Budapest a week after Karol Wojtyla, the Archbishop of Cracow, had been elected pope in October 1978. The Catholic world was euphoric at the unpredicted choice of a bishop from the communist world. The Hungarian bishop did not share the prevailing mood of optimism. His reason was that he feared that no one who had functioned as a bishop under the communist regimes of the Eastern Bloc would have the objectivity to provide the leadership needed to deal with the contemporary challenges facing the Church globally. He explained that, in a situation where the Church was under constant threat from the regime, success was judged by one's ability to preserve and to hand on the structures that you had inherited. In practice this required establishing a strong identity and high boundaries. It did not allow you to address problems in a more open and creative way. In western societies the threat of increasing secularization, the 'surfing' from congregation to congregation and the 'believing but not belonging' phenomena observed by Robert Putnam[138] have given rise to a growth in religious communities that assert their truth claims with more vigour and define their boundaries with higher fences.

In every age, and within each religious tradition, there are outstanding examples of individuals who have managed by thought and example to cross the cultural and religious boundaries, and by so doing have given witness to the essential transcendent nature of religion. To paraphrase the words of a nineteenth-century Russian Orthodox hierarch, the differences between faiths do not reach up to heaven. The example of the thirteenth-century Sultan of Egypt, al-Kamil, is a good illustration. His reputation as a 'just, civilised, man of peace' was confirmed clearly when he chose to enter into a dialogue on faith with Francis of Assisi at a time when the crusading Christians were besieging his territories. The Sultan's religious advisors saw Francis as a threat to their beliefs that should be eliminated, al-Kamil recognized in the person and commitment of this humble, unpretentious friar an essential goodness that should be engaged and protected.[139] He demonstrated a style of leadership capable of recognizing and responding to the 'adaptive challenges' of his time. Sister Eustochia Nata, a sixty-year-old Indonesian Catholic nun on the island of Flores is a good contemporary example of someone who has the depth of faith and awareness to make a similar kind of 'adaptive leap' that is necessary to prevent the inter-religious communal strife that is claiming thousands of lives on other islands in the region. Faced with the dangers of intolerance leading to violence against Muslims on this predominantly Christian island, Sister Eustochia took matters into her own hands and formed 'Truk 4', an inter-faith human rights group that enables young people to work together on some of the social issues that beset the island.[140] She is a good example of someone who recognized the need to take a leadership role despite the fact that she had no particular authority within either community to do so.

The crisis of terrorist violence the world faces today has its roots in the inequality of our global structures and the intolerance inherent in the competing truth claims of the different religious traditions. Whether or not we are successful in dealing with this crisis will depend not only on the abilities of our contemporary political and religious leadership but also the willingness of individuals to exercise a quality of leadership that transcends cultural and religious boundaries. The problem of inequality and poverty is partly a 'technical problem' and partly an 'adaptive challenge'. The world has both the 'know-how' and the resources to respond to the technical problem. On several occasions in the past decade we have seen how the western powers have been able to mobilize the resources and personnel to fight war when western interests appeared threatened. It remains to be seen, despite the declarations of good intent, whether or not the same leaders have the political will to address the fight against poverty and to effect the adaptive changes that will be necessary to implement a more just world order, and especially fairer trade practices between the rich and poorer nations.

The challenges facing religious leaders are also 'technical' and 'adaptive' in nature, and call for both political will and personal courage on their part if they are to take their respective communities beyond tolerance and enable them to discover the goodness in 'the other'. The 'technical' task is to provide opportunity for communities to be fully educated in their faith traditions and in particular to open up dialogue on the interpretation of texts. By focusing on those parts of their traditions that at least implicitly acknowledge the right of others to believe and to act differently, they will be challenging the fears and prejudices that have driven relationships between the diverse traditions for several centuries. This is part of the 'adaptive challenge', which to be handled effectively requires the willingness to deal with inevitable resentment and protest from within their constituencies, as people fear that their established identities are being threatened by what is being asked of them. It will also require a willingness to encourage and protect the voices of leadership that will emerge from within their communities as these new challenges are being addressed. The temptation to neutralize within the community the challenges of 'creative deviants' like, for example, Francis of Assisi in the interests of maintaining internal unity and balance should be resisted for as Heifetz and Laurie point out, 'buried inside a poorly packaged interjection may lie an important intuition that needs to be teased out and considered'.[141] Implicit in the teachings of all the religions that I have referred to in this chapter is the belief that when others are prevented from bearing witness as they see it there is a real danger of closing one's ears to an authentic though unusual source of revelation or truth.[142]

6

The Struggle for the Global Soul

The post 9/11 American-led war on terrorism appears to be driven by the belief that this is a temporary phenomenon that can be defeated by the combination of fire power and know-how. First in Afghanistan, and then in Iraq, we have witnessed a massive display of force used against regimes accused of supporting terrorism. This has been followed by efforts to establish in each country a western-style democracy. It is obvious from this response that some of the western leaders look upon the crisis facing the world today as if it were a 'technical problem' that can be dealt with in the old authoritarian style of providing answers from 'the top down'. However, a terrorism that is religiously inspired can be curtailed but cannot be defeated in this way. The military response and impositions of solutions may provide temporary comfort for those who feel threatened but these actions are equally likely to evoke a combination of religious zeal and anger that will only guarantee the enlistment of a whole new generation of faith-based terrorists, ready and willing to wage a life and death struggle for the global soul. This reaction is not confined solely to the Muslim world. It was while serving as a sharpshooter during the first Gulf War that America's homegrown religiously motivated terrorist, Timothy McVeigh, developed a taste for terror.[1]

A terrorism that is fired by deep religious convictions presents a more fundamental challenge that requires a more nuanced and multilevel response than bombs and ballot boxes. To deal with the real threat that this style of terrorism presents to the whole of civilization the global political authorities first need to recognize the true nature of the problem. Political repression, social injustice, unemployment and poverty create fertile feeding grounds for terrorists, but such conditions in themselves are not the prime reason why people feel compelled to kill in the name of their God.

The political and social milieu may act as a trigger but the roots of the religious intolerance and militancy are embedded in the history and sacred texts of each of the world faiths. Today's extremists can find in their own traditions sufficient texts and in their own religious history sufficient exemplars to justify their adoption of a world view that allows them to annihilate those who think or act differently. Those who have grown to accept uncritically the secularization thesis that has shaped western political thinking for the best part of the last century find it extremely difficult to understand that belief and theology can, and indeed do, form people's political judgements and actions. Their impoverished notion of religion that has allowed them to dismiss it as an epiphenomenon or to reduce it to mere doctrine and ritual has ill equipped them to provide an accurate analysis of the present crisis. To see religion as no more than a passive agent waiting to be ignited into a political flame by some unscrupulous political or tribal chauvinist is seriously to underestimate the destructive potential that lies in texts and traditions susceptible to contradictory interpretations. I fear that the reductionist mindset is so pervasive in western political thinking today that leaders of various backgrounds are now determining the response to religious terrorism as if it were merely a technical problem.

Addressing grievances, heightened security, good intelligence, detection, and the closure of funds and arms supplies are all necessary measures in the fight against terrorism whatever its motivation. These measures are in themselves, however, insufficient to eliminate the contemporary threat of faith-based terrorism and the continuing phenomenon of religious violence. These problems cannot be solved in a solely coercive way. Success, however that may be measured, will require a change of mindset among political and religious leaders. They first need to acknowledge that religion can, and does, play a role in causing and sustaining violent conflict. This requires an 'adaptive leap' in thinking and action as it can call into question basic beliefs and assumptions. It also requires political and religious authorities to recognize and encourage leadership at different levels within both these communities.

The international political community's record of conflict prevention and resolution is far from impressive. Its initiatives are frequently too late to prevent or to stop violence, and its focus is almost entirely on the political elites. The results are rarely viable and durable solutions as we can see from the current collapse in the peace processes in Northern Ireland and Israel/Palestine, and possibly Sri Lanka. Sustainable peace has to be rooted in a willingness at a local level to find ways to co-exist in a manner that will allow trust to develop over time between the warring parties. The failure to understand and therefore to address the aspirations, prejudices and fears of either party, no matter how misguided these may appear to be, is to put them beyond diplomacy, and by so doing to sow the seeds of potential conflict further down the line. Peace cannot be fabricated in 'a bubble' created to fit the agendas of the international fixers. A peace process that fails to take time to engage local communities and to build bridges both within and between them, religious and secular, is unlikely to survive the tensions festering below the surface in either community.

In Northern Ireland I learnt that the republicans had a clear strategy of keeping their constituency, the Catholic nationalist community, fully informed at each stage of the process, and consequently most Catholics found the final agreement acceptable. There was no such strategy among unionists I was told, the result being that most Protestants today are either uneasy or openly hostile to the Good Friday Agreement. In Sri Lanka I detected a similar problem. I met with Sinhalese and Tamils who were resentful of the fact that they were feeling excluded from the process of negotiation that has already begun at the top leadership level. The total collapse of the peace process in Israel/Palestine is hardly surprising, as I met no one at a community level on either side who felt in any way a part of the Oslo and Camp David meetings.

There is a clear and urgent need to strengthen the local peace-building capacity at a street level in parallel with the initiation of political talks at the top leadership level. From my thirty years of experience in the field of conflict resolution, I am convinced that this is the only way of guaranteeing a durable solution at the end of a peace process. Religious communities ought to be directly engaged, especially since religion is itself such a salient factor in the conflict. As Scott Appleby rightly observed, 'while the religious extremist is often integrated into a well-organized movement, armed to the teeth, expertly trained, lavishly financed, ideologically disciplined, and involved in a kind of "ecumenical" collaboration with other violence-prone organisations, the non-violent religious actor is relatively isolated, under-financed, unskilled in the techniques of conflict transformation.'[2] The United Nations and the European Union ought to play an important role by helping to develop the peace-building capacity of local communities by funding and organizing programmes aimed at helping to develop, especially in potential conflict areas, the leadership skills of those community activists that are willing to engage in cross-cultural and inter-religious dialogue.

Little, if indeed anything, is achieved by organizing meetings of top religious leaders like the World Peace Summit of Religious and Spiritual Leaders that took place at the United Nations in August 2000. The same I fear is true when such meetings happen at a national level. Throughout the thirty years of the Northern Ireland conflict the senior Catholic and

Protestant bishops and Free Church moderators met regularly but their meetings and statements failed to have any impact on their co-religionists who continued in their pursuit of a violent solution. The same is true I understand in Sri Lanka. Dr Theivandran, a distinguished medical doctor in Jaffna, told me that he compared such meetings of the religious hierarchy in his country to a ten-storey building where on the top floor leaders were discussing peace while the ground floor was on fire. When I suggested to a top United Nations official in New York that the organization should be more proactive in promoting dialogue and cross-cultural and religious training courses for leaders at the street level in conflict areas, his immediate reaction was that the UN could not support programmes that appear to have religious links. It would seem in this respect at least that the UN is trapped in the time warp of the late 1940s when Eleanor Roosevelt and her team felt it necessary to bracket any mention of God to guarantee the safe passage of the Universal Declaration on Human Rights. The world, however, has drastically changed since then. Religion has witnessed a rebirth in Russia and many of the other countries that once had outlawed or barely tolerated its existence. The United Nations cannot afford to remain within a secularist-reductionist mindset, failing to comprehend the potency of religion, if the organization is to be capable of developing a relevant and credible response to the ongoing phenomenon of religiously motivated communal strife and faith-based terrorism. The same applies to the European Union and to national governments like Norway, Britain and the United States and to the many NGOs that pursue their own independent efforts at conflict resolution and peacemaking. Peace agendas that exclude the relevancy of the religious factor or focus solely on the top religious leadership and political elites are likely to lack the broader and deeper foundations upon which a durable peace can be constructed. Voltaire believed that differences between religions constituted the single most important cause for strife in the world, but many of his heirs, today's political and social scientists, who help shape contemporary political thinking still seem to suffer from a myopia with regard to religion. The urgent need to build up at the street level credible cross-culture, cross-religious infrastructures that provide training in leadership and negotiation skills that can help communities to deal with their conflicting interests without resorting to violence is still to be recognized at the official level.

Religious leaders also need to be more proactive in addressing the sources of the violence that emanates from within their own communities. They can no longer disown their co-religionist extremists by simply dismissing their actions as being unreflective of the real values of their faith tradition. Deviations in belief and practice are not without roots, and the extremists, as I set out to demonstrate in this book, can seek justification for the atrocities that they pursue in the name of their God by appealing to ambivalence towards violence that is found in each of the different faith traditions. Hindus, Buddhists, Jews, Muslims and Protestants do not have a central doctrinal authority like that of the Catholic Church, and therefore it is more difficult for these traditions to speak with one voice. None the less, in each tradition there is a hierarchical pecking order, a fact that is clearly demonstrated at inter-faith gatherings. With a clear, unambiguous declaration of the true values of their traditions, the leaders of these hierarchical, clerical structures need urgently to develop a sense of co-responsibility for the actions of their own co-religionists, and to challenge their communities that are caught up in communal strife or global terrorism. Assent to a belief in the sacredness of life and the right to religious diversity, two fundamental beliefs to which the faith traditions examined in this book adhere, at least in principle, needs to top the faith agenda in this age of conflict, especially if religion is to cease to be a source of the problem and become part of the solution. Religious leaders need to encourage their adherents to rediscover their true origins, especially the fact that none of their traditions developed in complete isolation; indeed, there always has been a direct link or interplay between or among the various religious traditions. This realization might help to curb the feelings of superiority or absolutism that have marred relationships between believers over the centuries, but ignorance, however benign, cannot be allowed to go unchallenged in an age that is capable of inflicting destruction on a catastrophic scale.

To be a part of the solution to the contemporary global problem of indiscriminate violence for which religion is at least partly responsible, religious leaders need to embark upon 'an adaptive leap' that will require them to re-examine some of their own fundamental beliefs and loyalties. The realization that no single tradition is capable of comprehending the truth alone – in all its fullness – can be both painful to an adherent and threatening, especially if he/she has to communicate that awareness to others. And yet this is precisely the nature of the challenge that religion is facing today. The 'exclusivists' within each tradition who insist that 'there is only one way of understanding reality and interpreting the sacred' need to be enlightened, encouraged and supported along the path to becoming 'pluralists', disciples totally committed to their tradition but who recognize that 'a diversity of communities and traditions is not an obstacle to be overcome but an opportunity for energetic engagement and dialogue.'[3] Accusations of relativism or indifferentism should not deter religious leaders, at whatever level they are operating within their traditions, from responding to a crisis that could threaten the very survival of humanity. This is not an academic exercise. It is a mission that needs to be undertaken with a sense of urgency and responsibility that reaches beyond the boundaries of their own faith enclaves.

Pluralism is a threat to those whose faith has never matured beyond the cultural or cultic levels. Cultural religion thrives behind high fences as it depends upon the words of the creed, the actions of the cult, the letter of the code, and the sense of belonging to community to shape the identity of its adherents. None of these aspects of religion should be seen as an end in themselves. The prime purpose of religious dogmas, worship, laws and community is to enable people to discover the transcendent nearness – the divine presence – in the midst of human experience. They are props, as it were, meant to point the way to or sharpen our awareness of the transcendent in our lives. Only when people reach the mystical level of belief are they able to deal with the plurality of life without feeling threatened. In *Cultures in Conflict in an Age of Discovery*, Bernard Lewis is right, I believe, when he claims that the Jews were expelled from the reconquered parts of Spain before Muslims because, even though they did not have an army or political influence they were a greater threat to Christian identity and the unity of the kingdom because Jews believed that adherents of other faiths could find their own path to God. The non-missionary, pluralistic world view of fifteenth-century Judaism appears to have been more threatening than the competing claims to exclusive truth posed by Islam.

Some days after 9/11 when it became clear that the perpetrators were acting out of religious conviction, the British Prime Minister Tony Blair declared that the attacks were 'no more a reflection of true Islam than the Crusades were of true Christianity'.[4] The truth, as unpalatable as it may seem, is that both the Crusaders and the 9/11 hijackers sought religious justification for their violence in the foundational texts of their faith. The selective use of scripture or holy texts has provided, and continues to provide, religious militants with the moral authority to act outside acceptable human norms of behaviour. Texts, as we have seen, can be used either to promote pluralism and a respect for differences, or to endorse claims of exclusivity and spiritual superiority. In every tradition there are those who vehemently oppose anything other than a strictly literalist interpretation of the text. John Wansbrough's attempt to promote an informed debate on the origins and meaning of the Qur'an met with predictable outrage. His book *Quranic Studies: Sources and Methods of Scriptural Interpretation* was interpreted by one Muslim critic as a conspiracy to promote the global domination of the West. To question 'the historical authenticity or doctrinal autonomy of the Qur'anic revelation' is for a Muslim, the critic argued, to 'abdicate his universal mission'.[5] It took Catholicism the best part of nineteen hundred years to appreciate that even the literal sense of texts in both the Hebrew and Christian Scriptures is not always obvious. Prior to 1943, as mentioned earlier in this book, the hierarchical teaching authority, anxious to defend its understanding of the Bible as the verbatim word of God, staunchly condemned anything other than a literalist interpretation of the text regardless of its obvious cosmographical and historical errors. Those who questioned this normative approach were severely censured. Regardless of these predictable reactions it is essential to initiate an informed and open dialogue on the nature of revelation and the interpretation of texts both within and between the different religious traditions. Textual scholars need to be given the freedom to pursue their academic studies without fear of censure. An understanding of the historical context and the social and cultural milieus in which these foundational texts were first written is crucial to safeguard against the misinterpretation or the deliberate misuse of ambiguous verses.

In launching his call for a 'Dialogue among Civilizations' the President of the Islamic Republic of Iran, Seyed Mohammad Khatami, declared: 'Leaders, scholars and thinkers in our world today play a key role in nurturing the common human yearning for truth, understanding and compassion, and in freeing us all from historically conditioned prejudice.'[6] Key to any meaningful dialogue is the need for all the participants to re-examine the stereotypes they have of each other. Despite post 9/11 efforts to promote a better understanding of Islam in Europe and the United States, the views of the conservative Protestant televangelist, Pat Robinson, who described Islam as a violent religion that wants to 'dominate and then, if need be, destroy'[7] are not uncommon. Political leaders like Margaret Thatcher and Silvio Berlusconi have also contributed to the reinforcement of negative and monolithic images of Islam by claiming it to be the greatest threat to western security since the fall of communism.[8]

The image of Islam that still prevails in the West is that of a 'rigidly defined' faith that expects uniformity in belief and practice from all its adherents. Particular expressions of Islam have been generalized to the extent that all Muslims, whatever their cultural and ethnic differences, are judged according to a negative stereotype. The diversity that already exists within Islam and its potential for change are not generally recognized, especially in the western media.

I was invited recently to participate in a conference in New York, the purpose of which was to promote a greater dialogue and understanding between the Muslim and non-Muslim worlds. The theme of the first session was: 'Listening to the Muslim Worlds'. The aim was to allow the Muslim scholars who were present to share their thoughts on what was happening within their faith communities. Some of the western participants, however, seemed unable to resist intervening and before long I found myself listening to western interpretations of what was happening within the Muslim worlds. It struck me that what I was witnessing at the micro-level within the conference room has been, and still is, happening all the time at the macro or global level. The West needs to rediscover the art of listening to the Muslim worlds. The tendency to interpret rather than to listen to what Muslims have to say is driven, I fear, by the unconscious prejudice that Islam has nothing to offer the West. We seem to have forgotten how much Islam has contributed over the centuries to the development of western thought and culture. A true dialogue could prove to be mutually enriching.

At the beginning of chapter three, I quoted from an address given by a disciple of the nineteenth-century Hindu mystic, Ramakrishna, at a meeting of the Parliament of Religions in Chicago in 1893. He advocated as a remedy for the sectarianism and bigotry that had caused so much bloodshed in the world a unity rooted in pluralism that allowed for 'mutual influence and enrichment'. He believed engagement to be the antidote to religiously inspired violence. 'If anyone here hopes that this unity will come by triumph of any one of these religions and the destruction of the others, to him I say, Brother, yours is an impossible hope,' he declared. ' ... The Christian is not to become a Hindu or a Buddhist nor a Hindu or a Buddhist to become a Christian. But each must assimilate the spirit of the others and yet preserve its own individuality and grow according to its own law of growth.'9 If those words had been acted upon the twentieth century may have been less confrontational and bloody.

Notes

Foreword

1. Jonathan Fox, 'The Salience of Religious Issues in Ethnic Conflicts: A Large-N Study', *Nationalism and Ethnic Politics*, Vol. 3, No. 3 (Autumn 1997), pp. 1–19.
2. *States in Armed Conflict 2001*, Department of Peace and Conflict Research, Uppsala University.
3. See 'Rage of Luton Muslims', *The Times*, 30 October 2001.
4. See *The New York Times*, 7 April 2002.
5. *The Guardian*, 'Powell attacks Christian right', 15 November 2002.
6. *Harvard Magazine* (July–August 2002), pp. 64–5.
7. *The Westminster Dictionary of Christian Theology*, edited by Alan Richardson and John Bowden (Philadelphia: The Westminster Press, 1983), p. 498.
8. *ibid.*, p. 496.
9. Gabriel Marcel, *Creative Fidelity*, translated by Robert Rosthal (Fordham University Press, 2002), pp. 210–21.
10. *Dictionary of Art*, edited by Jane Turner, Vol. 18 (Macmillan Publishers Limited, 1996), pp. 464–7.

Chapter 1. The Clash of Paradigms

1. Samuel P. Huntington, *The Clash of Civilizations and the Remaking of World Order* (Simon & Schuster Touchtone, 1997 edn), p. 43.
2. *ibid.*, p. 254.
3. *ibid.*, p. 96.
4. *ibid.*, p. 209.
5. *ibid.*, p. 211.
6. *ibid.*, p. 211.
7. *ibid.*, p. 321.
8. *The Wall Street Journal*, report on the World Economic Forum, March 2002.
9. 'A Head-On Collision of Alien Cultures?' *The New York Times*, 20 October 2001.
10. Imam Khomeini, *Islam and Revolution*, translated by Hamid Algar (Berkeley: Mizan Press, 1981), pp. 55–81.
11. Olivier Roy, *The Failure of Political Islam*, translated by Carol Volk (Harvard University Press, 1996) pp. 36–8.
12. Sayyid Qubt, *Milestones*, Chapter 4 'Jihaad in the Cause of God', Section 122. The full text is available at http://www.youngmuslims.ca/online_library/books/milestones/index.htm.

13. A *fatwa* is a legal opinion issued by a private religious scholar as opposed to a judge in a law court (Esposito).

14. Abdullahi Ahmed An-Na'im, *Toward an Islamic Revolution, Civil Liberties, Human Rights, and International Law* (Syracuse University Press, 1990), p. 98, also cf. pp. 47–68 and 97–100.

15. John L. Esposito, *Islam and Politics*, fourth edition (Syracuse University Press, 1998), p. 140.

16. Roy, *The Failure of Political Islam*, p. 123.

17. Cf. Jeane J. Kirkpatrick and Albert L. Weeks, 'The Modernizing Imperative', *Foreign Affairs* (Sept./Oct. 1993).

18. Cf. Statement of the Millennium World Peace Summit of Religious and Spiritual Leaders, 28 August 2000.

19. Cf. Wheaton: http://www.wheaton.edu/polsci/kellstedt/apsa97h.htm.

20. Cf. Huntington, *The Clash of Civilizations*, p. 158.

21. Ancient church law held that there could only be one diocese and one bishop in a given geographical area.

22. Georges Florovsky, *Ecumenism 1, A Doctrinal Approach*, The Collected Works, Volume 13 (Vaduz: Buchervertriebsanstalt).

23. Although 1054 is the traditional date for the schism between the Eastern (Orthodox) and Western (Roman) Churches, it is difficult to determine the exact timing. The causes for the formal split are extremely complex with misunderstandings over philosophical terms, liturgical language and practice, papal authority and external political pressures contributing to a growing sense of alienation between the two Churches over a much longer period of time.

24. Cf. The Apostolic Letter *Orientalis Lumen*, Pope John Paul II, Vatican City, May 1995.

25. Cf. Fred Halliday, *Islam and the Myth of Confrontation: Religion and Politics in the Middle East* (New York: St Martin's Press, 1996).

26. Cf. Robert Bartley, 'The Case for Optimism', *Foreign Affairs* 72 [4], pp. 15–18.

27. Cf. Jonathan Fox, 'Two Civilizations and Ethnic Conflict: Islam and the West', *Journal of Peace Research*, vol. 38, no. 4 (2001), pp. 459–72. 'During both periods, about 38% of ethnic conflicts were civilizational. In addition, only a very small minority of ethnic conflicts was between the Islamic and Western civilizations, about 5.6% during the Cold War and about 6.7% after the Cold War [about 14.6% and 18.3% of civilizational conflicts, respectively]. Islamic groups were involved in 109 ethnic conflicts during the post Cold War period, 38 as the minority group, 33 as the majority group, and 38 in which both groups are Islamic. Of these conflicts, about 62.4% were civilizational. The results for the Cold War period are similar, with about 63.5% of 85 ethnic conflicts involving Islamic groups being civilizational', p. 463.

28. Errol A. Henderson and Richard Tucker, 'Clear and Present Strangers: The Clash of Civilizations and International Conflict', *International Studies Quarterly* (2001) 45, pp. 317–8.

29. Cf. *ibid.*, p. 332.

30. Cf. Huntington, *The Clash of Civilizations*, pp. 308–13.

31. Cf. Paul Collier and Anke Hoeffler, *Greed and Grievance in Civil War*, A World Bank Report 2001.

32. This finding runs contrary to the presumption that rapid growth is more likely to be a cause of conflict. In acknowledging this Collier argues that the average developing country faces an 11 per cent risk of having civil war in any five-year period. Each time a percentage point is added to the rate of growth, he claims, this reduces the risk of civil war by a percentage point. Cf. 'The Economic Agendas of Civil Wars', *Peace Colloquy* {I} (Spring 2002).

33. To support his theory that a country's dependence on primary commodities greatly increases the risk of conflict, Collier argues that in a country with no primary commodity exports at all, the risk of conflict is 1 per cent in a five-year period. This compares to a country with high dependence on primary commodities, which for him means that if about 30 per cent of its national income comes from these commodities, the risk is around 23 per cent.

34. Collier, 'Doing Well out of War: An Economic Perspective' in *Economic Agendas in Civil Wars, Greed and Grievance*, edited by Mats Berdal and David Malone (Boulder: Lynne Rienner, 2000), p. 9.

35. Cf. Elbadawi and Sambanis, *How Much War Will We See? Estimating the Incidence of Civil War in 161 Countries*, World Bank Reports No. 2253, p. 18.

36. Indra de Soysa, in 'The Resource Curse: Are Civil Wars Driven by Rapacity or Paucity?', argues that the abundance of natural resources in a country can be used equally to support grievance as a motive for civil conflict as total reliance on the exports of these primary commodities frequently means that governments fail to allocate capital for other areas of development and especially job creation in the manufacturing sector. The failure to innovate economically and politically, he claims, can hinder institutional development that prevents capricious behaviour and bad governance that gives rise to legitimate grievances. Cf. *Greed and Grievance, Economic Agendas in Civil Wars*, edited by Mats Berdal and David M. Malone, pp. 113–15.

37. Collier and Hoeffler restricted their research to internal conflicts that fit within the widely recognized definition of a civil war. The conditions they apply are at least 1000 combat-related deaths, with both an identifiable rebel organization and government forces suffering at least 5 per cent of these causalities. They identified within this definition 78 civil wars over the period 1960–99. Other conditions include the challenge of the authority of an internationally recognized state that is also one of the principle combatants in the conflict.

38. Cf. Ted Robert Gurr, 'Peoples Against States: Ethno political Conflict and the Changing World System', *International Studies Quarterly* (1994) 38, pp. 347–77. In this article Gurr defines these competing theories: the primordial explanation is based on the view that ethnic identities are more fundamental and persistent than loyalties to larger social units. The instrumental explanation holds that ethnic identities are no more salient than any other kind of identity; they only become significant when mobilized by political entrepreneurs in the pursuit of material or political benefits for the group or the region.

39. The communal criteria used by groups according to Gurr's findings may include any combination of identity markers such as shared culture, common history, fate or place of residence, nationality, language, religion or race. Gurr regards such identities as 'constructions' that are reinforced through encounters with other groups. None the less these are built around an enduring core of shared culture and experiences.

40. Ted Robert Gurr, *Peoples versus States, Minorities at Risk in the New Century* (United States Institute of Peace Press, 2000), p. 6.

41. Cf. Mark Juergensmeyer, *The New Cold War, Religious Nationalism Confronts the Secular State* (University of California Press, 1993).

42. Cf. *ibid.*, p. 358.

43. Gurr, *Peoples versus States, Minorities at Risk in the New Century*, p. 370.

44. Cf. *ibid.*, p. 359.

45. *ibid.*, p. 73.

46. *ibid.*, p. 68.

47. Cf. *ibid.*, pp. 78–9.

48. 'Frames' is a term used in the social and political sciences to describe such ideas as

self-determination, and indigenous and minority rights that are used to empower people and to justify their actions in achieving such goals. Cf. *ibid.*, pp. 72–4.

49. *From Voting to Violence, Democratisation and Nationalist Conflict* (New York: W.W. Norton & Company, 2000), p. 18.
50. *ibid.*, p. 15.
51. *ibid.*, p. 37.
52. *ibid.*
53. Tanja Ellingsen, 'Colorful Community or Ethnic Witches' Brew?' *Journal of Conflict Resolution*, vol. 44, no. 2 (April 2000), pp. 228–49.
54. Beverly Crawford and Ronnie D. Lipschutz (eds.), *The Myth of Ethnic Conflict* (Berkeley, 1998), p. 4.
55. *ibid.*, p. 12.
56. *ibid.*, p. 12.
57. *ibid.*, p. 532.

Chapter 2. Religion Matters

1. See Patrick Grant, *Northern Ireland: Religion and the Peace Process*, unpublished paper.
2. *ibid.*
3. Full Text of Notes Found After Hijackings, *The New York Times*, 29 September 2001.
4. Alan Aldridge, *Religion in the Contemporary World, A Sociological Introduction* (Cambridge: Polity Press, 2000), p. 2.
5. J.P. Clayton, *The Westminster Dictionary of Christian Theology*, edited by Alan Richardson and John Bowden (Philadelphia: The Westminster Press, 1983), p. 471.
6. *ibid.*, pp. 471–2.
7. Aldridge, *Religion in the Contemporary World*, p. 4.
8. *ibid.*, pp. 89–122.
9. *ibid.*, p. 2.
10. *ibid.*, p. 3.
11. See N.J. Demerath III, *Crossing the Gods* (Rutgers University Press, 2001), p. 122.
12. See *The Economist*, 16 November 2002.
13. See *The Economist*, 17 March 2001.
14. Aldridge, *Religion in the Contemporary World*, p. 3.
15. In 'The Religious Factor in World Politics', an address given at the University of Zurich, 2001.
16. Gilles Kepel, The *Revenge of God*, translated by Alan Braley (The Pennsylvanian State University Press, 1994), p. 2.
17. *ibid.*, p. 4.
18. *ibid.*, p. 192.
19. *ibid.*, p. 192.
20. Gilles Kepel, *Jihad: The Trail of Political Islam* (Cambridge: Harvard University Press, 2002), p. 375.
21. *ibid.*, p. 373.
22. *ibid.*, p. 376.
23. *ibid.*, p. 17.
24. 'Portrait of the Arab As a Young Radical', *The New York Times*, 22 September 2002.
25. Article by Rosie Cowan, *Guardian*, 21 December 2002.
26. Mark Juergensmeyer, *Terror in the Mind of God* (University of California Press, 2000), pp. 24–30.
27. See 'Holy War in the Spice Islands', *The Economist*, 17 March 2001; 'Settling the War of God and Gold', 2 February 2002; 'The Black Bats Strike Back', 11 August 2001.
28. *Religion in Kosovo*, ICG Report No. 105, January 2001.
29. Mitja Velikonja, 'In Hoc Signo Vinces: Religious Symbolism in the Balkan Wars

1991–1995', a paper presented in Paris at the international conference *Nationality and Citizenship in Post Communist Europe*, July 2001.

30. 'Rabin's Assassin', *The New York Times*, 5 November 1995.
31. Juergensmeyer, *Terror in the Mind of God*, p. 48.
32. Michael Karpin and Ina Friedman, *Murder in the Name of God* (New York: Henry Holt and Company, 1998), p. 9.
33. *ibid.*, p. 10.
34. Juergensmeyer, *Terror in the Mind of God*, p. 56.
35. Kepel, The *Revenge of God*, p. 164.
36. Demerath III, *Crossing the Gods*, p. 122.
37. See www. HinduUnity.org, the Nation of Hindutva.
38. *ibid.*
39. Ian Reader in *Cults, Religion and Violence*, edited by J. Gordon Melton and D.G. Bromly (Cambridge University Press, 2002), pp. 189–202.
40. Martin E. Marty, 'The Future of World Fundamentalisms', *Proceedings of the American Philosophical Society*, vol. 142, no. 3 (September 1998). The full results of The Fundamentalism Project have been published by the University of Chicago Press, edited by Martin E. Marty and R. Scott Appleby. The titles published between 1991 and 1995 are: *Fundamentalisms Observed; Fundamentalisms and Society; Fundamentalisms and the State; Accounting for Fundamentalisms;* and *Fundamentalisms Comprehended*.
41. *ibid.*, p. 373.
42. Martin E. Marty, 'Fundamentalism as a Precursor to Violence' in *Religion and Violence, Religion and Peace*, edited by Joseph H. Ehrenkranz (Sacred Heart University Press, 1998), pp. 53–75.
43. Juergensmeyer, *Terror in the Mind of God*, p. 139.
44. *ibid.*, p. 162.
45. *ibid.*, p. 190.
46. *ibid.*, p. 187.
47. *ibid.*, p. 217.
48. *ibid.*, p. 222.
49. Alice Miller, *The Truth Will Set You Free: Overcoming Emotional Blindness and Finding Your True Adult Self* (New York: Basic Books, 2001).
50. *ibid.*
51. *ibid.*, p. 190.
52. *ibid.*
53. *ibid.*
54. J. Gordan Melton and D.G. Bromly (eds.), *Cults, Religion and Violence*, p. 50.
55. *ibid.*, p. 59.
56. *ibid.*, p. 61.
57. *ibid.*, p. 62.
58. Reader in *Cults, Religion and Violence*, pp. 189–92.
59. *ibid.*, pp. 193–4.
60. *ibid.*, p. 195.
61. *ibid.*, p. 196.
62. *ibid.*, p. 202.
63. *ibid.*, p. 206.
64. *ibid.*, preface p. xiii.
65. 'Driving Al Qaeda: Religious Decrees', *International Herald Tribune*, 31 January 2002.
66. 'India Death Toll Rises in Religious Rioting', *The New York Times*, 1 March 2002.
67. 'Extremists in Nigeria', *International Herald Tribune*, 29 November 2002.
68. Peter L. Berger, 'Secularism in Retreat', *National Interest* (Winter 1996–7), 3–12.

69. 'Yes, This Is About Islam', *The New York Times*, 2 November 2001.
70. Olivier Roy, *The Failure of Political Islam* (Cambridge, Mass: Harvard University Press, 2002), pp. 61–2.
71. Velikonja, 'In Hoc Signo Vinces: Religious Symbolism in the Balkan Wars 1991–1995'.
72. Paul Mojzes, *Religion and the War in Bosnia* (Atlanta, Georgia: Scholars Press, 1998), p. 89.
73. Vjekoslav Perica, *Balkan Idols: Religion and Nationalism in Yugoslav States* (Oxford University Press, 2002).
74. See *Method and Theory in the Study of Religion, Islamic Origins Reconsidered: John Wansbrough and the Study of Early Islam*, edited by Herbert Berg, Volume 9–1 (1997).
75. Malise Ruthven, 'War on What?' *Analysis*, BBC Radio 4, 25 October 2001.
76. Perica, *Balkan Idols: Religion and Nationalism in Yugoslav States*, p. 221.

Chapter 3. Religion and the Legitimization of Violence

1. Cited by Kana Mitra in 'Outsiders-Insiders: Hindu Attitudes Toward Non-Hindus', in *Attitudes of Religions and Ideologies Toward The Outsider: The Other*, edited by Leonard Swidler and Paul Mojzes (Lewiston/Queenston/Lampeter: The Edwin Mellen Press, 1990), p. 113.
2. Voltaire, *Treatise on Tolerance and Other Writings*, edited by Simon Harvey (Cambridge University Press, 2000), p. ix.
3. See Anantanand Rambachan, 'Hindu violence against Muslims can't be justified', posted 3 April 2002 on TwinCities.com.
4. John Ferguson, *War and Peace in The World's Religions* (New York: Oxford University Press, 1978), p. 30.
5. *ibid.*, p. 31.
6. As quoted in *ibid.*, p. 30.
7. 'Hinduism and War', Hinduwebsite, July 2002.
8. David C. Rapoport, 'Fear and Trembling: Terrorism in Three Religious Traditions', *The American Political Science Review*, vol. 78, no. 3 (September 1984), p. 661.
9. *ibid.*, p. 661.
10. *ibid.*, pp. 662–3.
11. Martine Van Woerkens, *The Strangled Traveller, Colonial Imaginings and The Thugs of India* (Chicago and London: The University of Chicago Press, 2002), p. 7.
12. *ibid.*, pp. 149 and 288.
13. Mahatma K. Gandhi, *Non-violence in Peace and War* (Ahemedabad, 1948), vol. 1, p. 44.
14. Sulak Sivarksa, *Seeds of Peace; A Buddhist Vision of Renewing Society* (Berkeley, California: Parallax Press, 1992).
15. *ibid.*
16. Gelek Rinpoche, a Tibetan-born Buddhist teacher and writer, and Robert Thurman, a Professor of Religion and Buddhism at Columbia University who is also a thirty-year student of the Dalai Lama, both justify the limited use of force. See Dharma Justice, *The Osgood File* (CBS Radio Network): 15 April 2002, online at ACFNEW-SOURCE.
17. His Holiness The Dalai Lama, *Ethics for The New Millennium* (New York: Riverhead Books, 1999), p. 207.
18. *ibid.*, p. 212.
19. Ferguson, *War and Peace in the World's Religions*, p. 50.
20. *ibid.*, p. 52.
21. Sybil Thornton, 'Buddhist Chaplains in the Field of Battle', in *Buddhism in Practice*, edited by Donald S. Lopez Jr (Princeton University Press, 1995).

22. Yoichi Clark Shimatsu and Leeroy Betti, 'Buddhists caught up in Kashmir war', *The Baltimore Sun*, 5 August 2001.
23. *ibid.*, see also online World Tibet Network News.
24. Sulak Sivaraksa, 'Buddhism and Nonviolence, Choices, Living Consciously' on www.bodydharma.org.
25. Ferguson, *War and Peace in the World's Religions*, p. 55.
26. The Holy Bible, The New International Version (Zondervan Publishing House).
27. Rapoport, 'Fear and Trembling: Terrorism in Three Religious Traditions', pp. 668–9.
28. *ibid.*, p. 670, footnote on the Dead Sea Scrolls, the discovery of which have provided a new insight into the Zealots-Sicarii understanding of total war.
29. *ibid.*, p. 670.
30. Jona Lendering, 'First Century Judaism – the Messiah', www livius.org. See also Ferguson, *War and Peace in the World's Religions*, p. 100.
31. The Holy Bible, New International Version.
32. See footnote 7 in David Little, '"Holy War" Appeals and Western Christianity: A reconsideration of Bainton's Approach', in *Just War and Jihad*, edited by John Kelsay and James Turner Johnson (Greenwood Press, 1991).
33. Tertullian, quoted in John Helgeland, *Christians and the Military* (Minneapolis: Augsburg, 1985).
34. Ferguson, *War and Peace in the World's Religions*, p. 106.
35. Eusebius, *The conversion of Constantine, Library of Nicene and post Nicene Fathers*, second series, vol. 1 (New York: Christian Literature Company, 1990), pp. 489–91.
36. Ferguson, *War and Peace in the World's Religions*, p. 105.
37. Kelsay and Johnson, *Just War and Jihad*, pp. 7–10.
38. Ferguson, *War and Peace in the World's Religions*, p. 106.
39. *St Augustine of Hippo: Letters 189 (A.D. 418)*, electronic version copyright 1997 by New Advent, Inc.
40. Kelsay and Johnson, *Just War and Jihad*, pp. 12–13.
41. *Truce of God – Bishopric of Terouanne*, 1063, Internet Medieval Source Book, www.fordham.edu.
42. H.E.J. Cowdrey, *The Genesis of the Crusades in the Holy War* (Columbus: Ohio State University, 1976), p. 19.
43. *ibid.*, p. 20.
44. *ibid.*, p. 21.
45. Quoted by Malcolm Billings, *The Crusades* (Tempus with the British Library, edition 2000), p. 153.
46. Gesta Francorum, quoted by Cowdrey, *The Genesis of the Crusades in the Holy War*, p. 11.
47. Richard L. Crocker, 'Early Crusade Songs', in *ibid.*, pp. 96–7.
48. Billings, *The Crusades*, p. 110.
49. Adrian House, *Francis of Assisi* (London: Chatto & Windus), pp. 208–213.
50. Ferguson, *War and Peace in the World's Religions*, pp. 108–9.
51. *ibid.*, p. 115.
52. *ibid.*
53. Hans J. Hillerbrand, *The Reformation: A Narrative History Related by Contemporary Observers and Participants* (Grand Rapids: Baker Book House, 1981), p. 109.
54. Ferguson, *War and Peace in the World's Religions*, p. 116.
55. David Little, '"Holy War" Appeals and Western Christianity: A Reconsideration of Bainton's Approach', in *Just War and Jihad*, p. 130.
56. Ferguson, *War and Peace in the World's Religions*, pp. 114–15.
57. Mark R. Cohen, 'Anti-Jewish Violence and the Place of the Jews in Christendom and in Islam: a Paradigm' in *Religious Violence between Christians and Jews*, edited by Anna Sapir Abulafia (Palgrave, 2002), pp. 112–13.
58. Robert Chazan, 'The Anti-Jewish Violence of 1096: Perpetrators and Dynamics' in

ibid., pp. 21–43.

59. *ibid.*, p. 38.
60. Jeremy Cohen, 'Christian Theology and Anti-Jewish Violence in the Middle Ages', in *ibid.*, pp. 53–8.
61. Bernard Lewis, *Cultures in Conflict* (Oxford University Press, 1995), p. 34.
62. *ibid.*, p. 36.
63. Hassan Hathout, *Reading the Muslim Mind* (Indiana: American Trust Publications, 1996), p. 41.
64. *ibid.*, p. 10.
65. John L. Esposito, *Islam and Politics*, fourth edn (Syracuse University Press, 1998), p. 4.
66. The Qur'an, translated by Muhammad Zafrulla Khan (New York: Olive Branch Press, 1997), 2:31, p. 9.
67. Esposito, *Islam and Politics*, p. 4.
68. Hathout, *Reading the Muslim Mind*, pp. 63–74.
69. *ibid.*, p. 46.
70. W. Montgomery Watt, 'The Holy War', in *Islamic Conceptions of Holy War*, edited by Thomas Patrick Murphy (Ohio State University Press, 1976), pp. 141–2.
71. Esposito, *Islam and Politics*, p. 6.
72. Ferguson, *War and Peace in the World's Religions*, p. 126, and Montgomery Watt, p. 143.
73. Ferguson, *War and Peace in the World's Religions*, p. 126.
74. Esposito, *Islam and Politics*, p. 8.
75. *ibid.*, pp. 9–10.
76. *ibid.*, p. 12.
77. Montgomery Watt, 'The Holy War', p. 149.
78. Ferguson, *War and Peace in the World's Religions*, p. 127.
79. Qur'an 22:40–1.
80. Qur'an 4:75.
81. Montgomery Watt, 'The Holy War', p. 145.
82. Hathout, *Reading the Muslim Mind*, pp. 108–9.
83. Ferguson, *War and Peace in the World's Religions*, p. 130.
84. James Turner Johnson, *The Holy War Idea in Western and Islamic Traditions* (Pennsylvania University Press, 1997), p. 60.
85. Qur'an, 22:39–40.
86. See Hilmi M. Zawati, *Is Jihad a Just War, Peace and Human Rights under Islamic and Public International Law?* (New York: Mellen, 2001), p. 40.
87. Ferguson, *War and Peace in the World's Religions*, pp. 130–1.
88. Zawati, *Is Jihad a Just War, Peace and Human Rights under Islamic and Public International Law?*, pp. 41–5.
89. Lewis, *Cultures in Conflict*, pp. 126–7.
90. *ibid.*, p. 121.
91. *ibid.*, p. 27.
92. *ibid.*, pp. 32–3.
93. *ibid.*, p. 127.
94. Rapoport, 'Fear and Trembling: Terrorism in Three Religious Traditions', p. 666.
95. See Ghulam Ahmad, 'Review of Religions 1902', quoted on the website of the Ahmadiyya Muslim Community.
96. See Kahn, 'Biographies of Afghans' on www.afghanan.net/ biographies.
97. Ferguson, *War and Peace in the World's Religions*, p. 139.
98. *ibid.*, p. 141.
99. *ibid.*, p. 143.
100. *ibid.*, p. 147.

Chapter 4. Battles on Sacred Turf

1. John Darby, 'Conflict in Northern Ireland: A Background Essay', chapter 2 of *Facets of The Conflict in Northern Ireland*, edited by Seamus Dunn (Basingstoke: Macmillan Press Ltd, 1995).
2. Donald Harman Akenson, *God's Peoples, Covenant and Land in South Africa, Israel and Ulster* (Ithaca and London: Cornell University Press, 1992), pp. 103–11.
3. Darby in *The Conflict in Northern Ireland*, edited by Seamus Dunn.
4. John Whyte, *Interpreting Northern Ireland* (Oxford: Clarendon Press, 1990), p. vii.
5. *ibid.*, pp. 114–15.
6. *ibid.*, p. 16.
7. *ibid.*, p. 33.
8. *ibid.*, pp. 34–5.
9. *ibid.*, p. 43.
10. See the Irish Hierarchy's Statement on the New Ireland Forum in 1984 cited by Whyte, *Interpreting Northern Ireland*, p. 43.
11. *ibid.*, p. 45.
12. *ibid.*, p. 40.
13. Paul Brown, *Guardian*, 4 January 2002.
14. Joseph Liechty and Cecelia Clegg, *Moving Beyond Sectarianism* (Blackrock: The Columba Press, 2001), p. 12.
15. *ibid.*, p. 13.
16. *ibid.*, p. 14.
17. *ibid.*, p. 147.
18. John McGarry and Brendan O'Leary, *Explaining Northern Ireland: Broken Images* (Oxford: Blackwell, 1995), p. 173.
19. *ibid.*, p. 174.
20. *ibid.*, p. 197.
21. *ibid.*, p. 213.
22. Liechty and Clegg, *Moving Beyond Sectarianism*, p. 29.
23. Whyte, *Interpreting Northern Ireland*, p. 51.
24. John Hickey, Religion and The Northern Ireland Problem (Totowa: Gill and Macmillan, 1984).
25. *ibid.*, pp. 68–9.
26. Whyte, *Interpreting Northern Ireland*, p. 107.
27. See www. Free Presbyterian Church.
28. Whyte, *Interpreting Northern Ireland*, pp. 107–8.
29. Akenson, *God's Peoples, Covenant and Land in South Africa, Israel and Ulster*, pp. 39–41.
30. *ibid.*, p. 119.
31. *ibid.*, p. 42.
32. *Sri Lanka* (Michelin Travel Publications, 2001), p. 12.
33. I have chosen not to identify by name some of those whom I interviewed as I have no desire to put their role within their communities in jeopardy.
34. Lakshman Gunasekera, 'Sri Lanka', *Sunday Observer*, 17 November 2002.
35. K. M. de Silva, 'To Restore Peace to Sri Lanka's Fractured Polity', the official web site of the Sri Lankan Government's Secretariat for Coordinating the Peace Process.
36. Stanley Jeyaraja Tambiah, *Buddhism Betrayed? Religion, Politics and Violence in Sri Lanka* (Chicago and London: University of Chicago Press, 1992), pp. 42–57.
37. *ibid.*, p. 47.
38. *ibid.*, p. 48.
39. *ibid.*, p. 49.
40. *ibid.*, pp. 56–7.
41. *ibid.*, p. 63.

42. *ibid.*, pp. 70–5.
43. David Little, *Sri Lanka, The Invitation of Enmity* (Washington: United States Institute of Peace Press, 1994), p. 95.
44. Tessa J. Bartholomeusz, *In Defence of Dharma, Just-War ideology in Buddhist Sri Lanka* (London and New York: Routledge Curzon, 2002), pp. 5–7.
45. Tambiah, *Buddhism Betrayed? Religion, Politics and Violence in Sri Lanka*, pp. 23–8.
46. *ibid.*, p. 44.
47. *ibid.*, p. 61.
48. *ibid.*, p. 97.
49. *ibid.*, p. 98.
50. *ibid.*, p. 99.
51. Little, *Sri Lanka, The Invitation of Enmity*, p. 11.
52. History of Sri Lanka, Country Reports.org 2003.
53. Little, *Sri Lanka, The Invitation of Enmity*, p. 12.
54. *ibid.*, pp. 13–14.
55. George D. Bond, *The Buddhist Revival in Sri Lanka: Religious Tradition, Reinterpretation and Response* (Columbia: University of South Carolina Press, 1988), p. 22.
56. Little, *Sri Lanka, The Invitation of Enmity*, p. 18
57. Bond, *The Buddhist Revival in Sri Lanka*, p. 22.
58. Little, *Sri Lanka, The Invitation of Enmity*, pp. 21–5.
59. Bond, *The Buddhist Revival in Sri Lanka*, p. 54.
60. *ibid.*, p. 55.
61. Bartholomeusz, *In Defence of Dharma*, pp. 22–3.
62. *ibid.*, p. 165.
63. Little, *Sri Lanka, The Invitation of Enmity*, p. 33.
64. Bartholomeusz, *In Defence of Dharma*, p. 166.
65. Amos Oz, *In the Land of Israel* (San Diego: Harcourt Brace & Company, 1993), pp. 260–1.
66. Ian J. Bickerton and Carla L. Klausner, *A Concise History of the Arab–Israeli Conflict*, fourth edition (New Jersey: Prentice Hall, 2002), p. 4.
67. *ibid.*, p. 8.
68. *ibid.*, pp. 6–10.
69. *ibid.*, p. 17.
70. *ibid.*, p. 20.
71. *ibid.*, p. 25.
72. *ibid.*, p. 26.
73. *ibid.*, pp. 42–4.
74. *ibid.*, p. 47.
75. *ibid.*, p. 52.
76. *ibid.*, pp. 75–6.
77. *ibid.*, p. 87.
78. *ibid.*, p. 104.
79. *ibid.*, p. 112.
80. *ibid.*, p. 154.
81. Milton Viorst, *What Shall I do With This People? Jews and the Fractious Politics of Judaism* (New York: The Free Press, 2002), p. 216.
82. *ibid.*, p. 217.
83. *ibid.*, p. 220.
84. *ibid.*, p. 188.
85. *ibid.*, p. 189.
86. *ibid.*, p. 190.
87. *ibid.*, pp. 190–1.

88. *ibid.*, p. 193.
89. *ibid.*, p. 194.
90. *ibid.*, p. 195.
91. Cited in *ibid.*, pp. 198–9.
92. *ibid.*, p. 201.
93. *ibid.*, p. 205.
94. *ibid.*, p. 206.
95. *ibid.*, pp. 207–8.
96. *ibid.*, pp. 229–30.
97. *ibid.*, p. 237.
98. *ibid.*, p. 239.
99. *ibid.*, p. 240.
100. Samantha M. Shapiro, 'The Unsettlers', *The New York Times Magazine*, 16 February 2003.
101. James Bennet, 'Israel's Religious Parties See Battle for Government's Soul', *The New York Times*, 26 January 2003.
102. On the significance of the water issue see Bickerton and Klausner, pp. 192–3.
103. Bickerton and Klausner, *A Concise History of the Arab-Israeli Conflict*, p. 163.
104. *ibid.*, p. 164.
105. Magnus Ranstrop and Magnus Norell, *Terrorism in the Middle East*, p. 176.
106. *ibid.*, p. 179.
107. *ibid.*, p. 180.
108. *ibid.*, pp. 182–3.
109. *ibid.*, p. 186.
110. *ibid.*, p. 189.
111. Nadim N. Rouhana, 'Reconciliation in Protracted National Conflict: Identity and Power in the Israeli-Palestinian Case', a paper given in 2001 at the Weatherhead Center for International Affairs at Harvard University and which was due to be published in 2001.
112. *ibid.*, p. 19.
113. *ibid.*, p. 21.

Chapter 5. Poverty, Tolerance, Leadership

1. Quoted by Alan B. Krueger and Jitka Maleckova in 'The Economics and Education of Suicide Bombers', *New Republic*, 24 June 2002.
2. UN General Assembly Report, 11 November 2002.
3. Quoted by Martin Wolf, *Financial Times*, 10 October 2001.
4. See Biden's speech to the Senate, 20 December 2001, and Albright's article in the *Financial Times*, 17 July 2002.
5. BBC News online, 22 March 2002.
6. Mark Juergensmeyer, *Terror in the Mind of God* (University of California Press, 2000), p. 191.
7. Krueger and Maleckova, 'The Economics and Education of Suicide Bombers'.
8. Interview with Radio Free Europe, 27 November 2002.
9. Beverly Crawford and Ronnie D. Lipschutz (eds.), *The Myth of Ethnic Conflict* (Berkeley, 1998), p. 38.
10. Kofi A. Annan, 'Trade and Aid in a Changed World', *The New York Times*, 19 March 2002.
11. Robert F. Drinan SJ, *The Mobilization of Shame* (New Haven and London: Yale University Press 2001), p. 123.
12. *The Economist*, 16 June 2001.
13. Geneive Abdo, *No God But God, Egypt and The Triumph of Islam* (Oxford University Press, 2000), p. 5.

14. Susan Sechler, *The Chronicle of Philanthropy*, 7 February 2002. Also Drinan, *The Mobilization of Shame*, p. 128.
15. *Financial Times*, 17 July 2002.
16. Juergensmeyer, *Terror in the Mind of God*, p. 162.
17. Cited by Drinan, *The Mobilization of Shame*, p. 123.
18. See Edward Langerak, 'Disagreement: Appreciating the Dark Side of Tolerance', in *Philosophy, Religion and the Question of Intolerance*, edited by Mehdi Amain Razavi and David Ambuel (State University of New York Press, 1997).
19. See Michael Ignatieff, 'Whose Universal Values? The Crisis in Human Rights', Praemium Erasmianum Essay 1999, p. 44. See also Steiner and Alston, *International Human Rights in Context* (Oxford, 2000), pp. 56–135.
20. W. F. Adeney, 'Toleration', in *Encyclopedia of Religion and Ethics*, edited by James Hastings (New York: Charles Scribner's Sons, 1961), p. 364.
21. John Locke, *A Letter concerning Toleration*, edited by James Tully Hackett (Indianapolis, 1983), p. 27.
22. Richard H. Dees, 'The Justification of Toleration' in Razavi and Ambuel (eds.), *Philosophy, Religion and the Question of Intolerance*, p. 135.
23. Cited in Adeney, 'Toleration', in *Encyclopedia of Religion and Ethics*, p. 364.
24. J. B. Schneewind, 'Bayle, Locke, and the Concept of Toleration', in Razavi and Ambuel (eds.), *Philosophy, Religion and the Question of Intolerance*, p. 6.
25. *ibid.*, p. 6.
26. Adeney, 'Toleration', in *Encyclopedia of Religion and Ethics*, p. 365.
27. Voltaire, *Treatise on Tolerance*, edited and translated by Simon Harvey (Cambridge University Press, 2000), p. 5.
28. *ibid.*, p. 22.
29. *ibid.*, p. xv.
30. *ibid.*, p. 49.
31. *ibid.*, p. 83.
32. *ibid.*, pp. 20–1.
33. *ibid.*, p. 89.
34. *Tertullian Ad Scapulam*, c.2, cited by John Linnan in *The New Dictionary of Theology* (Michael Glazner Inc., 1988), p. 577.
35. See Nicholas Wolterstorff, 'Tertullian's Enduring Question', in *The Best Christian Writing 2000*, edited by John Wilson (San Francisco: Harper, 2000), pp. 304–30.
36. John Witte Jr, *Religious Human Rights in Global Perspective* (The Hague: Martinus Nijhoff, 1996), p. xx.
37. Harold Coward, *Pluralism in the World Religions* (Oxford: Oneworld, 2000), p. 102.
38. *ibid.*, p. 129.
39. *Tertullian Ad Scapulam*, c.2, cited by John Linnan in *The New Dictionary of Theology*, p. 577.
40. Cited by James Carroll, *Constantine's Sword* (Boston: Houghton Mifflin Company, 2001), p. 207.
41. *Tertullian Ad Scapulam*, c.2, cited by John Linnan in *The New Dictionary of Theology*, p. 578.
42. Cited in The *New Catholic Encyclopaedia*, second edition (Thompson/Catholic University of America, 2003), vol. 5, p. 949.
43. *ibid.*, p. 947.
44. *Tertullian Ad Scapulam*, c.2, cited by John Linnan in *The New Dictionary of Theology*, p. 578.
45. The *New Catholic Encyclopaedia*, p. 948.
46. *ibid.*, p. 498.
47. *ibid.*, p. 949.
48. *Pacem in Terris*, Encyclical Letter of Pope John XXIII, Vatican City, 1963.

49. See Walter Abbot SJ (gen. ed.), *The Documents of Vatican II*, translations directed by Joseph Gallagher (New York: Herder and Herder/Association Press, 1966), Declaration on Religious Liberty, paras. 2 and 6.

50. The *New Catholic Encyclopaedia*, p. 948.

51. See the discussion on this topic in *The Westminster Dictionary of Social Ethics* (Philadelphia: Westminster Press, 1986), pp. 465–6.

52. The *New Catholic Encyclopaedia*, p. 946.

53. 'Vatican Rebukes a Theologian', *The New York Times*, 28 February 2001.

54. See D.R. Finch and M. Hillar (eds.), *Essays in the Philosophy of Humanism*, Vol. 10 (Center for Socinian Studies, Humanist Society of Huston, 2002), pp. 31–56.

55. Adeney, 'Toleration', in *Encyclopedia of Religion and Ethics*, p. 363.

56. *ibid.*, p. 364.

57. *ibid.*, p. 364.

58. John Hick, *An Interpretation of Religion* (Yale University Press, 1989), pp. 375–6.

59. *The Wall Street Journal*, 8 February 2002.

60. 'Monks vow to wage spiritual war to prevent eviction', *The Associated Press*, 16 January 2003.

61. Demetrios J. Constantelos, 'The Attitude of Orthodox Christians toward Non-Orthodox and Non-Christians', in *Attitudes of Religions and Ideologies Toward The Outsider: The Other*, edited by Leonard Swidler and Paul Mojzes (The Edwin Mellen Press, 1990), p. 67.

62. *ibid.*, pp. 67–8.

63. *ibid.*, pp. 77–9.

64. Genesis 9:1–17.

65. Dan Cohn-Sherbok, *Judaism and Other Faiths* (Palgrave/Macmillan, 1994), p. 29.

66. Rabbi Daniel Polish, 'Attitudes of Judaism Toward Non-Jews' in *Attitudes of Religions and Ideologies Toward The Outsider*, edited by Swidler and Mojzes, p. 53.

67. Coward, *Pluralism in the World Religions*, p. 3; see also Leviticus 17–26 and Ezekiel 40–8.

68. Nehemiah 10.

69. Coward, *Pluralism in the World Religions*, p. 5.

70. Cohn-Sherbok, *Judaism and Other Faiths*, pp. 36–7.

71. Moses Mendelssohn, *Jerusalem*, translated by Alfred Josepe Ktav (New York, 1969), p. 66.

72. Juergensmeyer, *Terror in the Mind of God*, pp. 51–3. See also Ian S. Lustick, *For Land and the Lord: Jewish Fundamentalism in Israel Council on Foreign Relations* (New York, 1988), pp. 93–100.

73. Jonathan Sacks, *The Dignity of Difference, How to Avoid The Clash of Civilizations* (London: Continuum, 2002), p. 5.

74. *ibid.*, p. 17.

75. *ibid.*, p. 19.

76. *ibid.*, p. 20.

77. *ibid.*, p. 21.

78. Khalid Duran, 'Muslims and Non-Muslims' in *Attitudes of Religions and Ideologies Toward The Outsider*, edited by Swidler and Mojzes, p. 82.

79. See Muhammad Iqbal, *The Reconstruction of Religious Thought in Islam, Muhammad Ashraf*, (1930). See also Iqbal, 'The Thinker Poet of Islam', via Google online.

80. Duran, 'Muslims and Non-Muslims' in *Attitudes of Religions and Ideologies Toward The Outsider*, edited by Swidler and Mojzes, pp. 82–5.

81. *ibid.*, p. 88.

82. *ibid.*, pp. 91–3.

83. *ibid.*, p. 94.

84. Qur'an 2:256.
85. Qur'an 10:99, 100.
86. Qur'an xlii 13–14.
87. T. W. Arnold, *Toleration* (Muhammadan), p. 366.
88. *ibid.*, p. 366.
89. Cited by Arnold, *Toleration*, p. 367.
90. Maria Rosa Menocal, *The Ornament of the World, How Muslims, Jews and Christians Created A Culture of Tolerance in Medieval Spain* (Boston: Little, Brown and Company, 2002), pp. 32–4.
91. *ibid.*, p. 11.
92. *ibid.*, pp. 328–9.
93. *ibid.*, p. 43.
94. Arnold, *Toleration*, p. 368.
95. *ibid.*, pp. 368–9.
96. John L. Esposito, *What Everyone Needs to Know About Islam* (Oxford University Press, 2002), p. 41.
97. *ibid.*, p. 50.
98. *ibid.*, p. 51.
99. Jane Perlez, 'An Islamic Scholar's Lifelong Lesson: Tolerance', *The New York Times*, 16 March 2002.
100. Kana Mitra, 'Outsiders-Insiders: Hindu Attitudes Toward Non-Hindus', in *Attitudes of Religions and Ideologies Toward The Outsider*, edited by Swidler and Mojzes, p. 106.
101. Coward, *Pluralism in the World Religions*, p. 124.
102. For helpful insights on Hindu thought and terminology, see James C. Livingston, *Anatomy of the Sacred* (Upper Saddle River NJ: Prentice Hall, 1998).
103. Coward, *Pluralism in the World Religions*, p. 125.
104. Mitra in 'Outsiders-Insiders: Hindu Attitudes Toward Non-Hindus', in *Attitudes of Religions and Ideologies Toward The Outsider*, edited by Swidler and Mojzes, p. 110.
105. S. Radhakrishnan, *Eastern Religions and Western Thought*, Clarendon Press Oxford, 1939 p. 21; cited by Coward, *Pluralism in the World Religions*, p. 116.
106. Coward, *Pluralism in the World Religions*, pp. 118–9.
107. Mitra in 'Outsiders-Insiders: Hindu Attitudes Toward Non-Hindus', in *Attitudes of Religions and Ideologies Toward The Outsider*, edited by Swidler and Mojzes, p. 112.
108. Address at the Parliament of Religions Sept. 11th 1893. Cited in *ibid.*, p. 113.
109. *ibid.*, p. 114.
110. Uli Schmetzr, *The Chicago Tribune*, 29 October 1999.
111. L. Jayasooriya, *Buddhism For The Inquiring Mind* (Sri Lanka, 2001), p. 58.
112. *ibid.*, pp. ix–xi.
113. *ibid.*, p. x.
114. *ibid.*, pp. 57–67.
115. Coward, *Pluralism in the World Religions*, p. 129.
116. Chatsumarn Kabilsingh, 'The Attitude of Buddhists Towards Non-Buddhists', in *Attitudes of Religions and Ideologies Toward The Outsider*, edited by Swidler and Mojzes, p. 118.
117. *ibid.*, p. 120.
118. *ibid.*, p. 122.
119. Sacks, *The Dignity of Difference*, p. 9.
120. John Stuart Mill, *On Liberty*, edited by Elizabeth Rapaport (Indianapolis: Hackett Publishing Co., 1978), pp. 9, 50.
121. *Tertullian Ad Scapulam*, c.2, cited by John Linnan in *The New Dictionary of Theology*, pp. 576–8.
122. Razavi and Ambuel (eds.), *Philosophy, Religion and the Question of Intolerance*, p. vii.

123. The *New Catholic Encyclopaedia*, p. 102.
124. Razavi and Ambuel (eds.), *Philosophy, Religion and the Question of Intolerance*, pp. xi–xiv.
125. Robert D. Putman, *Bowling Alone: The Collapse and Revival of American Community* (Simon & Schuster, 2000), pp. 354–8.
126. Gabriel Marcel, *Creative Fidelity*, translated by Robert Rosthal, (New York: The Noonday Press, 1964), pp. 210–21.
127. The summary provided here has been based on the writings of Ron Heifetz, Marty Linsky and Don Laurie. See: 'The Work of Leadership', by Ronald A. Heifetz and Don Laurie, *Harvard Business Review* (Jan.–Feb. 1997); *Leadership Without Easy Answers* by Ronald A. Heifetz (Cambridge, Mass.: The Belknap Press, 1994); *The Real Work of Leaders* by Donald L. Laurie (Cambridge Mass.: Perseus Publishing, 2000); *Leadership On The Line* by Ronald A. Heifetz and Marty Linsky (Boston: Harvard Business School Press, 2002).
128. Laurie, *The Real Work of Leaders*, pp. 20–2.
129. Heifetz and Linsky, *Leadership On The Line*, pp. 13–14.
130. *ibid.*, p. 15.
131. *ibid.*, pp. 20–30.
132. Heifetz, *Leadership Without Easy Answers*, p. 20.
133. Heifetz and Linsky, *Leadership On The Line*, p. 53.
134. *ibid.*, p. 191.
135. Walter M. Abbott (ed.), *The Documents of Vatican, The Constitution on the Church*, (London: Geoffrey Chapman, 1966).
136. Clericalism in The *New Catholic Encyclopaedia*, p. 802.
137. Esposito, *What Everyone Needs to Know About Islam*, pp. 35–6.
138. Putman, *Bowling Alone*, p. 74.
139. Adrian House, *Francis of Assisi* (London: Chatto and Windus, 2000), pp. 210–13.
140. Jane Perlez, 'On an Indonesian Island, a Reverence for Tolerance', *The New York Times*, 11 March 2003.
141. 'The Work of Leadership' by Ronald A. Heifetz and Don Laurie, *Harvard Business Review*, p. 129.
142. J. Philip Wogaman, *Christian Social Ethics*, edited by J.F. Childress and J. Macquarrie (Philadelphia: The Westminster Press, 1986), p. 466.

Chapter 6. The Struggle for the Global Soul
1. Mark Juergensmeyer, *Terror in the Mind of God* (University of California Press, 2000), pp. 30–6, 189.
2. R. Scott Appleby, 'Building Peace to combat Religious Terror', *The Chronicle Review*, 28 September 2001.
3. Diana Eck, *Encountering God: A Spiritual Journey from Bozeman to Banaras* (Boston: Beacon Press 1993), p. 13.
4. Quoted by James Carroll, *The Boston Globe*, 9 October 2001.
5. S. Parvez Manzoor, quoted by Ibn Warraq in *What the Koran really says* (Prometheus Books, 2002), p. 113.
6. Seyed Mohammad Khatami, Seton Hall University, New York, 10 November 2001.
7. Associated Press, 22 February 2002.
8. 'War on Terror: Berlusconi', *New Statesman*, 8 October 2001.
9. Mitra in 'Outsiders-Insiders: Hindu Attitudes Toward Non-Hindus', in *Attitudes of Religions and Ideologies Toward The Outsider*, edited by Swidler and Mojzes, p. 113.

Bibliography

Abdo, Geneive. *No God But God: Egypt and the Triumph of Islam*, New York, Oxford University Press, 2000

Abulafia, Anna Sapir. *Religious Violence Between Christians and Jews: Medieval Roots, Modern Perspectives*, New York, Palgrave Publishers, 2002

Akenson, Donald Harman. *God's People: Covenant and Land in South Africa, Israel, and Ulster*, Ithica, New York, Cornell University Press, 1992

Aldridge, Alan. *Religion in the Contemporary World*, Cambridge, UK, Polity Press, 2000

Ambuel, David and Razavi, Mehdi Amin. *Philosophy, Religion, and the Question of Intolerance*, New York, State University of New York Press, 1997

Appleby, R. Scott. *The Ambivalence of the Sacred: Religion, Violence, and Reconciliation*, New York, Rowman & Littlefield Publishers Inc., 2000

Arinze, Francis Cardinal. *Religions for Peace: A Call for Solidarity to the Religions of the World*, New York, Doubleday, 2002

Armstrong, Karen. *The Battle for God: Fundamentalism in Judaism, Christianity and Islam*, Hammersmith, London, HarperCollins Publishers, 2000

Bartolomé, Lilia I. and Macedo, Donald. *Dancing with Bigotry*, New York, Palgrave, 1999

Bartholomeusz, Tessa J. *In Defense of Dharma, Just-war ideology in Buddhist Sri Lanka*, London and New York, Routledge Curzon, 2002

Berdal, Mats and Malone, David M. *Greed & Grievance: Economic Agendas in Civil Wars*, Boulder, Colorado, Lynne Rienner Publishers, 2000

Bickerton, Ian J. and Klausner, Carla L. *A Concise History of the Arab-Israel Conflict*, Upper Saddle River, New Jersey, Prentice Hall, 2002

Billings, Malcolm. *The Crusades*, Charleston, South Carolina, Tempus Publishing Inc., 2000

Binder, Leonard. *Islamic Liberalism: A Critique of Development Ideologies*, Chicago, Illinois, The University of Chicago Press, 1988

Bond, George D. *The Buddhist Revival in Sri Lanka: Religious Tradition, Reinterpretation and Response*, Columbia, South Carolina, University of South Carolina Press, 1988

Bromley, David and Melton, J. Gordon. *Cults, Religion, and Violence*, New York, Cambridge University Press, 2002

Carroll, James. *Constantine's Sword: The Church and the Jews*, New York, Houghton Mifflin Company, 2001

Chromsky, Noam. *9-11*, New York, Seven Stories Press, 2001

Clegg, Cecelia and Liechty, Joseph. *Moving Beyond Sectarianism, Religion, Conflict, and Reconciliation in Northern Ireland*, Dublin, Ireland, Colour Books Ltd, 2001

Coward, Harold. *Pluralism in the World Religions*, Boston, Massachusetts, Oneworld Publications, 2000

Crawford, Beverly and Lipschutz, Ronnie D. (eds.). *The Myth of Ethnic Conflict: Politics, Economics and Cultural Violence*, University of California, 1998

Dalai Lama. *Ethics for a New Millennium*, New York, Riverhead Books, 1999

Demerath III, NJ. *Crossing the Gods: World Religions and Worldly Politics*, New Brunswick, New Jersey, Rutgers University Press, 2001

Drinan, Robert F., SJ. *The Mobilization of Shame*, New Haven, Connecticut, Yale University Press, 2001

Eck, Diana L. *Encountering God: A Spiritual Journey from Bozeman to Banaras*, Boston, Massachusetts, Beacon Press, 1993

Ehrenkranz, Joseph H. *Religion and Violence, Religion and Peace*, Fairfield, Connecticut, Sacred Heart University Press, 2000

Esposito, John L. *Islam and Politics*, New York, Syracuse University Press, 1984

 What Everyone Needs to Know About Islam: Answers to Frequently Asked Questions, From One of America's Leading Experts, New York, Oxford University Press, 2002

Esposito, John L. and Voll, John O. *Islam and Democracy*, New York, Oxford University Press, 1996

Ferguson, John. *War and Peace in the World's Religions*, New York, Oxford University Press, 1978

Field, Michael. *Inside the Arab World*, Cambridge, Massachusetts, Harvard University Press, 1994

Friedman, Ina and Karpin, Michael. *Murder in the Name of God*, New York, Henry Holt and Company, 1998

Gopin, Marc. *Holy War, Holy Peace: How Religion Can Bring Peace to the Middle East*, New York, Oxford University Press, 2002

Graubard, Stephen R. *Daedalus*, Cambridge, Massachusetts, American Academy of Arts and Sciences, Fall 2000

Gurr, Ted Robert. *People Versus Statues: Minorities at Risk in the New Country*, Washington, DC, United States Institute of Peace Press, 2000

Halliday, Fred. *Two Hours that Shook the World*, London, UK, Saqi Books, 2002

Harvey, Simon (ed.). *Treatise on Tolerance*, Cambridge, United Kingdom, Cambridge University Press, 2000

Heifetz, Ronald A. and Linsky, Marty. *Leadership on the Line: Staying Alive through the Dangers of Leading*, Boston, Massachusetts, Harvard Business School Press, 2002

Helmick, Raymond G., SJ, and Peterson, Rodney. *Forgiveness and Reconciliation: Religion, Public Policy, and Conflict Transformation*, Philadelphia, Pennsylvania, Templeton Foundation Press, 2002

Hickey, John. *Religion and the Northern Ireland Problem*, Totowa, New Jersey, Barnes & Noble Books, 1984

Hodge, James F. and Rose, Gideon. *How Did This Happen?: Terrorism and the New War*, New York, Public Affairs, 2001

Horton, John and Nicholson, Peter. *Toleration: Philosophy and Practice*, Vermont, Ashgate Publishing Company, 1992

House, Adrian. *Francis of Assisi*, London, UK, Chatto & Windus, 2000

Huntington, Samuel P. *The Clash of Civilizations and the Remaking of World Order*, New York, Simon & Schuster Inc., 1996

Jayasooriya, L. *Buddhism for the Inquiring Mind*, Mount Lavinia, Sri Lanka, Tharanjee Prints

Johnson, James Turner. *The Holy War Idea in Western and Islamic Traditions*, University Park, Pennsylvania, The Pennsylvania State University Press, 1997

Johnson, James Turner and Kelsey, John. *Just War and Jihad: Historical and Theoretical*

Perspectives on War and Peace in Western and Islamic Traditions, New York, Greenwood Press, 1991

Juergensmeyer, Mark. *Terror in the Mind of God: Global Rise of Religious Violence*, Berkeley, California, University of California Press, 2001

Karetzky, Patricia Eichenbaum. *The Life of the Buddha: Ancient Scriptural and Pictorial Traditions*, New York, University Press of America, 1992

Kaufman, Daniel J., Nielsen, Suzanne C. and Parker, Jay M. *Through Alternative Lenses: Current Debates in International Relations*, New York, The McGraw-Hill Companies, Inc., 2000

Kepel, Gilles. *Jihad: The Trial of Political Islam*, Cambridge, Massachusetts, Harvard University Press, 2002

Kepel, Gilles. The *Revenge of God*, University Park, Pennsylvania, The Pennsylvania State University Press, 1994

Küng, Hans. *The Catholic Church: A Short History*, London, UK, Weidenfeld and Nicolson, 2001

Laurie, Donald L. *The Real Work of Leaders, A Report from the Front Lines of Management*, Cambridge, Massachusetts, Perseus Publishing, 2000

Lewis, Bernard. *The Assassins: A Radical Sect in Islam*, London, UK, Weidenfeld and Nicolson, 1967

Cultures in Conflict: Christians, Muslims, and Jews in the Age of Discovery, New York, Oxford University Press, 1995

The Multiple Identities of the Middle East, New York, Schocken Books, 1998

What Went Wrong: Western Impact and Middle Eastern Response, New York, Oxford University Press, 2002

Little, David. *Sri Lanka: The Invention of Enmity*, Washington, DC, United States Institute of Peace Press, 1994

Lopez Jr, Donald S. *Buddhism in Practice*, Princeton, New Jersey, Princeton University Press, 1995

MacArthur, John. *Terrorism, Jihad, and the Bible*, USA, W. Publishing Group, 2001

Marin, David. *Does Christianity Cause War?* New York, Oxford University Press, 1997

Menocal, Maria Rosa. *The Ornament of the World: How Muslims, Jews, and Christians Created a Culture of Tolerance in Medieval Spain*, Boston, New York, London, Little, Brown and Company, 2002

Miller, Alice. *The Truth Will Set You Free*, Oxford, UK, The Perseus Press, 2001

Mojzes, Paul. *Religion and the War in Bosnia*, Atlanta, Georgia, Scholars Press, 1998

Mojzes, Paul and Swidler, Leonard (eds.). *Attitudes of Religions and Ideologies Toward the Outsider: The Other*, Lewiston, New York, The Edwin Mellen Press, 1990

Murphy, Thomas Patrick. *The Holy War*, Columbus, Ohio, Ohio State University Press, 1976

Nasr, Seyyed Hossein. *The Heart of Islam: Enduring Values for Humanity*, New York, HarperSanFrancisco, 2002

Newey, Glen. *Virtue, Reason and Tolerance*, George Square, Edinburgh, Edinburgh University Press Ltd, 1999

Oz, Amos. *In the World of Israel*, New York, Harvest in Translation, 1993

Peri, Yoram. *The assassination of Yitzhak Rabin*, Stanford, California, Stanford University Press, 2000

Perica, Vjekoslav. *Balkan Idols: Religion and Nationalism in Yugoslav States*, New York, Oxford University Press, 2002

Reinhart, Tanya. *Israel/Palestine: How to End the War of 1948*, New York, Seven Stories Press, 2002

Roy, Olivier. *The Failure of Political Islam*, Cambridge, Massachusetts, Harvard University Press, 1996

Rubin, Barry. *The Tragedy of the Middle East*, Cambridge, United Kingdom, Cambridge University Press, 2002

Sachedina, Abdulaziz. *The Islamic Roots of Democratic Pluralism*, New York, Oxford University Press, 2001

Sacks, Jonathan. *The Dignity of Difference: How to Avoid the Clash of Civilizations*, New York, Continuum, 2002

Schwartz, Regina M. *The Curse of Cain*, Chicago, Illinois, University of Chicago Press, 1997

Seligmann, Elisabeth and Stern, Susan. *The End of Endurance*, London, UK, Nicholas Breakey Publishing, 2002

Silk, Mark. *Religion on the International News Agenda*, Hartford, Connecticut, Trinity College, 2000

Snyder, Jack. *From Voting to Violence*, New York, W.W. Norton & Company, 2000

Stern, Jessica. *The Ultimate Terrorist*, Cambridge, Massachusetts, Harvard University Press, 1999

Swartley, Willard M. *Violence Renounced*, Telford, Pennsylvania, Pandora Press US, 2000

Tambiah, Stanley Jeyaraja. *Buddhism Betrayed?: Religion, Politics, and Violence in Sri Lanka*, Chicago, Illinois, The University of Chicago Press, 1992

Taylor, Charles. *Varieties of Religion Today*, Cambridge, Massachusetts, Harvard University Press, 2002

Taylor, Mark C. *Critical Terms for Religious Studies*, Chicago, Illinois, The University of Chicago Press, 1998

Viorst, Milton. *What Shall I Do With This People?: Jews and the Fractious Politics of Judaism*, New York, The Free Press, 2002

Volf, Miroslav. *Exclusion and Embrace: The Theological Exploration of Identity, Otherness, and Reconciliation*, Nashville, Tennessee, Abington Press, 1996

Waardenburg, Jacques. *Muslim Perceptions of Other Religions: A Historical Survey*, New York, Oxford University Press, 1999

Wansbrough, John. *Quranic Studies: Sources and Methods of Scriptural Interpretation*, New York, Oxford University Press, 1977

Whyte, John. *Interpreting Northern Ireland*, Oxford, UK, Clarendon Press, 1990

Woerkens, Martine Van. *The Strangled Traveler: Colonial Imaginings and the Thugs of India*, Chicago, Illinois, The University of Chicago Press, 2002

Index